The Seven C's of Creativity

Series Editor
Todd Lubart
Université Paris Cité
Paris, France

This series explores a new framework for understanding creativity based on seven "C's": Creators (characteristics of creative people), Creating (the process of creating), Collaborations (creativity in dyads, teams, groups), Context (the environment for creativity), Creations (the nature of creative productions), Consumption (the uptake of creative productions, adoption of creative ideas by the public), Curricula (the development and teaching of creativity).

Comprising seven edited volumes, one for each C, the series will be first comprehensive overview of the Seven C's framework and will bring together leading international scholars to study creativity-related phenomena with an interdisciplinary lens. Topics covered will include: group creativity; leadership and creativity in the workplace; consumer creativity; language as a creative consumption medium; writing, screen writing, and filmmaking; creative products in education, music, science, and engineering; creativity and AI; creativity in school and learning; creativity training.

Zorana Ivcevic
Editor

Creators

What Makes Individuals Creative

palgrave
macmillan

Editor
Zorana Ivcevic
Yale Center for Emotional Intelligence
Yale University
New Haven, CT, USA

ISBN 978-3-032-09174-1 ISBN 978-3-032-09225-0 (eBook)
https://doi.org/10.1007/978-3-032-09225-0

Cover credit: DrAfter123

This Palgrave Macmillan imprint is published by the registered company Springer Nature Switzerland AG.
The registered company address is: Gewerbestrasse 11, 6330 Cham, Switzerland

For Ravenna Helson, Frank Barron, Donald MacKinnon, Harrison Gough, and all the pioneers of the study of creative personality at the Institute for Personality Assessment and Research at the University of California at Berkeley on whose shoulders we stand.

Acknowledgments

I would like to thank the series editor, Todd Lubart, as well as Clelia Petracca and Tikoji Rao Mega Rao at Palgrave for their hard work and guidance in helping this book become a reality. Editing of this book was funded by the Fundación Botín, Santander, Spain (Emotions, Creativity and the Arts grant; Principal investigator: Zorana Ivcevic).

Contents

Notes on Contributors

Baptiste Barbot is a psychology professor at UCLouvain, Psychological Sciences Research Institute. His research mainly focuses on creativity development in adolescence and its relationships with identity development. He has extensively written on creativity in adolescence, measurement issues, individual differences in creativity, and held several editorial roles in the main creativity journals.

Denis Dumas is Associate Professor of Educational Psychology at the University of Georgia. His work focuses on the psychology of human creativity, including its development over the lifespan, instructional support in schools, and measurement using psychometric assessments. His work has been funded by the Institute of Education Sciences, the Naval Research Lab, the National Academy of Education, and the NeuroArts Blueprint and he serves on the editorial boards of *Journal of Educational Psychology*, *Review of Educational Research*, *Contemporary Educational Psychology*, *Thinking Skills and Creativity*, and *Journal of Creative Behavior*.

Molly Holinger is Assistant Professor of Creativity and Change Leadership at SUNY Buffalo State. She received her PhD in Educational Psychology with an emphasis in Giftedness, Creativity, and Talent Development from the University of Connecticut and her M.S. in Creative Studies from the Center for Applied Imagination at SUNY Buffalo State. Her research and teaching focus on the positive outcomes of creativity, such as engagement, meaning, and positive emotions. Molly has published in research journals such as *Gifted and Talented International*, *Translational Issues in Psychological Science*, and the *Journal of Creative*

Behavior. She has also written chapters in the *Cambridge Handbook of Creativity and Emotions*, the *Cambridge Handbook of Creativity Across Domains*, and the *Cambridge Handbook of Instructional Feedback*.

Zorana Ivcevic is a senior research scientist at the Yale Center for Emotional Intelligence. She studies the role of emotion, emotional intelligence, and self-regulation in creativity and well-being, as well as how to use the arts (and art-related institutions) to promote emotion and creativity skills. Dr. Ivcevic has edited the *Cambridge Handbook of Creativity and Emotion* (with Jessica Hoffmann and James Kaufman), and *Crisis, Creativity, and Innovation* (with Roni Reiter-Palmon, Magdalena Grohman, and Min Tang), and she is the author of *The Creativity Choice: The Science of Making Decisions to Turn Ideas into Action*.

Sofiia Kagan is a PhD student in the Department of Educational Psychology at the University of Georgia, focusing on the psychology of creativity and creative education.

Hansika Kapoor is a research author at the Department of Psychology, Monk Prayogshala, Mumbai, India. She holds a PhD from IIT, Bombay. Her research interests lie in creativity, socio-moral psychology, and behavioral science. She is the recipient of the Fulbright-Nehru Post-Doctoral Research Fellowship (2019–2020) and is an Affiliate at the University of Connecticut. She won the 2025 Daniel E. Berlyne Award from Division 10 of the American Psychological Association for outstanding research by an early-career scholar. She is an author, practicing psychologist, and has diverse experiences in research consultancy in behavioral and cognitive science. Dr. Kapoor has been featured in the book *31 Fantastic Adventures in Science: Women Scientists in India*.

Shengjie Lin is Assistant Professor of Educational Psychology at the University of New Mexico. His research adopts a social-contextual approach to examine the intersection of motivation, emotion, and creativity. First, he studies how students' motivation is shaped by cultural context and by socializers, such as parents and siblings. Second, he investigates the roles of motivation and emotion in individuals' creativity. Shengjie obtained his PhD in Educational Psychology from the University of Texas at Austin and completed postdoctoral training at the Yale Center for Emotional Intelligence.

Jean E. Pretz is Professor of Psychology at Elizabethtown College. She received her PhD from Yale University under the supervision of Dr. Robert Sternberg. Her research is focused on the relationship between creativity and success in college, and she evaluates the effectiveness of teaching for creativity in her courses. Dr. Pretz teaches courses on cognition, intelligence and creativity, leadership, senior seminar, and advanced research methods at Elizabethtown.

Sarah Rezaei is a research assistant at the Department of Psychology, Monk Prayogshala, Mumbai, India. Her work spans creativity, morality, deception, and misinformation, with a focus on how socio-moral and affective factors shape creativity and creative deception. Her broader research interests extend to socio-moral decision-making and applied behavioral science. She also writes for the *Non-WEIRD Science* blog at *Psychology Today*, focusing on cross-cultural psychology in non-WEIRD contexts.

Rebekah Rodriguez-Boerwinkle is a researcher at the Yale Center for Emotional Intelligence. Her work examines psychological processes underpinning creative behavior and art engagement, especially in applied and virtual settings. Her work is committed to promoting open science practices and tackling methodological challenges facing research in the arts.

Lakshmi Sithambaram is a Licensed Mental Health Counselor Associate in Washington State and the founder of Inner Canopy Therapy, PLLC, Bothell, WA. She holds a Master's in Applied Psychology and a Master's in Creativity and Change Leadership from Buffalo State University. Her work integrates creativity, mindfulness, and trauma-informed approaches to support healing and resilience.

Jean Urbaniak is a PhD candidate in psychology at UCLouvain (Belgium), under the supervision of Baptiste Barbot. His research focuses on creativity development in educational contexts, with a particular emphasis on the effects of school evaluation on students' creative potential and engagement. Before pursuing an academic career, he taught natural sciences in secondary school for ten years.

CHAPTER 1

Introduction: In Search of the Creative Person

Zorana Ivcevic

This book asks a fundamental question in creativity studies: How can we describe creative individuals? Underneath this seemingly straightforward question is a host of others and each one has to be answered before we can come back to our main focus. We need to answer how to identify creative individuals. Next, we should know whether it is appropriate to talk about different kinds of creative individuals interchangeably, whether we speak of different levels of creativity or different domains in which creativity is expressed. Other questions pertain to what we mean by describing creative individuals. Traditionally, this area of scholarship concerns the study

Author Note

I have no known conflict of interests to disclose.

The work on this chapter was funded by the Fundación Botín, Santander, Spain (Emotions, Creativity and the Arts grant, Principal investigator: Zorana Ivcevic).

Correspondence concerning this article should be addressed to: Zorana Ivcevic, Yale Center for Emotional Intelligence, Yale University, 350 George St., New Haven, CT 06511, United States.

Z. Ivcevic (✉)
Yale Center for Emotional Intelligence, Yale University, New Haven, CT, USA
e-mail: Zorana.ivcevic@yale.edu

Z. Ivcevic (ed.), *Creators*, The Seven C's of Creativity,
https://doi.org/10.1007/978-3-032-09225-0_1

of creative personality. But then, picking up any personality psychology textbook will show that there are many perspectives on how personality could and should be defined and empirically examined.

A single volume like this cannot answer all the questions. But what it can do is provide a cross-section of important areas to consider in the study of creators and creative personality. In doing this, it is worth looking back into the history of creativity scholarship. Ravenna Helson (1996) summarized several decades of research on creative individuals at the Institute for Personality Assessment and Research (IPAR) at the University of California at Berkeley. There, the history of creativity and history of personality were tightly related. New measures of personality, including the California Psychological Inventory (Gough, 1956) and the Adjective Check List (Gough, 1960), were developed and used to describe traits of different samples of creative individuals, including writers, architects, scientists, engineers, mathematicians, and others. These early decades of research were marked by intensive assessments; each of the samples was studied through a combination of self-report inventories, performance tests, and observations of behavior. Many of these samples were brought to a former fraternity house on the Berkeley campus for a weekend and observed by psychologists not only in laboratory contexts, but also daily activities and interactions. This enabled the breadth and depth of assessment that has not been matched since.

We have learned much. In a creativity series presentation at Buffalo State College, Donald MacKinnon (1964), long-time director of IPAR, identified openness as a central attribute of creative personality and one that enables creative individuals to stand "aside from the social collectivity and sometimes in conflict with it". He likened openness to courage,

> It is in perceptions of the outer world and of his own inner life that the courage of the creative person is again clearly to be seen. It manifests itself in his perceptual openness to experience of the inner life, as well as of the outer environment and culture.

Several decades later, we can affirm with great reliability afforded by multiple meta-analyses (Feist, 1998; Puryear et al., 2017) that openness is a trait dimension most strongly associated with creative individuals and that it describes creative personality regardless of domain.

Chapters in this volume recognize important debates in creativity studies that have implications for understanding creative individuals and provide reviews and integration of existing research on key topics in the study of creative personality. In Chap. 2, Razaei and Kapoor start the discussion about the nature of the creative person by describing creativity as a spectrum of expression. They examine the implications of 4c's of creativity for defining the creative person and argue that each of the four levels of expression and creative achievement describes not only products, but different kinds of personal engagement and personal identity investment. They also examine other key debates about the nature of creativity in the context of the creative person, such as specificity vs. generality and light vs. dark creativity.

Rodriguez-Boerwinkle (Chap. 3) reviews scholarship on personality traits of creative individuals. The ubiquity of the Big Five model makes the study of traits synonymous with personality for many casual observers. She acknowledges the power of structural models of major personality traits and discusses traits of creative individuals both from the lens of the Big Five and the HEXACO model. But she also acknowledges that descriptions in terms of these broad traits are crude sketches only and that the study of narrower traits, such as tolerance of ambiguity, risk-taking, or curiosity, promise to add detail in the form of incremental prediction. The chapter concludes by considering big questions in how we approach describing creative individuals. Rather than portraying them abstracted from their social environment and domains, it is becoming clear that we need to study them in interaction with these contexts of creativity.

Pretz (Chap. 4) dives into the research on the creative self. She discusses both the role of general self-evaluations (evident in one's self-esteem) and creativity-specific self-evaluations (evident in global creative self-efficacy and domain-specific self-perceptions) in the study of creative people. This chapter draws attention to challenges to accurate self-perception that stem from both erroneous beliefs (e.g., equating creativity with artistic endeavors or genius) and limited personal experience with and feedback for creativity. Understanding these obstacles to accurate self-perceptions can inform both theoretical approaches to the creative self and potential educational interventions.

Lin (Chap. 5) starts with the big question of what motivates creative people. He reviews relevant research from several major theoretical traditions in motivation science, such as intrinsic vs. extrinsic motivation, goal orientation models, and self-determination theory, as well as creativity-native motivational constructs (e.g., creative self-efficacy, creative values and attitudes). This discussion echoes research on personality traits in the context of creativity—there is value on broad dimensions of motivation (e.g., intrinsic motivation), but also narrower motives studied in different creativity domains (e.g., emotion and prosocial motives in artists and scientists). Future research will be most informative when it integrates different approaches.

No description of creative individuals would be complete without understanding their thinking. Dumas and Kagan (Chap. 6) challenge the field to look beyond traditional emphasis on divergent thinking abilities. They argue that we have learned much about these abilities, but also that they could be better understood as attributes of creative potential than key cognitive attributes of highly creative individuals. If we want to understand creators, especially at professional levels, we need to learn about their thinking in real-life contexts in which they create. Dumas and Kagan integrate past research and identify five specific cognitive attributes of highly creative individuals: domain knowledge, epistemic cognition, relational reasoning, problem-finding, and evaluation ability. These are not the only creativity-relevant cognitive attributes, but they address the full process from ideas to realization, and as such can describe crucial aspects of creative individuals' thinking action. Future research can examine profiles of cognitive abilities of creators across domains. Could it be that artists are strongest on relational thinking and problem-finding, whereas creative scientists require greater domain knowledge, epistemic cognition, and ability to evaluate their own ideas?

Urbaniak and Barbot (Chap. 7) take a developmental approach to understanding creative individuals. This chapter asks how creative individuals have become creative. The authors take a two-fold approach. First, they review development of creative potential from the individual difference perspective. Recognizing importance of sociocultural influences on development, they put a particular emphasis on the effects of school in shaping individual resources for creativity. And second, they address identity development as both a creative process and a product.

Hollinger and Sithambaram (Chap. 8) review what we know about mental health and well-being of creative individuals. They note that this discussion has to pay attention to types of creative individuals across levels from mini-c to little-c, Pro-c, and finally Big-C. At lower levels, creative individuals are characterized by well-being, whereas at Pro-c levels creators might be better described by a profile of both high strengths and vulnerabilities, and at Big-C level there is a higher likelihood of mental health disorders for creators in some domains (e.g., mood disorders in artists). The authors also discuss personality traits that are related to both creativity and mental health and well-being, contributing to the discussion about whether the relationship between creativity and mental health is due to creative action itself or because of shared influences.

The final chapter has a goal of integration. It pulls the strings from all the contributing topics and asks a unifying question about what we know when we know creative people. This chapter reviews potential answers or part answers to this question based on major theoretical approaches in personality psychology and argues for future research that does not pick a single approach, but rather acknowledges their complementary nature. To achieve a comprehensive description of creative individuals, scholars will have to assess and examine in the same time attributes of different personality functions—emotion and motivation, cognition, social action, self-regulation—and also address both core and surface personality attributes (i.e., key dispositional traits and features of the self-concept).

All chapters in this volume have something in common. They conclude that the description of creative individuals needs to be reframed to refer to plural personalities, depending on creativity domain, level of analysis, and interaction between individual and their environment. A call for a new generation of research on creative individuals rooted in their sociocultural realities is loud and clear. The chapters that follow review their respective areas of scholarship to highlight what we have learned and what we still need to learn.

References

Feist, G. J. (1998). A meta-analysis of personality in scientific and artistic creativity. *Personality and Social Psychology Review, 2*(4), 290–309. https://doi.org/10.1207/s15327957pspr0204_5

Gough, H. G. (1956). *California psychological inventory*. Consulting Psychologists Press.

Gough, H. G. (1960). The adjective check list as a personality assessment research technique. *Psychological Reports, 6*, 107–122. https://doi.org/10.2466/PR0.6.1.107-122

Helson, R. (1996). In search of the creative personality. *Creativity Research Journal, 9*(4), 295–306. https://doi.org/10.1207/s15326934crj0904_1

MacKinnon, D. (1964, June 23). *The creative personality* [Invited address] Alex Osborn Creative Studies Collection. Archives & Special Collections Department, E. H. Butler Library, SUNY Buffalo State. https://digitalcommons.buffalostate.edu/cs-speakers/1

Puryear, J. S., Kettler, T., & Rinn, A. N. (2017). Relationships of personality to differential conceptions of creativity: A systematic review. *Psychology of Aesthetics, Creativity, and the Arts, 11*(1), 59–68. https://doi.org/10.1037/aca0000079

CHAPTER 2

What Is the Nature of the Creative Person?

Sarah Rezaei and Hansika Kapoor

What Is the Nature of the Creative Person?

In 1914, Thomas Edison's laboratory caught fire. All his years of work, together with his irreplaceable prototypes and numerous notes, vanished in minutes. Rather than despair, Edison famously turned to his son and said, "Go get your mother and all her friends. They'll never see a fire like this again." The next day, he began rebuilding, almost as if undeterred by the loss. Within months, Edison not only managed to recreate much of what was lost but also developed new ideas inspired by the catastrophe.

Edison's resilience highlights a central truth about creativity: it often thrives under constraints, setbacks, and unexpected challenges. We wonder—was Edison's response to adversity unique to his genius level of creativity, or can we find such adaptability in everyday contexts? What

S. Rezaei
Department of Psychology, Monk Prayogshala, Mumbai, India
e-mail: sr@monkprayogshala.in

H. Kapoor (✉)
Department of Psychology, Monk Prayogshala, Mumbai, India

Neag School of Education, University of Connecticut, Storrs, CT, USA
e-mail: hk@monkprayogshala.in

Z. Ivcevic (ed.), *Creators*, The Seven C's of Creativity,
https://doi.org/10.1007/978-3-032-09225-0_2

circumstances let Edison turn disaster into opportunity? And would others in his position have acted differently?

Creativity can show up in surprising ways. Yet, not all creative individuals think, feel, or act alike (Arenius et al., 2021; Chen et al., 2023). Some showcase their creativity through technical innovations, others through artistic breakthroughs, and still others through everyday problem-solving. Creativity may emerge during moments of crisis, but it can also develop gradually and quietly over years of persistence and refinement. This diversity in creativity raises fundamental questions: Are creative people born or made? Is creativity shaped more by internal drive or by external circumstances? And importantly, does creativity always serve a constructive purpose, or can it also be used for darker, more self-serving goals?

In this chapter, we explore these questions by examining the multifaceted nature of creativity and the people who express it. Here is a brief outline: each section describes classical theories and literature associated with the nature of the creative act and the creative person. We start by describing the levels at which creativity can be displayed, followed by revisiting debates on whether creativity is only reserved for geniuses. We then discuss the domain generality and specificity of creativity, tied in with relatively recent scholarship on the dark side of creativity. Our concluding sections focus on the challenges encountered when sustaining creative pursuits, especially in less welcoming environments, and how the conceptualization of the creative person can be expanded to creative people in different contexts.

Creativity as a Spectrum of Expression

Many often see creativity as a rare and mysterious trait. Something possessed only by a small number of artists, scientists, and inventors who make a significant contribution to history. This limited view of creativity, however, puts one at risk of ignoring the myriad ways creativity appears in everyone, from top professionals to regular problem-solvers. Being creative is not limited to ground-breaking accomplishments; it can also be found in the little, routine inventions that improve the quality, efficiency, and meaning of life.

Researchers use the scope and societal influence of creativity as one way to understand it. This is seen in the "Four C" model of creativity (Kaufman & Beghetto, 2009), which emphasizes the range of human creativity and how it manifests itself. The model describes four types of creativity: ***mini-c*** creativity, which refers to personal insights and learning moments that may not be publicly recognized but are meaningful to the individual; for example, a child discovering a new way to build with blocks. Then we have *little-c* creativity, which includes everyday problem-solving and innovation, such as a teacher developing a creative way to explain a lesson or a chef improvising with new ingredients. Third, we have *Pro-c* creativity, which represents professional-level expertise and innovation within a given field. It emerges after years of dedication, whether in music composition, scientific research, or business entrepreneurship. Last, there is *Big-C* creativity, which refers to groundbreaking achievements that transform entire disciplines, such as Einstein's theory of relativity or Picasso's development of Cubism.

By acknowledging these distinctions, we move beyond seeing creativity as a binary trait—"creative" vs "non-creative"—but recognize it as a basic human quality; a quality that manifests itself in different ways and at varying levels in people, transcending who they are and what they do.

Little-c Creativity: *Everyday Ingenuity*

For many, creativity thrives in the realm of what is known as *little-c creativity*—the small but ingenious ways we solve problems and adapt to challenges in daily life. Although these acts may not have life-altering and mind-blowing consequences for the world, they, in some way, enrich our experiences and those of the people around us.

Consider a teacher who explains fractions through storytelling in an attempt to make math more engaging for students, or a parent who invents an indoor game to entertain their children on a rainy day. Speaking of parents, another innovative example of everyday ingenuity in parenting is *Horizontal Parenting*. There is even a book on it that essentially is a how-to book on how (exhausted) parents can entertain their kids while lying down. The reel showcased a mom drawing a racing track on the dad's white T-shirt so the kids could roll cars over his back while he was lying down. These everyday innovations may not bring fame or recognition (although the reel now has about a million views), but they embody creativity in its most accessible and universal form. Importantly, *little-c creativity* isn't limited to those who see themselves as "creative." In fact, even individuals who don't consider themselves artistic or innovative engage in these acts daily, and research suggests that *little-c creativity* is closely tied to positive emotions, personal fulfillment, and problem-solving (Silvia et al., 2014). These examples tell us that the significance of a creative act does not necessarily lie in its scale or societal impact but rather in its originality and meaning.

Little-c creativity is more than just creative problem-solving; it is an extension of the individual engaging in it. A parent who invents a game to entertain their children on a rainy day expresses adaptability and resourcefulness by reflecting their capacity to transform everyday challenges into moments of joy. *Little-c* creativity is not just an incidental act, it's a reflection of the person's emotional state and personality, where research shows that traits like openness to experience and conscientiousness influence everyday creative problem-solving (Silvia et al., 2014). This highlights how deeply rooted these acts are in individual characteristics.

Despite its importance and evident presence in our lives, *little-c creativity* is sometimes misunderstood or undervalued. Researchers (Ilha Villanova & Pina e Cunha, 2020) argue that *little-c* plays a crucial role in personal growth and adaptation to life's challenges, yet this remains underexplored in academic literature. Others point out a paradox: the term *little-c creativity* is sometimes seen as overly inclusive, while other times, it seems to exclude nuanced expressions of everyday ingenuity (Helfand et al., 2016; Kaufman & Beghetto, 2009). However, its greatest strength lies in its universality and accessibility, which reminds us that creativity is not the privilege of a select few but a resource available to everyone.

Big-C Creativity*: The Creative Genius*

At the other end of the spectrum lies *Big-C Creativity,* which is often associated with revolutionary thinkers and artistic trailblazers—individuals whose contributions leave a lasting impact on history. This rare level of creative achievement is exemplified by figures like Marie Curie, whose pioneering work in physics and chemistry reshaped science, or Beethoven, whose symphonies continue to inspire many even centuries later. What sets *Big-C Creators* apart is not just their talent but their ability to think divergently, persist through challenges, and push the boundaries of their fields. Their ideas don't just introduce something new, they transform entire disciplines. But reaching this level of creativity often requires an individual to devote years to master their knowledge and skill and also show resilience in the face of failure, rejection, and societal skepticism.

Creativity at this scale is rarely the product of a single moment of inspiration. For example, while Thomas Edison is credited with inventing the (first commercially practical) light bulb, his success came after hundreds of failed experiments, collaborative insights, and countless incremental improvements. This level of genius is often a result of a cumulative effort rather than an isolated stroke of brilliance. Though *little-c* and *Big-C Creativity* may seem worlds apart, they share certain fundamental similarities. Research suggests that both forms rely on cognitive and emotional processes such as divergent thinking and adaptability (Simonton, 2012). A person designing a clever way to organize their workspace demonstrates the same underlying creative processes that an architect might use to design a groundbreaking building—the difference is in scale and recognition.

Our favorite example that typifies the relationship between *little-c* and *Big-C Creativity* is the story of the Post-it Note. The *Big-C Creativity* of Spencer Silver led to the discovery of a low-tack adhesive while working at 3M—a scientific breakthrough that, at the time, seemed to lack a clear application. Many called it a solution without a problem. Years later, his colleague at 3M, Art Fry, demonstrated *little-c creativity* by using the adhesive to bookmark pages in his church hymnal. His simple yet ingenious idea transformed Silver's invention into one of the most successful office products in history. This collaborative and incremental nature of the creative process highlights how everyday creativity can complement and amplify groundbreaking discoveries!

Commonplace vs Genius Creativity

Imagine a world where only a handful of people were considered truly creative. Whereas, the rest of us are mere spectators. But is that really how creativity works? Creativity research has long explored both extraordinary and everyday creativity, though emphasis has varied by tradition. Historiometric analyses (e.g., Simonton, 2016) have extensively examined creative genius, while cognitive and social-psychological approaches have provided rich insights into the everyday creative acts we see in education, work, and daily life (Kaufman & Beghetto, 2009; Runco, 2004), what we can call commonplace creativity. For example, a mother improvises a meal by ingeniously using leftovers or substitutes ingredients when something is missing, or an employee finds a clever shortcut to finish tasks quickly—these may not receive the same recognition or have the same impact as a scientific discovery or a world-class painting, but these acts also embody creativity in meaningful ways.

In contrast, genius creativity is found in the rare, historic breakthroughs (e.g., Beethoven's ability to compose masterpieces even after losing his hearing, or Da Vinci's mastery of painting, anatomy, and engineering). The former is often praised in the traditional view of creativity, which feeds into what we refer to as the "genius bias"—the idea that creativity is a unique gift that only a select few possess. Creativity research has been influenced by this bias, which has resulted in an excessive focus on this "genius" side of creativity with individuals such as Einstein, Picasso, and Curie, often cited as examples (Simonton, 2014, 2016; Weisberg, 2010). But why is it that we celebrate Picasso's Guernica but overlook the everyday artist sketching a beautiful mural in a café? Why is it that many often associate creativity with brilliance when innovation has, more often than not, come from persistence, trial, and error? Focusing only on genius-level creativity disregards the wide spectrum of creativity, which extends beyond the historically recognized geniuses to commonplace problem-solving and innovation.

The Full Spectrum of the Creative Person: Revisiting the Four C's

To fully understand the creative person, however, we need to look beyond this familiar polarity of everyday and genius creativity. The Four-C Model of Creativity (Kaufman & Beghetto, 2009) offers a more comprehensive lens through which to view the rich variety of creative expression. The model doesn't just classify creative outcomes; it also helps us understand the creative person behind those outcomes. Each level represents not only different scales of impact but different kinds of engagement, identity, and recognition.

At the heart of each level lies the creative person, whose creativity is shaped by experience, motivation, opportunity, and context. *Mini-c* creativity represents the earliest, most personal form of creative expression. These are novel and meaningful insights that arise during learning or discovery, often invisible to others but transformative for the individual. For instance, a child experimenting with colors to express an emotion in art class, or a student discovering a unique way to solve a maths problem; these moments may never receive public attention, but they are foundational for the individual's creative development (Beghetto & Kaufman, 2007). Research shows that *mini-c* moments are crucial for identity formation and for building the confidence to engage in future creative acts (Beghetto, 2013).

Little-c creativity involves everyday creative problem-solving and innovation, something most people engage in regularly, whether or not they identify as creative. As discussed earlier, this includes acts like finding new ways to explain a concept, creating a novel recipe, or devising an innovative workaround to a logistical challenge. These creative acts provide personal fulfillment (Karwowski & Barbot, 2016) and are often recognized within one's immediate social environment —family, friends, or colleagues—who are typically the first to witness, appreciate, or benefit from them.

Pro-c creativity emerges when individuals dedicate themselves to honing expertise in a field over time. These creative persons (whether writers, scientists, educators, designers, business leaders, or working in any other domain) may not be household names, but their work shapes communities, industries, and disciplines. This level of creativity often reflects years of deliberate practice (Ericsson et al., 1993) and is typically supported by formal education, professional training, and a network of peers. Many *Pro-c* creators may never ascend to *Big-C* status, but their contributions are no less vital to the creative landscape.

Big-C Creativity represents the rare, iconic breakthroughs that shift paradigms and leave a lasting cultural or historical impact. Achieving this level often requires not only extraordinary talent and vision but also perseverance, risk-taking, and resilience in the face of failure or rejection (Simonton, 2017).

What is crucial to understand is that these categories are not rigid. People may move between levels across different domains and over the course of their lives. For example, someone may exhibit *Pro-c* creativity in their professional work as a scientist while expressing *little-c* creativity in cooking at home, and may have once experienced *mini-c* moments as they first discovered their passion for science in school. Even those who achieve *Big-C* status often begin with countless *mini-c* and *little-c* experiences, shaped by opportunity, feedback, and cultural context. In describing creative individuals, levels of creativity refer to peak creativity, often in one specific domain, but not the only level of creativity that describes all their contributions.

Research suggests that creative self-beliefs, that is, how people perceive their own creative potential, play a critical role in whether they continue to move along this developmental trajectory (Karwowski, 2009). Moreover, social and cultural influences, including mentorship and access to resources, can shape the extent to which individuals actualize their creative potential at higher levels (Glăveanu, 2013).

By recognizing the full spectrum of the *Four Cs*, we not only challenge the myth of the "lone genius" but also affirm that creativity is a dynamic, accessible, and developmental process that unfolds differently for each person. Creativity, in this view, is not an exclusive trait of a privileged few, but a deeply human capacity that can be nurtured, expressed, and recognized in many forms.

The Myth of the "Mad Genius"

Another related, but interesting idea within the genius-centered view of creativity is the "mad genius" stereotype—the belief that extraordinary creativity is inherently linked to mental illness (Schlesinger, 2009). This stereotype has been popularized by cultural myths and historical tales that are highly romanticized. A well-known example of this is Vincent van Gogh, whose extraordinary artistic talent in painting is often discussed along with his mental health struggles, and sometimes in a manner that suggests his suffering is what made him an exceptional artist. Although some highly creative artists and innovators may struggle with mental health, there is no scientific evidence to substantiate that there is a clear causal link between creativity and mental illness (Fisher, 2015; Schlesinger, 2009; Silvia & Kaufman, 2010). Some studies have found correlations between mild psychopathological traits (such as schizotypal thinking or bipolar tendencies) and certain types of creative output, but severe mental illness is more often a hindrance to creativity than a catalyst (Abraham, 2014). In fact, psychological well-being and resilience are more favorable for sustained creative work (Silvia & Kaufman, 2010). Historical biases and selective reporting may be more to blame for the "mad genius" stereotype's enduring popularity than actual factual data (Fisher, 2015).

While the idea of the "mad genius" remains culturally pervasive, researchers have looked at more empirical ways to study creativity and creative achievement. Traditionally, historiometric methods were used to study creativity. These methods look at historical writings, biographies, and cultural factors to find patterns in creative work (Simonton, 1999). According to Simonton (2017), genius-level creativity frequently results from a broader socio-cultural effect rather than something that develops in a person independently. For example, Leonardo da Vinci's artistic and scientific achievements were vastly influenced by the intellectual atmosphere of the Renaissance and his relationships with his peers.

On the other hand, researchers who believe that creativity is a universal quality often evaluate creativity in the general population and across domains using psychometric instruments such as the Kaufman Domains of Creativity Scale (K-DOCS) (Kaufman, 2012). Further, Karwowski (2009) found that most people consider themselves creative in modest ways (*mini/little-c*) but are usually reluctant to identify themselves as *Big-C* creators. This shows that people can intuitively recognize these distinctions in their self-perceptions of creativity, which confirms that creativity is not just restricted to historically acknowledged geniuses and that there is a diverse range of creative expression that ranges from artistic pursuits to scientific problem-solving.

By combining the two viewpoints, we challenge the myth that only a select few are born with the ability to be creative. Even the most well-known creative people, according to Simonton (2012), do not have any different cognitive processes from regular people; rather, opportunity, perseverance, and acknowledgment from others all work together to shape their creativity. Furthermore, creativity is not just for those formally educated. While some research suggests that formal education can, in certain situations, unintentionally stifle creativity (Moore, 2007; Plucker et al., 2011; Simonton, 2017), it is important to note that in many domains, particularly in the sciences and other fields requiring specialized expertise, formal education and sustained training are essential stepping stones to achieving *Pro-c* and *Big*-C creativity.

Interestingly, research has shown that constraints sometimes act as catalysts for creativity. Moderate levels of constraints have been found to increase both the quantity and quality of solutions in creative tasks (Ehls et al., 2021). Particularly, financial constraints can lead to more creative outcomes while using fewer resources (Scopelliti et al., 2014). Such findings show us that ingenuity is not only accessible to those with privilege or formal training but can emerge under conditions of scarcity and constraint, too. Knowing this variety helps us to embrace creativity as a necessary component of the human experience that is accessible to everybody, and to reject the myth of the genius.

Specific and General

To become a creative genius, surely one will have to excel in one particular domain, perhaps at the expense of others. Maybe that's why Marie Curie is an anomaly—not only because she was the first woman to win a Nobel prize, but because she continues to be the *only* woman to win Nobel awards in two separate domains: physics and chemistry. This brings us to a salient debate related to the creative person: whether creativity is domain-general or domain-specific (Qian et al., 2019).

This debate gained considerable attention in creativity research during the 2000s, with several key scholars arguing both sides. One influential volume from this period, *Creativity: From Potential to Realization* (Sternberg et al., 2004), brought together a range of perspectives exploring how creativity might operate differently across domains or whether it reflects a more general cognitive ability. This work, among others, highlighted the complexity of the question and suggested that creativity may not fit neatly into either category. Ivcevic and Mayer (2006) found that when creativity is assessed across a broader range of life domains, the picture becomes more nuanced: for some individuals, creative behavior is domain-specific, while for others it is more generalized.

Proponents of the domain-general view argue that creativity relies on broad higher-order cognitive skills like problem-solving, divergent thinking, and associative reasoning that are not restricted to specific domains (e.g., Plucker & Beghetto, 2004). On the other end of the spectrum are researchers who argue that domain specificity is central to creativity theory (e.g., Baer, 2012). These opposing positions are closely tied to how creativity is measured (Qian et al., 2019; Silvia et al., 2009) and how creative training programs are designed and implemented. For instance, a creative writing course can focus on overarching and transferable skills like divergent thinking and lateral thinking (domain-general) or more nuanced skills like generating and using original prompts for storytelling (domain-specific).

If this sounds like a false dichotomy, that's because it probably is. It may be simpler to conceive of creativity as a composite of domain-general *and* domain-specific skills, which are emphasized in different proportions based on the social context (Amabile, 1983, 1996; Plucker & Beghetto, 2004). Sternberg (2009) suggests that generality-specificity is moderated by having a creative attitude toward life, the extent of one's area-specific knowledge, and environments that allow creativity to flourish. For instance, for creative persons who seek new experiences and enjoy coming up with ideas, across various domains like furniture rearrangement and word puzzles, and in different contexts like work and home, creativity is more likely to be *domain-general.*

In an attempt to bridge this divide, Baer and Kaufman (2005) proposed the amusement park theoretical model of creativity. Using the analogy of an amusement park, they illustrated how generality and specificity in creativity can be connected through four stages: initial requirements (which are very broad and general, like the motivation to be creative), general thematic areas (such as verbal skills), domains (such as journalism), and micro-domains (which are very specific, like an Indian metal music journalist). Highlighting a more developmental trajectory, the specialization-differentiation hypothesis (Barbot & Tinio, 2015) suggests that although there may be domain-general skills that form the base for creativity, specialization in certain domains will be associated with differentiated skills specific to that domain. Suppose you were painting a wall; domain-general skills would form your primer, specialization in certain domains would comprise your wallpaper, and a high level of differentiated expertise in a domain would be the framed artwork on your wall (see also Baer, 2015).

What can we conclude about whether creativity is domain-general or domain-specific? The jury is still out, but we infer that the creative person uses a combination of skills, at differing levels of expertise and knowledge, based on the environments in which they operate, with limited transferability of highly specialized skills across domains. In sum, we wouldn't have expected Einstein to paint the ceiling of the Sistine Chapel, would we?[1]

Bright and Dark

Till now, we have discussed the different levels at which one can be creative, the nature of the creative person ranging from a layperson to a genius, and the general and/or specific nature of creativity itself. You may assume that all of the above creative pursuits were toward useful goals, or at least not harmful ones—notice how we did not mention crime (for example) as a specific domain of creativity. This assumption would largely be correct—a vast majority of creativity scholarship has focused on how creativity is a positive force, meant for doing good and promoting good. This perspective also aligns with the contemporary idea of transformational creativity, which prescriptively suggests that the wisest use of creativity is for the common good; in other words, for society at large to benefit from creative endeavors (Sternberg, 2021).

However, steadily over the past few decades, the dark side of creativity has emerged (e.g., Cropley et al., 2010; Kapoor, 2023; McLaren, 1993), where the creative person, depending on certain dispositional and situational factors, could use the creative process for self interest or outright

[1] That said, some very interesting work on polymathy and creativity suggests similar processes underlying artistic and scientific creativity (Root-Bernstein & Root-Bernstein, 2004).

harm (Kapoor & Khan, 2020; Runco, 2010). The creative person can use the creative process to move toward bright, useful, helpful, positive, and benevolent ends, but can also use the same process to move toward dark, harmful, unhelpful, negative, and malevolent ends. The progression of research on the dark side of creativity has been rapid (Zhou et al., 2023) and in diverse areas, such as social exclusion (Baas et al., 2019), revenge ideation (Perchtold-Stefan et al., 2021), and forming anti-immigration online communities (de Saint Laurent et al., 2020).

The AMORAL model of dark creativity (Kapoor & Kaufman, 2022a) proposes how antecedents like power can prompt someone with certain individual traits like moral flexibility to engage in dark creativity, within a socio-cultural milieu. The realization of the act can vary based on several factors, such as the nature of the target or even the role that moral chance plays in the creative behavior. The creative act itself leads to immediate aftereffects and a long-term legacy, tying into the Big-C genius levels of creativity, but from a darker lens. For instance, suppose a person feels wronged by a romantic partner for cheating on them. Their response, varied by valence and creativity, can include any of the following options:

- Creating pornographic deepfakes of the ex-partner and sending those to their employer anonymously (evil and creative)
- Starting an original rumor about themselves and their sexual prowess with their ex-partner to gain future relationships (self-interested and creative)
- Obsessively following the ex-partner's social media posts to find some resolution for themselves (ambiguous and not creative)
- Sending a note to the ex-partner with a few examples of the cute quirks they have in relationships, wishing them the best for the future (noble and creative)

Therefore, morality, or lack thereof, plays an important role in the manifestations of dark creativity (Kapoor & Kaufman, 2023). In this context, research has examined moral foundations (Kapoor et al., 2024), moral emotions (Fu & Zhang, 2022), moral reasoning (Zhao et al., 2022), and moral disengagement (Shi et al., 2023). In general, findings support the notion that the creative person is adept at justifying their moral transgressions, especially when those moral missteps benefit themselves. Yet, not every creative individual will resort to using their original ideation in evil ways; consider this to be a moral handbrake or dispositional speedbump.

One's belief system will or will not permit them to use deception for nefarious purposes (Kapoor & Khan, 2017), implying that there are several permutations and combinations of individual and contextual factors that interact to produce bright or dark creative behavior. For instance, if individuals are unable to effectively take the perspective of others, they may behave in morally questionable ways if they are creative as well (Hui et al., 2021). Extending this, higher dark personality traits, like psychopathy, sadism, and Machiavellianism, amplify malevolent creativity associated with lower morality (Kapoor & Kaufman, 2022b).

Challenges and Barriers

Do all circumstances support creativity? The answer is a resounding no. Although creativity may be inherent in humans, it is often constrained by external and internal barriers (e.g., Sternberg & Kaufman, 2010). Cultural and institutional norms frequently stifle creativity by enforcing rigid structures and discouraging deviation from established conventions. Research suggests that "tight" cultures, or those with strict social norms, tend to limit creative engagement and suppress unconventional thinking (Chiu & Kwan, 2010; Chua et al., 2014). For instance, collectivist societies may value harmony over the disruptive nature of innovation, whereas individualist cultures may encourage bold ideas but neglect the collaborative aspects of creativity. Similarly, rigid institutional structures—whether in education or the workplace—often prioritize measurable outcomes over exploratory thinking, which may often curb the free flow of ideas. Additionally, cultural values influence the acceptance of creative ideas, often leading to environments where originality is undervalued (Kwan et al., 2018; Leung & Koh, 2018).

On an individual level, psychological factors like fear of failure and perfectionism can suppress creativity (Goulet-Pelletier et al., 2022; Lin et al., 2023). Fear of criticism or rejection discourages people from sharing unconventional ideas, while perfectionism can lead to paralysis, where nothing seems "good enough" to present. Additionally, sustained creative efforts are emotionally taxing, often resulting in burnout, particularly in environments that fail to reward innovation. Research in organizational settings has shown that workers who do not receive enough recognition for their creativity are less likely to continue producing creative work over the long term (Baer et al., 2003; Mdhlalose, 2024). Moreover, when workplace motivation is low, burnout inhibits creative engagement and overall has a detrimental effect on innovative work behavior (Drafahl, 2020). Despite these barriers, creating safe spaces where failure is accepted as part of the learning process can encourage risk-taking (Klinger & Bajestani, 2018). Fostering psychological safety and embracing diversity gives individuals the freedom to take creative risks and engage in innovative thinking without fear of negative repercussions (Rosario, 2024).

Creativity cannot be fully understood by looking only at the individual; it must also be seen as a product of interaction with the environment. The creative person does not exist in isolation; their ability to generate original and meaningful ideas is shaped by how well their environment supports or stifles their creative potential. The creative person, therefore, is not simply someone with innate talent or personality traits, but someone whose creativity is dynamic—continuously shaped by opportunity, support, challenge, and context. Some individuals may flourish when encouraged to take risks or explore unconventional ideas, while others may have their creative capacities diminished in rigid or judgmental environments. Ultimately, understanding the creative person means recognizing this ongoing interaction between individual agency and external conditions. The potential for creative growth lies not only in personal qualities like resilience or curiosity but also in the capacity to adapt to, seek out, and even reshape environments that either enable or constrain creative expression.

A Creative Person or Creative People?

This chapter has now reached its crescendo—it seems that the nature of the creative person is characterized by differing levels, domains, task-appropriate general and specific skills, and a motive to create, to name a few. Yet, is the creative person an individual entity, or can we conceive of people, economies, countries, and collectives as being creative as well? If we were to rely on Rhodes' (1961) four Ps conception, the creative person is just that—a person. However, as the nature of the creative actor has evolved (Glăveanu, 2013), so has the composition of the actor. Today, with the democratization of creative expression (Karwowski et al., 2022; Schröter, 2019), a creative person doesn't even have to be a human being! This brings us back to the chapter's title: What then is the nature of the creative person?

As a first step, we propose expanding the construct of the creative person to a broader conceptualization of creative people. We argue that it may be beneficial to reframe the singular nature of a creative person to multiple natures of creative people, which takes into account their contexts, cultures, and circumstances (see also Glăveanu, 2013). This departure from a single kind of creative person also allows us to consider their malleability, as creative persons interact with their environment in a social constructivist manner (Vlasceanu et al., 2018). For instance, consider the story of Sam—they are creative, love playing around with new ideas, are an engineer by profession, and like to knit over the weekends. Sam decides to start a new venture of creating customized science-inspired knit kits (picture a 3D knitted microscope) after receiving encouraging feedback from family and friends. The next step is to formalize the venture, apply for a business license, and start selling. But,

1. In one scenario, Sam lives in a nation where bureaucratic red tape and a rigid regulatory environment prevent them from starting up a business.
2. In another, it is much easier to incorporate and sustain a local enterprise, and Sam can hire a small team, diversify into selling finished products, and learn how to crochet.

Did Sam's nature as a creative person change? Maybe not. But their ability to continuously engage in creative activities through multiple avenues did. Scholarship has reviewed how social and cultural institutions shape creative expression and the differences between what is valued and devalued cross-culturally concerning the originality and usefulness of new ideas (Barth & Stadtmann, 2024; Shao et al., 2019). In addition to the value that a culture or cohort places on creativity, multiple other contextual and social factors can influence the trajectory of a creative person. Therefore, the nature of creative people is ever-changing and dynamic, operating within certain boundaries wherein some kinds of creativity are allowed to emerge as compared to others.

Consider the emergence of creativity by generative artificial intelligence (AI). Although spirited debates ensue regarding the true nature of AI creativity (see also Cropley, 2023; Medieros et al., 2024), these systems are capable of producing divergent responses. However, we would hesitate to include AI in a discussion on the nature of a creative person; after all, it is a machine. Yet, human-AI co-creativity (Haase & Pokutta, 2024) may be fundamentally altering the nature of creative people, with creative individuals leveraging the computational prowess of AI systems to generate more original, more novel, more effective, and more surprising output than ever before.

In tracing the nature of the creative person, we come to realize that creativity is not a singular, fixed trait, but a living, changing, and context-dependent quality. From the everyday acts of ingenuity to the historical achievements that redefine disciplines, creativity represents a wide range of expressions. It is seen in the persistence of ordinary people and in the brilliance of well-known geniuses. Whether or not it develops across domains or within specialization, whether it's used for altruistic or more nefarious purposes, it's always characterized by the interaction of individual and socio-cultural factors.

Importantly, creativity does not exist in a vacuum. It is enabled or stifled by settings, defined by social expectation, and tinted by moral decisions. By broadening our perspective from an individual creative "person" to that of creative "people" within various contexts, we more accurately represent the actual complexity of creativity. Acknowledging this diversity in creativity is not merely an academic exercise; rather, it is a step toward nuturing creativity in all its forms, across individuals, communities, and cultures. By welcoming the many faces of creativity, we create opportunities for innovation, collaboration, and expansion in an increasingly interconnected world.

References

Abraham, A. (2014). Is there an inverted-U relationship between creativity and psychopathology? *Frontiers in Psychology, 5*. https://doi.org/10.3389/fpsyg.2014.00750

Amabile, T. M. (1983). The social psychology of creativity: A componential conceptualization. *Journal of Personality and Social Psychology, 45*(2), 357–376. https://doi.org/10.1037/0022-3514.45.2.357

Amabile, T. M. (1996). *Creativity in context: Update to "The social psychology of creativity"*. Westview Press.

Arenius, P., Chuah, S.-H., Coate, B., & Hoffmann, R. (2021). The economic psychology of creating and venturing: A comparative behavioural portrait of artists and entrepreneurs. *Small Business Economics, 57*(2), 721–737. https://doi.org/10.1007/s11187-020-00420-1

Baas, M., Roskes, M., Koch, S., Cheng, Y., & De Dreu, C. K. W. (2019). Why social threat motivates malevolent creativity. *Personality and Social Psychology Bulletin, 45*(11), 1590–1602. https://doi.org/10.1177/0146167219838551

Baer, J. (2012). Domain specificity and the limits of creativity theory. *The Journal of Creative Behavior, 46*(1), 16–29. https://doi.org/10.1002/jocb.002

Baer, J. (2015). The importance of domain-specific expertise in creativity. *Roeper Review, 37*(3), 165–178. https://doi.org/10.1080/02783193.2015.1047480

Baer, J., & Kaufman, J. C. (2005). Bridging generality and specificity: The amusement park theoretical (APT) model of creativity. *Roeper Review, 27*(3), 158–163. https://doi.org/10.1080/02783190509554310

Baer, M., Oldham, G., & Cummings, A. (2003). Rewarding creativity: When does it really matter? *The Leadership Quarterly, 14*, 569–586. https://doi.org/10.1016/S1048-9843(03)00052-3

Barbot, B., & Tinio, P. P. L. (2015). Where is the "g" in creativity? A specialization-differentiation hypothesis. *Frontiers in Human Neuroscience, 8*. https://doi.org/10.3389/fnhum.2014.01041

Barth, P., & Stadtmann, G. (2024). Creativity in the West and the East: A meta-analysis of cross-cultural differences. *Creativity Research Journal*, 1–47. https://doi.org/10.1080/10400419.2024.2369442

Beghetto, R. A. (2013). *Killing ideas softly? The promise and perils of creativity in the classroom.* (pp. xiii, 163). IAP Information Age Publishing.

Beghetto, R. A., & Kaufman, J. C. (2007). Toward a broader conception of creativity: A case for "mini-c" creativity. *Psychology of Aesthetics, Creativity, and the Arts, 1*(2), 73–79. https://doi.org/10.1037/1931-3896.1.2.73

Chen, Q., Christensen, A. P., Kenett, Y. N., Ren, Z., Condon, D. M., Bilder, R. M., Qiu, J., & Beaty, R. E. (2023). Mapping the creative personality: A psychometric network analysis of highly creative artists and scientists. *Creativity Research Journal, 35*(3), 455–470. https://doi.org/10.1080/10400419.2023.2184558

Chiu, C., & Kwan, L. Y.-Y. (2010). Culture and creativity: A process model. *Management and Organization Review, 6*(3), 447–461. https://doi.org/10.1111/j.1740-8784.2010.00194.x

Chua, R., Roth, Y., & Lemoine, J. F. (2014). The impact of culture on creativity. *Administrative Science Quarterly, 60*, 189–227. https://doi.org/10.1177/0001839214563595

Cropley, D. H. (2023). Is artificial intelligence more creative than humans?: ChatGPT and the Divergent Association Task. *Learning Letters, 2*, 13. https://doi.org/10.59453/ll.v2.13

Cropley, D. H., Cropley, A. J., Kaufman, J., & Runco, M. (2010). *The dark side of creativity.* https://books.google.co.uk/books?hl=en&lr=&id=KTQ_NFcyB7wC&oi=fnd&pg=PR1&dq=crime+and+creativity+&ots=B7GjCgtNDl&sig=h3_uai_9PNAGIZcYE9simg-p340

de Saint Laurent, C., Glaveanu, V., & Chaudet, C. (2020). Malevolent creativity and social media: Creating anti-immigration communities on Twitter. *Creativity*

Research Journal, 32(1), 66–80. https://doi.org/10.1080/10400419.2020.1712164

Drafahl, B. (2020). The influences burnout and lack of empowerment have on creativity in nursing faculty. *Nursing Education Perspectives, 41*(1), 33–36. https://doi.org/10.1097/01.NEP.0000000000000545

Ehls, D., Lakhani, K. R., & Lane, J. (2021). A field experiment on the role of constraints in creative problem-solving. *Academy of Management Proceedings, 2021*(1), 12221. https://doi.org/10.5465/AMBPP.2021.12221abstract

Ericsson, K. A., Krampe, R. T., & Tesch-Römer, C. (1993). The role of deliberate practice in the acquisition of expert performance. *Psychological Review, 100*(3), 363–406. https://doi.org/10.1037/0033-295x.100.3.363

Fisher, J. E. (2015). Challenges in determining whether creativity and mental illness are associated. *Frontiers in Psychology, 6*. https://doi.org/10.3389/fpsyg.2015.00163

Fu, H., & Zhang, Z. (2022). The inhibitory effect of moral emotions on malevolent creativity: Exploring the mediation role of emotional valence and prosocial behavior. *Frontiers in Psychology, 13*, 945848. https://doi.org/10.3389/FPSYG.2022.945848/BIBTEX

Glăveanu, V. P. (2013). Rewriting the language of creativity: The Five A's framework. *Review of General Psychology, 17*(1), 69–81. https://doi.org/10.1037/a0029528

Goulet-Pelletier, J.-C., Gaudreau, P., & Cousineau, D. (2022). Is perfectionism a killer of creative thinking? A test of the model of excellencism and perfectionism. *British Journal of Psychology (London, England: 1953), 113*(1), 176–207. https://doi.org/10.1111/bjop.12530

Haase, J., & Pokutta, S. (2024). *Human-AI co-creativity: Exploring synergies across levels of creative collaboration* (No. arXiv:2411.12527). arXiv. https://doi.org/10.48550/arXiv.2411.12527

Helfand, M., Kaufman, J. C., & Beghetto, R. A. (2016). The four-c model of creativity: Culture and context. In V. P. Glăveanu (Ed.), *The Palgrave handbook of creativity and culture research* (pp. 15–36). Palgrave Macmillan UK. https://doi.org/10.1057/978-1-137-46344-9_2

Hui, P. P., Chiu, W. C. K., Pang, E., Coombes, J., & Tse, D. Y. P. (2021). Seeing through and breaking through: The role of perspective taking in the relationship between creativity and moral reasoning. *Journal of Business Ethics, 0123456789*. https://doi.org/10.1007/s10551-021-04876-3

Ilha Villanova, A. L., & Pina e Cunha, M. (2020). Everyday creativity: A systematic literature review. *The Journal of Creative Behavior, 55*(3), 673–695. https://doi.org/10.1002/jocb.481

Ivcevic, Z., & Mayer, J. D. (2006). Creative types and personality. *Imagination, Cognition and Personality, 26*(1), 65–86. https://doi.org/10.2190/0615-6262-g582-853u

Kapoor, H. (2023). Shining a light on dark creativity. *Creativity Research Journal*, 1–6. https://doi.org/10.1080/10400419.2023.2224689
Kapoor, H., & Kaufman, J. C. (2022a). The evil within: The AMORAL model of dark creativity. *Theory and Psychology, Sec, 8.* https://doi.org/10.1177/09593543221074326
Kapoor, H., & Kaufman, J. C. (2022b). Unbound: the relationship among creativity, moral foundations, and dark personality. *The Journal of Creative Behavior, 56*(2), 182–193. https://doi.org/10.1002/jocb.523
Kapoor, H., & Kaufman, J. C. (2023). *Creativity and morality*. Elsevier. https://doi.org/10.1016/C2020-0-02810-0
Kapoor, H., & Khan, A. (2017). Deceptively yours: Valence-based creativity and deception. *Thinking Skills and Creativity, 23*, 199–206. https://doi.org/10.1016/J.TSC.2016.12.006
Kapoor, H., & Khan, A. (2020). Creators and presses: The person–situation interaction in negative creativity. *The Journal of Creative Behavior, 54*(1), 75–89. https://doi.org/10.1002/jocb.346
Kapoor, H., Mahadeshwar, H., Rezaei, S., Reiter-Palmon, R., & Kaufman, J. C. (2024). The ties that bind: Low morals, high deception, and dark creativity. *Creativity Research Journal*, 1–20. https://doi.org/10.1080/10400419.2024.2306447
Karwowski, M. (2009). I'm creative, but am I creative? Similarities and differences between self-evaluated small and big-C creativity in Poland. *The International Journal of Creativity & Problem Solving, 19*(2), 7–26.
Karwowski, M., & Barbot, B. (2016). Creative self-beliefs: Their nature, development, and correlates. In J. C. Kaufman & J. Baer (Eds.), *Creativity and reason in cognitive development* (pp. 302–326). Cambridge University Press.
Karwowski, M., Zielińska, A., & Jankowska, D. M. (2022). Democratizing creativity by enhancing imagery and agency: A review and meta-analysis. *Review of Research in Education, 46*(1), 229–263. https://doi.org/10.3102/0091732X221084337
Kaufman, J. (2012). Counting the muses: Development of the Kaufman domains of creativity scale (K-DOCS). *Psychology of Aesthetics, Creativity, and the Arts, 6*, 298. https://doi.org/10.1037/a0029751
Kaufman, J. C., & Beghetto, R. A. (2009). Beyond big and little: The four c model of creativity. *Review of General Psychology, 13*(1), 1–12. https://doi.org/10.1037/a0013688
Klinger, R., & Bajestani, M. F. (2018). Psychological safety. In *Management*. Oxford University Press. https://doi.org/10.1093/obo/9780199846740-0154
Kwan, L. Y.-Y., Leung, A. K.-Y., & Liou, S. (2018). Culture, creativity, and innovation. *Journal of Cross-Cultural Psychology, 49*(2), 165–170. https://doi.org/10.1177/0022022117753306

Leung, A. K. Y., & Koh, B. (2018). The role of culture in creative cognition. In *Handbook of culture and creativity: Basic processes and applied innovations* (pp. 3–32). https://doi.org/10.1093/oso/9780190455675.003.0001

Lin, S.-Y., Hirst, G., Wu, C.-H., Lee, C., Wu, W., & Chang, C.-C. (2023). When anything less than perfect isn't good enough: How parental and supervisor perfectionistic expectations determine fear of failure and employee creativity. *Journal of Business Research, 154*, 113341. https://doi.org/10.1016/j.jbusres.2022.113341

McLaren, R. B. (1993). The dark side of creativity. *Creativity Research Journal, 6*(1–2), 137–144. https://doi.org/10.1080/10400419309534472

Mdhlalose, D. (2024). An examination of employee rewards and work environment on employee creativity and innovation. *SEISENSE. Journal of Management, 7*(1), 21–34. https://doi.org/10.33215/rewfe541

Medieros, K., Cropley, D. H., Marrone, R. L., & Reiter-Palmon, R. (2024). *Human-AI co-creativity: Does ChatGPT make us more creative?* https://doi.org/10.31234/osf.io/98hdk

Moore, E. (2007). How to Kill creativity — ten easy steps. *Industry and Higher Education, 21*(5), 337–343. https://doi.org/10.5367/000000007782311876

Perchtold-Stefan, C. M., Fink, A., Rominger, C., & Papousek, I. (2021). Failure to reappraise: Malevolent creativity is linked to revenge ideation and impaired reappraisal inventiveness in the face of stressful, anger-eliciting events. *Anxiety, Stress, & Coping, 0*(0), 1–13. https://doi.org/10.1080/10615806.2021.1918682

Plucker, J., Waitman, G., & Hartley, K. (2011). Education and creativity. *In Elsevier eBooks* (pp. 435–440). https://doi.org/10.1016/b978-0-12-375038-9.00086-8

Plucker, J. A., & Beghetto, R. A. (2004). Why creativity is domain general, why it looks domain specific, and why the distinction does not matter. In R. J. Sternberg, E. L. Grigorenko, & J. L. Singer (Eds.), *Creativity: From potential to realization* (pp. 153–167). American Psychological Association. https://doi.org/10.1037/10692-009

Qian, M., Plucker, J. A., & Yang, X. (2019). Is creativity domain specific or domain general? Evidence from multilevel explanatory item response theory models. *Thinking Skills and Creativity, 33*, 100571. https://doi.org/10.1016/j.tsc.2019.100571

Rhodes, M. (1961). An analysis of creativity. *The Phi Delta Kappan, 42*(7), 305–310.

Root-Bernstein, R., & Root-Bernstein, M. (2004). Artistic scientists and scientific artists: The link between polymathy and creativity. In *Creativity: From potential to realization* (pp. 127–151). American Psychological Association. https://doi.org/10.1037/10692-008

Rosario, S. (2024). Fostering creativity in the workplace: Unlocking the power of diversity through psychological safety. In *Creativity and change leadership grad-*

uate student master's projects. https://digitalcommons.buffalostate.edu/creativeprojects/382

Runco, M. A. (2004). Creativity. *Annual Review of Psychology, 55*, 657–687. https://doi.org/10.1146/annurev.psych.55.090902.141502

Runco, M. A. (2010). Creativity has no dark side. *The Dark Side of Creativity, 9780521191*, 15–32. https://doi.org/10.1017/CBO9780511761225.002

Schlesinger, J. (2009). Creative mythconceptions: A closer look at the evidence for the "mad genius" hypothesis. *Psychology of Aesthetics, Creativity, and the Arts, 3*(2), 62–72. https://doi.org/10.1037/A0013975

Schröter, J. (2019). Artificial intelligence and the democratization of art. In *The democratization of artificial intelligence. Net politics in the era of learning algorithms* (pp. 297–311). https://doi.org/10.25969/MEDIAREP/13546

Scopelliti, I., Cillo, P., Busacca, B., & Mazursky, D. (2014). How do financial constraints affect creativity? *Journal of Product Innovation Management, 31*(5), 880–893. https://doi.org/10.1111/jpim.12129

Shao, Y., Zhang, C., Zhou, J., Gu, T., & Yuan, Y. (2019). How does culture shape creativity? A mini-review. *Frontiers in Psychology, 10*, 1219. https://doi.org/10.3389/fpsyg.2019.01219

Shi, Z., Zhou, Z., Tian, L., Zhu, Y., Liu, C., & Xu, L. (2023). What causes malevolent creative people to engage in malevolent behaviors? Mediating role of moral disengagement and moderating effects of conscience. *Thinking Skills and Creativity, 49*(May), 101329. https://doi.org/10.1016/j.tsc.2023.101329

Silvia, P. J., & Kaufman, J. C. (2010). Creativity and mental illness. In J. C. Kaufman & R. J. Sternberg (Eds.), *The Cambridge handbook of creativity* (1st ed., pp. 381–394). Cambridge University Press. https://doi.org/10.1017/CBO9780511763205.024

Silvia, P. J., Kaufman, J. C., & Pretz, J. E. (2009). Is creativity domain-specific? Latent class models of creative accomplishments and creative self-descriptions. *Psychology of Aesthetics, Creativity, and the Arts, 3*(3), 139–148. https://doi.org/10.1037/a0014940

Silvia, P. J., Beaty, R. E., Nusbaum, E. C., Eddington, K. M., Levin-Aspenson, H., & Kwapil, T. R. (2014). Everyday creativity in daily life: An experience-sampling study of "little c" creativity. *Psychology of Aesthetics, Creativity, and the Arts, 8*(2), 183–188. https://doi.org/10.1037/a0035722

Simonton, D. K. (1999). *Origins of genius: Darwinian perspectives on creativity.* Oxford University Press USA.

Simonton, D. K. (2012). Creative genius as a personality phenomenon: Definitions, methods, findings, and issues. *Social and Personality Psychology Compass, 6*(9), 691–706. https://doi.org/10.1111/j.1751-9004.2012.00455.x

Simonton, D. K. (2014). Chapter 2—Creative genius in literature, music, and the visual arts. In V. A. Ginsburgh & D. Throsby (Eds.), *Handbook of the Economics of Art and Culture* (Vol. 2, pp. 15–48). Elsevier. https://doi.org/10.1016/B978-0-444-53776-8.00002-7

Simonton, D. K. (2016). Genius and creativity. In H. S. Friedman (Ed.), *Encyclopedia of mental health* (2nd ed., pp. 269–276). Academic Press. https://doi.org/10.1016/B978-0-12-397045-9.00204-4

Simonton, D. K. (2017). Big-c versus little-c creativity: Definitions, implications, and inherent educational contradictions. In R. A. Beghetto & B. Sriraman (Eds.), *Creative contradictions in education: Cross disciplinary paradoxes and perspectives* (pp. 3–19). Springer International Publishing. https://doi.org/10.1007/978-3-319-21924-0_1

Sternberg, R. J. (2009). Domain-generality versus domain-specificity of creativity. In P. Meusburger, J. Funke, & E. Wunder (Eds.), *Milieus of Creativity* (Vol. 2, pp. 25–38). Springer. https://doi.org/10.1007/978-1-4020-9877-2_3

Sternberg, R. J. (2021). Transformational creativity: The link between creativity, wisdom, and the solution of global problems. *Philosophies, 6*(3), 75. https://doi.org/10.3390/philosophies6030075

Sternberg, R. J., & Kaufman, J. C. (2010). Constraints on creativity: Obvious and not so obvious. In J. C. Kaufman & R. J. Sternberg (Eds.), *The Cambridge handbook of creativity* (pp. 467–482). Cambridge University Press. https://doi.org/10.1017/CBO9780511763205.029

Sternberg, R. J., Grigorenko, E. L., & Singer, J. L. (Eds.). (2004). *Creativity: From potential to realization* (1st ed.). American Psychological Association.

Vlasceanu, M., Enz, K., & Coman, A. (2018). Cognition in a social context: A social-interactionist approach to emergent phenomena. *Current Directions in Psychological Science, 27*(5), 369–377. https://doi.org/10.1177/0963721418769898

Weisberg, R. (2010). The study of creativity: From genius to cognitive science. *International Journal of Cultural Policy, 16*(3), 235–253. https://doi.org/10.1080/10286630903111639

Zhao, J., Xu, X., & Pang, W. (2022). When do creative people engage in malevolent behaviors? The moderating role of moral reasoning. *Personality and Individual Differences, 186*(PB), 111386. https://doi.org/10.1016/j.paid.2021.111386

Zhou, J., Zhao, B., & Zhang, M. (2023). Hotspots and research trends of the 'dark side of creativity' in the last decade. *Heliyon, 9*(10), e20392. https://doi.org/10.1016/j.heliyon.2023.e20392

CHAPTER 3

Personality Traits of the Creative Person

Rebekah Rodriguez-Boerwinkle

> Many reasons exist for an individual's failure to develop ideas or to translate ideas into action, but one of the more important influences appears to be the individual's unique personality. (p. 34; Mumford & Gustafson, 1988)

Creativity has long been recognized as an important human capacity: an enabler great scientific genius, artistic achievements, and everyday problem-solving alike. But what makes some people more creative than others? Beyond cognitive abilities, environment, and motivation, research into personality traits is central to understanding human creativity, and especially so when our goal is to describe who are the creators.

At its core, creativity involves the production of ideas or products that are both novel and appropriate (Runco & Jaeger, 2012). While novelty captures the originality of an idea, appropriateness—sometimes framed as usefulness, effectiveness, or even beauty (for a discussion of this criterion's nuances across levels of creative activity, see Ivcevic & Kaufman, 2024)—grounds creativity in its social or functional value. Creative individuals can be found in every domain of human activity, from music to science to social engineering. Understanding the attributes of creative individuals

R. Rodriguez-Boerwinkle (✉)
Yale Center for Emotional Intelligence, Yale University, New Haven, CT, USA
e-mail: rebekah.rodriguez-boerwinkle@yale.edu

Z. Ivcevic (ed.), *Creators*, The Seven C's of Creativity,
https://doi.org/10.1007/978-3-032-09225-0_3

has been a central question in psychology since at least the 1950s (Guilford, 1987) and personality has always been part of the story (e.g., MacKinnon, 1962; MacKinnon, 1975), though its prominence has varied over time.

In the early and mid-twentieth century, personality-based approaches dominated creativity research. In several early studies of the creative personality, Frank Barron examined traits related to dispositional originality in US Air Force personnel (Barron, 1955, 1957). Shortly after, MacKinnon conducted intensive personality investigations of highly creative people, including artists, writers, architects, or mathematicians (MacKinnon, 1962). Together, these studies demonstrated that creative people tend to systematically differ from their less creative peers, not just in terms of cognitive ability but in personality traits that shape how they perceive and interact with the world.

This early work formed the foundation for the strong focus in individual differences that creativity research has today bolstered by the development of comprehensive trait models such as the Big Five (Costa & McCrae, 1992; Goldberg, 2013) and the HEXACO frameworks (Ashton & Lee, 2007). These models have provided structure to a previously disconnected literature and allowed researchers to compare findings across studies (such as Feist, 1998). Yet even as we recognize the contributions to creative personality of broad personality dimensions—especially Openness to Experience—there is growing awareness that narrower traits, subdimensions, and dynamic patterns of personality also play a vital role.

In this chapter, I explore some of the personality traits that describe creative individuals by surveying both well-established and emerging research in the field. I begin with a focus on the broad trait dimensions of the Big Five traits, particularly Openness to Experience, and then expand the discussion to include the HEXACO model. Then, I turn to narrower traits that extend beyond these dimensions, such as playfulness, nonconformity, and tolerance for ambiguity. These traits have additional predictive power in understanding the creative personality but aren't always robustly captured by broader models. Finally, I end this chapter by discussing the future of personality and creativity research, including some of the field's most promising directions. Throughout, I draw on empirical findings and theoretical models to highlight how personality traits shape not only creative potential, but also creative expression, and achievement across domains.

Broad Structural Models of Personality and the Creative Person

The Big Five and Creativity

The Big Five model of personality traits—comprising Openness to Experience, Conscientiousness, Extraversion, Agreeableness, and Neuroticism—has become a dominant framework in psychological science (Rauthmann & Kuper, 2025). It offers a parsimonious yet flexible way to capture broad dimensions of individual differences between people. When it comes to creativity, one trait consistently stands out: Openness to Experience.

Openness to Experience

Openness to Experience (hereafter called Openness) is defined by imagination, intellectual curiosity, aesthetic sensitivity, and a preference for novelty and complexity (Connelly et al., 2014; McCrae, 1996; McCrae & Costa, 1997). It is, by far, the most robust personality correlate of creativity across multiple levels of analysis: from divergent thinking tasks and self-reported creative behavior to real-world artistic and scientific achievement (Feist, 1998; Puryear et al., 2017; Silvia et al., 2009b). People high in Openness tend to seek out new experiences, engage deeply with ideas, and appreciate ambiguity and nuance—all characteristics that support the exploration, flexibility, and originality required for creative thinking, activity, and achievement. Highly open individuals are more likely to engage in activities that foster creativity, such as visiting museums (Meyer et al., 2023; Schwaba et al., 2018), becoming absorbed while reading narrative fiction (Kuijpers et al., 2019), or picking up more creative hobbies (Wolfradt & Pretz, 2001).

Yet, despite its predictive power, Openness is not a unitary construct. Broad trait labels can conceal important differences in how individuals process the world and express creativity.

After the initial establishment of the Big Five, recent research has clarified that Openness to Experience is best understood as comprising two separable but correlated aspects: Intellect and Openness proper (DeYoung et al., 2005; DeYoung et al., 2007; Nusbaum & Silvia, 2011). Intellect describes a propensity for cognitive engagement with abstract, semantic information during activities such as logical reasoning and analytical problem-solving, whereas Openness reflects sensory and affective engagement with aesthetics, fantasy, and perceptual novelty. This distinction has meaningful implications for creative achievement: Intellect tends to predict scientific, technical, and problem-solving creativity, while Openness proper is more closely tied to artistic and expressive forms of creativity (Kaufman et al., 2016). The two aspects are correlated but not exactly interchangeable; individuals high in Intellect may be analytically brilliant but aesthetically indifferent, while those high in Openness may be highly imaginative but less drawn to logical abstraction. Measurement tools like the Big Five Aspect Scales (BFAS; DeYoung et al., 2007) now allow researchers to differentiate these components more precisely, enabling a more nuanced understanding of how personality traits support creative achievement in distinct domains.

Other Big Five Traits

Other Big Five traits show weaker or more complex associations with creativity-related outcomes. Conscientiousness, for example, tends to have a mixed relationship with creativity. On the one hand, individuals who are high in Conscientiousness, particularly those with strong perseverance and goal orientation, may be better equipped to sustain creative work overtime (Reiter-Palmon et al., 2009). On the other hand, high Conscientiousness in the form of dependability, which emphasizes self-discipline and organization, is negatively related to creative achievement (Reiter-Palmon et al., 2009). The effect may depend on domain: one might be likely to meet a conscientious scientist who has persevered through years of experimental failures, while meeting a highly structured poet, who struggles with creative block as a consequence of their personality, might be less likely.

Extraversion, too, has been linked to creative achievement in a variety of settings, particularly in expressive or social domains (McKay et al., 2017). Traits such as assertiveness, energy, and sociability can facilitate creative performance in fields that involve collaboration, self-promotion, or public presentation (Martindale & Dailey, 1996; Silvia et al., 2009a). For example, in team settings, members who are confident, sociable, and talkative be more likely to share their ideas, contributing to cross-fertilization (Baer et al., 2008; Pérez-Luño et al., 2024). In the workplace, this may manifest as employee "voice," when a person creatively challenges a coworker in a constructive and promoting manner rather than with the intent to criticize—a behavior that has been associated with Extraversion via meta-analysis (Zare & Flinchbaugh, 2019). Adding to this, extraverts tend to be more positive about their own creative abilities (also called creative self-concept; for a multidomain measure, see Kaufman, 2012), facilitating creative contributions in social spheres.

However, Extraversion's role in creative personality may have more to do with confidence and assertiveness than with gregariousness (Feist, 1999). While this distinction is theoretically compelling and aligns with some domain-specific predictions, it is not strongly supported by more current meta-analytic evidence (e.g., Puryear et al., 2017). One possibility is that existing research disproportionately emphasizes domains where Extraversion is less relevant (such as solitary artistic work or scientific research) leaving questions about its role in socially embedded or social performance-based forms of creativity underexplored. As such, the relationship between Extraversion and creativity may be more context-dependent than general, but further work is needed to test this claim across a broader range of creative settings and domains.

The role of Neuroticism is perhaps the most contested. In trait theory, Neuroticism reflects emotional instability, anxiety, and sensitivity to negative emotions (Widiger, 2009). On the surface, it might seem antithetical to creativity, because the negative rumination and worry associated with this trait can take up the cognitive resources necessary for flexible and divergent thinking (Davis & Nolen-Hoeksema, 2000). And indeed, omnibus analysis finds a negative correlation with creativity operationalized across a variety of tasks and measures (e.g., divergent thinking, ideation and production-based measures, self and externally reported measures; Puryear et al., 2017). Yet a more nuanced picture is emerging: in certain domains, especially those involving emotional expression, like advertising and visual art, some level of Neuroticism may be beneficial (Gelade, 1997; Haller & Courvoisier, 2010; Ivcevic et al., 2022).

A study by Leung et al. (2013) that produced a state of worry by asking participants to recall a worrisome past event before a creativity task resulted in higher creativity scores for participants high in Neuroticism. Highly neurotic participants in this study were also more likely to select worrisome over happy experiences prior to engagement in creative tasks, suggesting that the relationship between creativity and emotional worry is that of a tool for instrumental emotion regulation—that is, an emotion elicited by an individual to achieve a specific goal, rather than for hedonic purposes. Indeed, Perkins and colleagues (2015) theoretically proposed that Neuroticism drives greater creativity through the prevalence of self-generated thought (SGT). Their reasoning is that SGT, which encompasses experiences such as mind wandering and daydreaming, advances creative thought by allowing individuals to explore ideas without the constraints of the immediate environment. Without commenting on domain, they hold that people high in Neuroticism engage in SGT more frequently and with more persistence, facilitating creativity, but leading to greater unhappiness. This supposition, however, was sharply opposed in subsequent commentary by Pickering and colleagues, who contrasted the idea with evidence that this trait is negatively or not-at-all related to divergent thinking, insight problem-solving, everyday creative behavior, creative achievement in the sciences, self-assessed creativity, as well as science as a vocation and creativity in science (Pickering et al., 2016). This presentation of evidence across several domains suggests that while neurotic individuals may indeed experience more SGT, the content of these thoughts might not be high enough quality to have functional benefits to creativity.

Finally, Agreeableness shows the least consistent relationship with creativity. Agreeable individuals are cooperative, polite, and motivated to maintain social harmony (Graziano & Tobin, 2009). Traditionally, these traits may be at odds with the independence and norm-challenging nature of creative people, because they may lead to conformity and less idea-sharing when ideas seem to break with expectations, push boundaries, or defy group consensus (Hunter & Cushenbery, 2015). Meta-analysis of personality traits in artists and scientists finds no relationship with Agreeableness (e.g., Feist, 1998), although hostility, a component of low agreeableness, is higher among both professions. More recently, another meta-analysis by Puryear et al. (2017) reported a significant, but small, positive relationship between agreeableness and fluency on divergent thinking tasks. Similarly, another component of low Agreeableness, nonconformity, has also been linked to creativity (Hoffmann et al., 2021). However, the picture is not entirely empty: recent research preliminary supports a curvilinear relationship between Agreeableness in group settings. In team settings, higher Agreeableness among team members may facilitate collaboration (Curşeu et al., 2019) and crystallize abstract ideas (Chang et al., 2014) when present in moderate amounts. However, after peaking at a certain level, the slope of this relationship decreases (Chang et al., 2014; Curşeu et al., 2019). As with other Big Five traits, the impact of Agreeableness on the success and behaviors of creative people may depend less on absolute levels and more on fit between trait and domain.

As the research behind each of these traits solidifies, the Big Five offers a valuable starting point for understanding the personality of creative individuals, because it provides a broad, empirically validated framework that captures the sweeping, higher-level dimensions of personality trait differences among people. Openness to Experience remains the most consistently predictive trait and research into the role of Openness in creativity has moved into the narrower aspects of the trait, but the role of the other four have been examined more coarsely and have been shown to depend on domain, context, and the specific creative processes under examination.

The HEXACO Model

One prominent branch of personality research on creativity makes use of the HEXACO model (Ashton & Lee, 2007). The HEXACO retains much of the structure of the Big Five but builds on it by introducing a sixth factor, Honesty-Humility, which distinguishes features like sincerity, fairness, modesty, and lack of entitlement from the broader Big Five conception of Agreeableness. In the HEXACO, Agreeableness itself is reframed to emphasize tolerance, forgiveness, and flexibility, while Emotionality replaces Neuroticism but with a slightly different balance of anxiety, sentimentality, dependence than in the Big Five. Together, the refinements resulting in the Honesty-Humility, Agreeableness, and Emotionality facets of the HEXACO more explicitly capture social and moral (or "altruistic"; Ashton & Lee, 2007) dispositions than the Big Five does. Openness to Experience, Extraversion, and Conscientiousness, meanwhile, remain largely comparable between the two models, and thus won't be addressed in this section (Ashton & Lee, 2007).

At first glance, Honesty-Humility may seem unrelated to creativity, but it is increasingly recognized as important in collaborative and prosocial creative contexts, where creative work is directed toward benefiting others or improving collective well-being (references needed). Notably, the literature suggests that Honesty-Humility shows a negative relationship with traditional measures of creativity. For example, Silvia et al. (2011) examined the HEXACO traits in relation to several self-report measures of creative achievement and activity, and found that, under this model, Agreeableness had no relationship with creativity, but that Honesty-Humility was negatively related to scores on several self-reported measures of creative behavior and achievement. People high in Honesty Humility, it seems, lack the assertiveness relevant for some forms of creativity.

Recent work has extended this finding into the moral domain. Higher Honesty-Humility scores negatively predict both engaging in malevolent creativity (Fu & Zhang, 2024) and justifying unethical creative acts

(Ścigała et al., 2020). At the team level, however, Honesty-Humility can have a more complex role. While research on the creative contributions of individual team members remains limited, some evidence suggests that leader humility can promote greater team creativity by encouraging creative self-efficacy in the members (Wang et al., 2020). Future research on the Honesty-Humility facet of the HEXACO may examine forms of prosocial creativity, such as community arts, socially engaged design, social entrepreneurship, or other forms of interdisciplinary collaboration.

The HEXACO model also reconceptualizes Emotionality, distinguishing it from Neuroticism in meaningful ways. HEXACO Emotionality includes characteristics like emotional attachment, sentimentality, and anxiety about harm—traits that may resonate with forms of creativity rooted in emotional expression or empathetic insight. This raises intriguing parallels with the concept of emotional creativity (Averill, 1999), which refers to the ability to prepare and express novel, effective, and authentic emotional responses. Yet, despite this conceptual overlap, empirical work remains sparse. These constructs have not been examined in concert and, more generally, no clear relationship between HEXACO Emotionality and creativity has been established thus far (Silvia et al., 2011).

Moving beyond the Big Five and HEXACO models, researchers are increasingly turning to finer-grained traits to enrich understanding of creative personality. We turn to these topics in the next section.

Narrower Traits of Creative Individuals

While expansive structural models like the Big Five and HEXACO offer a solid foundation for understanding the creative personality in broad strokes, their dimensions can obscure important distinctions. Course-grained traits are valuable because they summarize large clusters of how we think, feel, and act in ways that are stable and replicable across many contexts. But they might also lack specificity. As Paunonen and Ashton (2001) demonstrated, narrower traits often have incremental validity, predicting specific behaviors above and beyond what is explained by broad factors alone. In other words, knowing someone is high in Openness to Experience is informative, but knowing that they have a *high degree of intellectual curiosity* or a strong *tolerance for ambiguity* may tell us more about their likelihood of engaging in creative behavior (e.g., Christensen et al., 2019). This point has been reinforced repeatedly in the personality literature (Ashton, 1998; Ashton et al., 2014): while broad traits provide conceptual parsimony, narrow traits offer predictive precision. The study of creative people, with their many interests and behaviors, is a prime example of a domain where the added resolution of narrow traits can illuminate how personality expresses itself in specific and highly varied contexts.

This section discusses several (but not all) narrow traits that are relevant to understanding creative individuals but not always well captured by broad structural models. Traits like tolerance for ambiguity, risk-taking, playfulness, curiosity, autonomy, and preference for complexity are more specific than the Big Five or HEXACO domains and closely tied to creativity. These narrower traits can be seen as related or adjacent to broader personality factors, particularly Openness to Experience and, to a lesser extent, Extraversion and Conscientiousness. However, each only partially maps onto existing models.

Tolerance for Ambiguity

For example, tolerance for ambiguity—comfort with uncertainty, contradiction, or lack of closure—includes elements of Openness and Neuroticism (Jach & Smillie, 2019) and has been highlighted as a key trait in creative individuals by creativity scholars (Stoycheva, 2010; Zenasni et al., 2008) but has also been at the center of notable debate. Empirically, this trait's relationship to creativity has been criticized for having an insufficient nomological pedigree (Merrotsy, 2013). In his critique, Merrotsy pointed out that wherever tolerance for ambiguity appears in empirical research on the creative personality, its origins are not well documented. He describes that some authors have referenced the work of Csikszentmihalyi, Vernon, or Guilford, but these citations have proved to be entirely incorrect or vaguely and indirectly derived, without a network of well-designed measures or empirical findings rigorously supporting it.

A recent theoretical examination of tolerance of ambiguity, however, contributes a more detailed account of the construct's conceptual and methodological development, and suggests that it may be key to capturing a creative individual's ability to suspend judgment (endure) and remain receptive to multiple possibilities (engage) (Stoycheva, 2025). Stoycheva (2025) suggests that people with a high tolerance for ambiguity tend to show greater intrinsic motivation for explorative and experimental aspects of the creative process as well as having greater ability to cope with the discomfort of uncertain, contradictory, or complex experiences recurrent during creative action. A study by Zenasni et al. (2008) supports this: in a study of adolescents, greater tolerance for ambiguity was correlated with several measures of creativity, such as a divergent thinking response uniqueness, and self-report measurements of creative attitudes and behavior, with divergent thinking task fluency, in particular, showing the most consistent results. Tolerance for ambiguity has also been positively linked to creative thinking ability in college-level architecture (Mahmoud et al., 2020) and engineering students (Balgiu, 2014).

Risk-Taking and Sensation-Seeking

Risk-taking and sensation-seeking may reflect facets of Extraversion or low Conscientiousness, yet in creative contexts they function as motivation, enabling people to depart from convention and pursue ideas with uncertain outcomes (Dewett, 2007). However, not all forms of risk-taking may support creativity; this association is most prominent in social risk-taking, as opposed to financial, health, or other domains (Tyagi et al., 2017). Building on this distinction, recent work highlights the importance of intellectual risk-taking, which describes the willingness to share tentative ideas, ask novel questions, and embrace the possibility of failure in the pursuit of knowledge. Beghetto, Karwowski, and Reiter-Palmon (2021) describe intellectual risk-taking as a moderating factor between creative confidence and actual creative behavior: even people who believe in their creative potential may hold back from acting on their ideas if they don't want to risk appearing wrong or inept.

Playfulness

Playfulness, another promising trait, is most commonly studied in children and is likely underestimated in terms of its unique predictive power in creativity research (Proyer, 2017). Playfulness at the trait level reflects a tendency toward engaging in activities that employ mental flexibility and divergent ideation for fun and enjoyment. Measures of playfulness have been shown to correlate with self-reported creativity as well as with fluency and originality in idea generation (Bateson & Nettle, 2014)—suggesting that this trait is not merely recreational, but important to the creative person. Relatedly, literature on pretend play behavior in children shows numerous links to creativity (for an in-depth discussion, see Russ, 2016), however trait-level playfulness, especially in adults, is continuing to solidify.

Playfulness may also have a role in problem-finding, an often overlooked but essential ability of creative individuals. In the classic study by

Csikszentmihalyi and Getzels (1971), playfulness distinguished more and less creative artists: artists who explored and "played" with objects before starting their still-life compositions produced works judged as more creative, suggesting that playful interaction with materials allows for the discovery of novel problems and possibilities. By speculatively extending this to adult trait playfulness, we might see how playful people approach tasks differently (e.g., experimenting more with ideas, more successfully reframing challenges, and frequently testing alternatives). Playfulness, then, becomes a descriptor for creative individuals by demonstrating their increased cognitive and motivational space for identifying more interesting, complex, or personally worthwhile problems.

Curiosity

Other traits, such as curiosity, fall in the domain of Openness but likely have incremental prediction power. Curiosity reflects an active desire to explore, ask questions, and seek new knowledge. Research has shown reasonably consistent links between trait curiosity and self-reported creative self-concepts and behaviors (Karwowski, 2012; Ren et al., 2026; Schutte & Malouff, 2020). One theory is that curiosity acts as a motivational element that ties novel or challenging situations to personal growth (Kashdan et al., 2004). However, much of the experimental work focuses on curiosity as a state or momentary process (e.g., curiosity triggered by surprising information) rather than as a stable personality disposition (e.g., Evans & Jirout, 2023; Gross et al., 2020; Ma & Wei, 2023). As a result, there is still a lack of strong behavioral evidence that trait curiosity, as opposed to situationally evoked curiosity, reliably predicts creative behavior and achievement.

Preference for Complexity

Preference for complexity, another narrow trait first formulated by Frank Barron (e.g., Barron, 1953; Barron & Welsh, 1952), captures an aesthetic or cognitive enjoyment of intricacy and layered, multifaceted ideas, which may distinguish creative individuals not only by how they think, but *what kinds* of stimuli and tasks they gravitate toward. This construct has been most heavily studied in relation to art and aesthetic experience where individuals who have high art expertise demonstrate a greater preference for complexity, tending to favor abstract, ambiguous, and richly detailed works of art over simple, highly structured, or immediately accessible pieces (Millis, 2001; Silvia, 2006). In the realm of domain-general creativity, higher preference for complexity has been shown to contribute to elaboration in divergent thinking tasks (Kharkhurin & Yagolkovskiy, 2019), as well as the ability to overcome rigid thought during drawing tasks (Kharkhurin & Charkhabi, 2021), making it a good candidate for further research into the creative person.

Autonomy

Finally, autonomy, a trait historically associated with creativity in both the arts and sciences (Crutchfield, 1962; Barron & Harrington, 1981), often appears within Big Five models as low Agreeableness or high Openness, but it speaks more directly to a willingness to pursue independent directions of thought and action (Barrick & Mount, 1993). Importantly, autonomy in this sense is not well captured by a single Big Five dimension. While it overlaps with Openness in how it values originality and novel ideas, and with low Agreeableness in a reduced concern for maintaining social harmony, autonomy as a trait reflects a broader disposition toward self-governance and independent, internal regulation of one's behavior (Ryan & Deci, 2024). This is conceptually distinct from situational autonomy, widely studied in organizational contexts as the degree of choice or freedom afforded to an employee, which consistently predicts higher creative performance (Orth & Volmer, 2017; Shalley & Gilson, 2004; Sia & Appu, 2015). By analogy, a dispositional tendency toward autonomy may similarly promote creativity by fostering intrinsic motivation, independent decision-making, and resistance to external pressures that allow nonconformity to flourish. Yet within personality research, autonomy has been used with varying meanings: as a situational affordance, a motivational state, and a trait-like disposition. The future of autonomy as a construct in the study of creativity would therefore benefit from greater conceptual precision among future studies.

The Future of Personality Traits and Creativity Research

Collectively, the traits discussed in this chapter highlight a broader issue: creative people are not described by any one trait, but by a collection of dispositions that interact dynamically with different phases of the creative process and different circumstances. As research on personality and creativity develops, the field is moving beyond static trait models toward more dynamic, contextualized, and fine-grained understandings of the creative individual. This section, therefore, offers a glance at a few promising directions for the future of the field.

Functional Approaches to Traits of the Creative Person

One promising direction involves asking a more precise question: what kinds of traits are essential for understanding the creative person? A functional approach focuses on the role a trait plays in enabling creativity, whether it's as a source of motivation, a cognitive resource, a social skill, or a self-regulation capacity. For instance, traits like playfulness and sensation-seeking may intrinsically motivate exploration and novelty-seeking, while tolerance for ambiguity may play a role in a person's affect throughout the creative process.

Although some models attempt to map traits onto various functional processes that influence creative thought and behavior (e.g., cognitive, social, motivational-affective, clinical; Feist, 2010; or energy development, knowledge guidance, executive management, and action implementation; Mayer, 2005), few studies have systematically examined how specific traits contribute to these different aspects of the person. Such models aim to capture the multiple capacities, resources, and orientations that together define an individual's creative potential, rather than reducing the creative person to a single set of traits. Understanding which traits align with what functional domains can clarify why people differ on overall level of creativity, as well as the ways they approach, sustain, and express it. This requires measurement strategies that capture enduring tendencies relevant to each domain: for example, the motivational drive to explore novel ideas, the social skill to build collaborative relationships, or the cognitive flexibility to reframe problems. A functional perspective can thus provide a richer, multidimensional account of the creative person, linking personality to the diverse roles and strengths that creativity can take across individuals.

Integrative Models of Traits and the Role of Context

Another useful idea emphasizes integrative models that account not only for traits but also for how they interact with contextual and task-related factors. Person × Context (Abraham, 2022; Shalley et al., 2015) models argue that the predictive power of traits like Openness or Extraversion depends on the environmental conditions under which creativity is expressed. To give an example, a highly open but introverted scientist might enjoy brainstorming unconventional research questions in the privacy of her office but choose safer, more conventional ideas when sharing them in a large departmental meeting, wary of potential social judgment. Expanding this idea further, Person × Task × Situation (Tromp & Sternberg, 2022) models suggest that traits may be more or less predictive of creativity depending on the demands of the task as well as the broader features of the situation. Going back to our introverted, but highly open scientist, her willingness to propose bold, risky research ideas may depend on the composition of the audience: whether she is talking with close collaborators in the department who value exploratory thinking or presenting in front of a department head or dean who favors more incremental work.

These interactions demonstrate the importance of viewing traits as capacities whose effects are shaped by environmental affordances (*How much freedom is there to express unconventional dining ideas?*), social norms (*What kinds of ideas are seen as acceptable or credible in this setting?*), and domain-specific demands (*Is the goal to generate novel possibilities or to present polished, feasible solutions?*). Moving forward, creativity research would benefit from frameworks that can accommodate these complex, multilevel interactions. These types of examples also highlight the importance of examining how personality interacts with the settings or demands of real-world professional experiences and everyday life. When we think about who is creative, we must also consider where and when.

Traits Across Creative Domains

Following another conceptual approach, the recognition that there is no single "creative personality" but rather distinct trait profiles that support creativity in different domains has deep roots in the history of personality and creativity research, and contemporary research on the creative person should build on these ideas using more recent statistical and modeling advancements. This idea can be seen in the work of the Institute of Personality Assessment and Research (IPAR) at Berkeley, beginning in the 1950s and extending through the 1970s and beyond. Ravenna Helson's award address to APA Division 10, *In Search of the Creative Personality* (published in manuscript form; Helson, 1996), synthesized decades of IPAR findings and longitudinal studies to demonstrate that artistic, scientific, and everyday creativity are supported by overlapping yet distinct constellations of traits. Artistic creativity, for example, is often externalized and norm questioning, associated with aesthetic sensitivity, emotional intensity, and nonconformity, while scientific creativity tends to be more internalizing and norm following, relying more heavily on intellectual curiosity, cognitive control, and a tolerance for complexity (Feist, 1998; Helson, 1996). Everyday creativity, in contrast, reflected traits like flexibility, social insight, and practicality, all of which enable adaptive problem-solving in daily life. Helson's longitudinal work further emphasized the dynamic developmental nature of these profiles over time, showing both continuity and change in how personality predicts creative achievement across the lifespan (Helson & Pals, 2000; Helson et al., 1995).

Research by Ivcevic and Mayer (2006) showed that creative profiles can be identified based on patterns of behavior, which can be then linked to personality traits. Similarly, Silvia et al. (2009a) identified latent classes relating to "uncreative" people, people with creative achievements in visual arts, and people with creative interests in performing arts, all three of which differed according to their Big Five traits. Recent psychometric advancements on creative behavior scales such as the Biographical Inventory of Creative Behaviors (BICB; Silvia et al., 2021), Creative Behavior Inventory (CBI; Rodriguez et al., 2023), and Kaufman Domains of Creativity Scales (K-DOCS; McKay et al., 2017) provide researchers with reliable tools for pursuing research that connects creative traits to behavior. Identifying and validating these trait constellations across domains represents an important step toward building a more differentiated and ecologically valid science of creative personality.

Paradoxical Trait Configurations

A final conceptual approach focuses on configurations of traits within individuals, particularly the presence of seemingly contradictory qualities. This idea traces back to Frank Barron's early observations of creative individuals at IPAR. Barron famously described creative personalities as "occasionally crazier and yet adamantly saner than the average person" (Barron, 1963, p. 224), suggesting that the hallmark of creativity may lie not in singular traits, but in unusual *combinations* of traits.

This theme continues in later work by Csikszentmihalyi (1996), whose interviews with Big C creators also revealed complex, even seemingly paradoxical, patterns, such as individuals exhibiting at once rebelliousness and responsibility, emotional sensitivity and rational detachment, or impulsivity paired with self-discipline. Eminent creative individuals were described as playful yet disciplined, introverted and extraverted, humble but proud—able to flexibly draw on opposing qualities depending on the demands of the task or context, as opposed to consistently demonstrating any one (or set of) creative trait(s). Such findings resonate with the idea that creativity is not merely the product of one or a set of facilitating traits, but an emergent property of dynamic tensions between traits that manifest differently to help the individual adapt to the open-ended needs of creative tasks.

More recently, Ivcevic et al. (2022) have extended this work by identifying psychological profiles of professional artists and non-artists based on both vulnerabilities and psychological resources. Their study found that artists were more likely to exhibit profiles that combined the types of paradoxes described by Barron and Csikszentmihalyi; in some people, moderately high psychological resources (such as hope and self-acceptance) were clustered with elevated psychological vulnerabilities (such as anxiety or self-doubt), yet these same individuals also reported more creative behavior. This work brings to mind the possibility that creativity may flourish not despite inner tensions, but *through* them, supported by complex configurations of traits that may seem maladaptive in isolation but productive in interaction.

The unifying feature of all the approaches touched on in this section is that a deeper understanding of creativity requires tools that are well suited to capture complexity: how do the traits of creative people combine, coexist, and interact over time and in different scenarios? Continuing this tradition of domain-sensitive and profile-based research will benefit from modern statistical and modeling tools, such as latent profile analysis, network modeling, and machine-learning approaches, to capture all the layers of creative personalities in ways that earlier methodological approaches could only hint at. By bringing contemporary methods to bear on the classic insights of earlier work, researchers can move past one-size-fits-all views of the creative person and instead trace the unique constellations of traits that give rise to creativity in its many forms, whether in the lab, the studio, or the everyday rhythms of life.

Conclusion

The study of the creative personality has come a long way from its start in mid-twentieth century. Contemporary structural models of personality traits, particularly the Big Five and HEXACO, offer reliable, replicable insights into how broad trait dimensions describe creative individuals. Yet as this chapter has shown, a fuller understanding of the creative personality (or personalities) requires looking beneath and beyond these broad dimensions to consider narrower traits, functional divisions, and contextual dynamics. Creative personality is not defined by a single trait, nor does it operate in isolation. It reflects the interaction of dispositions, environments, and tasks, and it is shaped by the domain in which the creative person works. Future work will benefit from a continued shift toward more integrative models: ones that recognize the specificity of traits, the complexity of functional approaches, and the need to move beyond one-size-fits-all personality profiles. As the science of personality grows increasingly dynamic and contextual, so too will our understanding of what it means to possess a creative personality.

References

Abraham, A. (2022). Creativity or creativities? Why context matters. *Design Studies, 78*, 101060. https://doi.org/10.1016/j.destud.2021.101060

Ashton, M. C. (1998). Personality and job performance: The importance of narrow traits. *Journal of Organizational Behavior, 19*(3), 289–303. https://doi.org/10.1002/(SICI)1099-1379(199805)19:3<289::AID-JOB841>3.0.CO;2-C

Ashton, M. C., & Lee, K. (2007). Empirical, theoretical, and practical advantages of the HEXACO model of personality structure. *Personality and Social Psychology Review, 11*(2), 150–166. https://doi.org/10.1177/1088868306294907

Ashton, M. C., Paunonen, S. V., & Lee, K. (2014). On the validity of narrow and broad personality traits: A response to Salgado, Moscoso, and Berges (2013). *Personality and Individual Differences, 56*, 24–28. https://doi.org/10.1016/j.paid.2013.08.019

Averill, J. R. (1999). Individual differences in emotional creativity: Structure and correlates. *Journal of Personality, 67*(2), 331–371. https://doi.org/10.1111/1467-6494.00058

Baer, M., Oldham, G. R., Jacobsohn, G. C., & Hollingshead, A. B. (2008). The personality composition of teams and creativity: The moderating role of team creative confidence. *The Journal of Creative Behavior, 42*(4), 255–282. https://doi.org/10.1002/j.2162-6057.2008.tb01299.x

Balgiu, B. A. (2014). Ambiguity tolerance in productional creativity. Logos, Universality, Mentality, Education, *Novelty. Section Social Sciences, 3*(1), 29–40

Barrick, M. R., & Mount, M. K. (1993). Autonomy as a moderator of the relationships between the Big Five personality dimensions and job performance. *Journal of Applied Psychology, 78*(1), 111–118. https://doi.org/10.1037/0021-9010.78.1.111

Barron, F. (1953). Complexity-simplicity as a personality dimension. *The Journal of Abnormal and Social Psychology, 48*(2), 163–172. https://doi.org/10.1037/h0054907

Barron, F. (1955). The disposition toward originality. *The Journal of Abnormal and Social Psychology, 51*(3), 478–485. https://doi.org/10.1037/h0048073

Barron, F. (1957). Originality in relation to personality and intellect 1. *Journal of Personality, 25*(6), 730–742. https://doi.org/10.1111/j.1467-6494.1957.tb01561.x

Barron, F. (1963). *Creativity and psychological health* (pp. x, 292). D. Van Nostrand.

Barron, F., & Harrington, D. M. (1981). Creativity, intelligence, and personality. *Annual Review of Psychology, 32*, 439–476. https://doi.org/10.1146/annurev.ps.32.020181.002255

Barron, F., & Welsh, G. S. (1952). Artistic perception as a possible factor in personality style: Its measurement by a figure preference test. *The Journal of Psychology, 33*(2), 199–203. https://doi.org/10.1080/00223980.1952.9712830

Bateson, P., & Nettle, D. (2014). Playfulness, ideas, and creativity: A survey. *Creativity Research Journal, 26*(2), 219–222. https://doi.org/10.1080/10400419.2014.901091

Beghetto, R. A., Karwowski, M., & Reiter-Palmon, R. (2021). Intellectual risk taking: A moderating link between creative confidence and creative behavior? *Psychology of Aesthetics, Creativity, and the Arts, 15*(4), 637–644. https://doi.org/10.1037/aca0000323

Chang, C. C., Wang, J. H., Liang, C. T., & Liang, C. (2014). Curvilinear effects of openness and agreeableness on the imaginative capability of student designers. *Thinking Skills and Creativity, 14*, 68–75. https://doi.org/10.1016/j.tsc.2014.09.001

Christensen, A. P., Cotter, K. N., & Silvia, P. J. (2019). Reopening openness to experience: A network analysis of four openness to experience inventories. *Journal of Personality Assessment, 101*(6), 574–588. https://doi.org/10.1080/00223891.2018.1467428

Connelly, B. S., Ones, D. S., & Chernyshenko, O. S. (2014). Introducing the special section on openness to experience: Review of openness taxonomies, measurement, and nomological net. *Journal of Personality Assessment, 96*(1), 1–16. https://doi.org/10.1080/00223891.2013.830620

Costa, P. T., & McCrae, R. R. (1992). Normal personality assessment in clinical practice: The NEO Personality Inventory. *Psychological Assessment, 4*(1), 5–13. https://doi.org/10.1037/1040-3590.4.1.5

Crutchfield, R. S. (1962). Conformity and creative thinking. In H. E. Gruber, G. Terrell, & M. Wertheimer (Eds.), *Contemporary approaches to creative thinking: A symposium held at the University of Colorado* (pp. 120–140). Atherton Press. https://doi.org/10.1037/13117-004

Csikszentmihalyi, M. (1996). *Creativity: Flow and the psychology of discovery and invention*. Harper Collins Publishers.

Csikszentmihalyi, M., & Getzels, J. W. (1971). Discovery-oriented behavior and the originality of creative products: A study with artists. *Journal of Personality and Social Psychology, 19*(1), 47–52. https://doi.org/10.1037/h0031106

Curşeu, P. L., Ilies, R., Vîrgă, D., Maricuţoiu, L., & Sava, F. A. (2019). Personality characteristics that are valued in teams: Not always "more is better"? *International Journal of Psychology, 54*(5), 638–649. https://doi.org/10.1002/ijop.12511

Davis, R. N., & Nolen-Hoeksema, S. (2000). Cognitive inflexibility among ruminators and nonruminators. *Cognitive Therapy and Research, 24*(6), 699–711. https://doi.org/10.1023/A:1005591412406

Dewett, T. (2007). Linking intrinsic motivation, risk taking, and employee creativity in an R&D environment. *R&D Management, 37*(3), 197–208. https://doi.org/10.1111/j.1467-9310.2007.00469.x

DeYoung, C. G., Peterson, J. B., & Higgins, D. M. (2005). Sources of openness/intellect: Cognitive and neuropsychological correlates of the fifth factor of personality. *Journal of Personality, 73*(4), 825–858. https://doi.org/10.1111/j.1467-6494.2005.00330.x

De Young, C. G., Quilty, L. C., & Peterson, J. B. (2007). Between facets and domains: 10 aspects of the Big Five. *Journal of Personality and Social Psychology, 93*(5), 880–896. https://doi.org/10.1037/0022-3514.93.5.880

Evans, N. S., & Jirout, J. J. (2023). Investigating the relation between curiosity and creativity. *Journal of Creativity, 33*(1), 100038. https://doi.org/10.1016/j.yjoc.2022.100038

Feist, G. J. (1998). A meta-analysis of personality in scientific and artistic creativity. *Personality and Social Psychology Review, 2*(4), 290–309. https://doi.org/10.1207/s15327957pspr0204_5

Feist, G. J. (1999). Autonomy and independence. *Encyclopedia of creativity, 1*, 157–163.

Fu, H., & Zhang, Z. (2024). The relationship between Honesty-Humility and malevolent creativity: Sequential mediation models with prosocial moral emotional traits and prosocial tendencies. *Current Psychology, 43*(8), 7424–7436. https://doi.org/10.1007/s12144-023-04941-2

Gelade, G. A. (1997). Creativity in conflict: The personality of the commercial creative. *The Journal of Genetic Psychology, 158*(1), 67–78. https://doi.org/10.1080/00221329709596653

Goldberg, L. R. (2013). An alternative "description of personality": The Big-Five factor structure. In *Personality and personality disorders* (pp. 34–47). Routledge.

Graziano, W. G., & Tobin, R. M. (2009). Agreeableness. In M. R. Leary & R. H. Hoyle (Eds.), *Handbook of individual differences in social behavior* (pp. 46–61). The Guilford Press.

Gross, M. E., Zedelius, C. M., & Schooler, J. W. (2020). Cultivating an understanding of curiosity as a seed for creativity. *Current Opinion in Behavioral Sciences, Curiosity (Explore vs Exploit), 35*, 77–82. https://doi.org/10.1016/j.cobeha.2020.07.015

Guilford, J. P. (1987). Creativity research: Past, present and future. In *Frontiers of creativity research: Beyond the basics* (pp. 33–65). Buffalo, NY: Bearly.

Haller, C. S., & Courvoisier, D. S. (2010). Personality and thinking style in different creative domains. *Psychology of Aesthetics, Creativity, and the Arts, 4*(3), 149–160. https://doi.org/10.1037/a0017084

Helson, R., & Pals, J. L. (2000). Creative potential, creative achievement, and personal growth. *Journal of Personality, 68*(1), 1–27. https://doi.org/10.1111/1467-6494.00089

Helson, R., Roberts, B., & Agronick, G. (1995). Enduringness and change in creative personality and the prediction of occupational creativity. *Journal of personality and social psychology, 69*(6), 1173–1183. https://doi.org/10.1037/0022-3514.69.6.1173

Helson, R. (1996). In search of the creative personality. *Creativity Research Journal, 9*(4), 295–306. https://doi.org/10.1207/s15326934crj0904_1

Hoffmann, J., Ivcevic, Z., & Feist, G. (2021). Personality, emotions, and creativity. In J. C. Kaufman and R. J. Sternberg (Eds.), *Creativity: An introduction* (pp. 152–175). Cambridge University Press.

Hunter, S. T., & Cushenbery, L. (2015). Is being a jerk necessary for originality? Examining the role of disagreeableness in the sharing and utilization of original ideas. *Journal of Business and Psychology, 30*(4), 621–639. https://doi.org/10.1007/s10869-014-9386-1

Ivcevic, Z., & Kaufman, J. C. (2024). Inside the box: Considering the role of appropriateness for creativity. In *Psychology of aesthetics, creativity, and the arts*. Advance online publication. https://doi.org/10.1037/aca0000703

Ivcevic, Z., & Mayer, J. D. (2006). Creative types and personality. *Imagination, Cognition and Personality, 26*(1), 65–86. https://doi.org/10.2190/0615-6262-G582-853U

Ivcevic, Z., Grossman, E., & Ranjan, A. (2022). Patterns of psychological vulnerabilities and resources in artists and nonartists. *Psychology of Aesthetics, Creativity, and the Arts, 16*(1), 3–15. https://doi.org/10.1037/aca0000309

Jach, H. K., & Smillie, L. D. (2019). To fear or fly to the unknown: Tolerance for ambiguity and Big Five personality traits. *Journal of Research in Personality, 79*, 67–78. https://doi.org/10.1016/j.jrp.2019.02.003

Karwowski, M. (2012). Did curiosity kill the cat? Relationship between trait curiosity, creative self-efficacy and creative personal identity. *Europe's Journal of Psychology, 8*(4), 547–558. https://doi.org/10.5964/ejop.v8i4.513

Kashdan, T. B., Rose, P., & Fincham, F. D. (2004). Curiosity and exploration: Facilitating positive subjective experiences and personal growth opportunities. *Journal of Personality Assessment, 82*(3), 291–305. https://doi.org/10.1207/s15327752jpa8203_05

Kaufman, J. C. (2012). Counting the muses: development of the Kaufman domains of creativity scale (K-DOCS). *Psychology of Aesthetics, Creativity, and the Arts, 6*(4), 298–308. https://doi.org/10.1037/a0029751

Kaufman, S. B., Quilty, L. C., Grazioplene, R. G., Hirsh, J. B., Gray, J. R., Peterson, J. B., & DeYoung, C. G. (2016). Openness to experience and intellect differentially predict creative achievement in the arts and sciences. *Journal of Personality, 84*(2), 248–258. https://doi.org/10.1111/jopy.12156

Kharkhurin, A. V., & Charkhabi, M. (2021). Preference for complexity and asymmetry contributes to an ability to overcome structured imagination: Implications for Creative Perception Paradigm. *Symmetry, 13*(2), 343. https://doi.org/10.3390/sym13020343

Kharkhurin, A. V., & Yagolkovskiy, S. R. (2019). Preference for complexity and asymmetry contributes to elaboration in divergent thinking. *Creativity Research Journal, 31*(3), 342–348. https://doi.org/10.1080/10400419.2019.1641687

Kuijpers, M., Douglas, S., & Kuiken, D. (2019). Personality traits and reading habits that predict absorbed narrative fiction reading. *Psychology of Aesthetics, Creativity, and the Arts, 13*(1), 74–88. https://doi.org/10.1037/aca0000168

Leung, A. K. Y., Kwan, L., Liou, S., Chiu, C. Y., Qiu, L., & Yong, J. C. (2013, June). The role of instrumental emotion regulation in the emotions-creativity link. How worries render neurotic individuals more creative. In *Proceedings of the 9th ACM Conference on Creativity & Cognition* (pp. 332–336). https://doi.org/10.1145/2466627.2466656

Ma, J., & Wei, W. (2023). Curiosity causes creativity? Revealing the reinforcement circle between state curiosity and creativity. *The Journal of Creative Behavior, 57*(4), 488–494. https://doi.org/10.1002/jocb.606

MacKinnon, D. W. (1962). The nature and nurture of creative talent. *American Psychologist, 17*(7), 484–495. https://doi.org/10.1037/h0046541

MacKinnon, D. W. (1975). IPAR's contribution to the conceptualization and study of creativity. In I. A. Taylor & J. W. Getzels (Eds.), *Perspectives in creativity* (pp. 60–89). Aldine Publishing Company.

Mahmoud, N. E., Kamel, S. M., & Hamza, T. S. (2020). The relationship between tolerance of ambiguity and creativity in architectural design studio. *Creativity Studies, 13*(1), 179–198. https://doi.org/10.3846/cs.2020.9628

Martindale, C., & Dailey, A. (1996). Creativity, primary process cognition and personality. *Personality and Individual Differences, 20*(4), 409–414. https://doi.org/10.1016/0191-8869(95)00202-2

Mayer, J. D. (2005). A tale of two visions: Can a new view of personality help integrate psychology? *American Psychologist, 60*(4), 294–307. https://doi.org/10.1037/0003-066X.60.4.294

McCrae, R. R. (1996). Social consequences of experiential openness. *Psychological Bulletin, 120*, 323–337. https://doi.org/10.1037/0033-2909.120.3.323

McCrae, R. R., & Costa, P. T., Jr. (1997). Conceptions and correlates of openness to experience. In R. Hogan, J. Johnson, & S. Briggs (Eds.). *Handbook of personality psychology* (pp. 825–847). Elsevier. https://doi.org/10.1016/B978-012134645-4/50032-9

McKay, A. S., Karwowski, M., & Kaufman, J. C. (2017). Measuring the muses: Validating the Kaufman domains of creativity scale (K-DOCS). *Psychology of Aesthetics, Creativity, and the Arts, 11*(2), 216–230. https://doi.org/10.1037/aca0000074

Merrotsy, P. (2013). Tolerance of ambiguity: A trait of the creative personality? *Creativity Research Journal, 25*(2), 232–237. https://doi.org/10.1080/10400419.2013.783762

Meyer, J., Thoma, G. B., Kampschulte, L., & Köller, O. (2023). Openness to experience and museum visits: Intellectual curiosity, aesthetic sensitivity, and creative imagination predict the frequency of visits to different types of museums. *Journal of Research in Personality, 103*, 104352. https://doi.org/10.1016/j.jrp.2023.104352

Millis, K. (2001). Making meaning brings pleasure: The influence of titles on aesthetic experiences. *Emotion, 1*(3), 320–329. https://doi.org/10.1037/1528-3542.1.3.320

Mumford, M. D., & Gustafson, S. B. (1988). Creativity syndrome: Integration, application, and innovation. *Psychological Bulletin, 103*, 27–43. https://doi.org/10.1037/0033-2909.103.1.27

Nusbaum, E. C., & Silvia, P. J. (2011). Are openness and intellect distinct aspects of openness to experience? A test of the O/I model. *Personality and Individual Differences, 51*(5), 571–574. https://doi.org/10.1016/j.paid.2011.05.013

Orth, M., & Volmer, J. (2017). Daily within-person effects of job autonomy and work engagement on innovative behaviour: The cross-level moderating role of creative self-efficacy. *European Journal of Work and Organizational Psychology, 26*(4), 601–612. https://doi.org/10.1080/1359432X.2017.1332042

Paunonen, S. V., & Ashton, M. C. (2001). Big Five factors and facets and the prediction of behavior. *Journal of Personality and Social Psychology, 81*(3), 524–539. https://doi.org/10.1037/0022-3514.81.3.524

Pérez-Luño, A., Aguilar-Caro, R., & Muñoz-Doyague, M. F. (2024). The influence of personality and team-member exchange on creativity: A gendered approach. *Gender in Management: An International Journal, 39*(1), 145–164. https://doi.org/10.1108/GM-01-2022-0023

Perkins, A. M., Arnone, D., Smallwood, J., & Mobbs, D. (2015). Thinking too much: self-generated thought as the engine of neuroticism. *Trends in Cognitive Sciences, 19*(9), 492–498. https://doi.org/10.1016/j.tics.2015.07.003

Pickering, A. D., Smillie, L. D., & DeYoung, C. G. (2016). Neurotic individuals are not creative thinkers. *Trends in Cognitive Sciences, 20*(1), 1–2. https://doi.org/10.1016/j.tics.2015.10.001

Proyer, R. T. (2017). A multidisciplinary perspective on adult play and playfulness. *International Journal of Play, 6*(3), 241–243. https://doi.org/10.1080/21594937.2017.1384307

Puryear, J. S., Kettler, T., & Rinn, A. N. (2017). Relationships of personality to differential conceptions of creativity: A systematic review. *Psychology of Aesthetics, Creativity, and the Arts, 11*(1), 59–68. https://doi.org/10.1037/aca0000079

Rauthmann, J. F., & Kuper, N. (2025). The landscape of personality psychology in the new millennium: A systematic keyword analysis of journal articles from 2000 to 2021. *Journal of Personality and Social Psychology, 128*(3), 722–763. https://doi.org/10.1037/pspp0000532

Reiter-Palmon, R., Illies, J. J., & Kobe-Cross, L. M. (2009). Conscientiousness is not always a good predictor of performance: The case of creativity. *The International Journal of Creativity & Problem Solving, 19*(2), 27–45.

Ren, Z., Chen, Q., Li, X., Wei, D., & Qiu, J. (2026). What doesn't kill the cat makes it creative: Complex interplay between trait curiosity and creativity. *Creativity Research Journal, 38*(1), 225–241. https://doi.org/10.1080/10400419.2024.2431785

Rodriguez, R. M., Silvia, P. J., Kaufman, J. C., Reiter-Palmon, R., & Puryear, J. S. (2023). Taking inventory of the Creative Behavior Inventory: An item response theory analysis of the CBI. *Creativity Research Journal, 35*(2), 143–153. https://doi.org/10.1080/10400419.2023.2183322

Runco, M. A., & Jaeger, G. J. (2012). The standard definition of creativity. *Creativity Research Journal, 24*(1), 92–96. https://doi.org/10.1080/10400419.2012.650092

Russ, S. W. (2016). Pretend play: Antecedent of adult creativity. *New Directions for Child and Adolescent Development, 2016*(151), 21–32. https://doi.org/10.1002/cad.20154

Ryan, R. M., & Deci, E. L. (2024). Self-determination theory. In F. Maggino (Ed.) *Encyclopedia of quality of life and well-being research* (pp. 6229–6235). Springer International Publishing.

Schutte, N. S., & Malouff, J. M. (2020). A meta-analysis of the relationship between curiosity and creativity. *The Journal of Creative Behavior, 54*(4), 940–947. https://doi.org/10.1002/jocb.421

Schwaba, T., Luhmann, M., Denissen, J. J., Chung, J. M., & Bleidorn, W. (2018). Openness to experience and culture-openness transactions across the lifespan. *Journal of Personality and Social Psychology, 115*(1), 118–136. https://doi.org/10.1037/pspp0000150

Ścigała, K. A., Schild, C., & Zettler, I. (2020). Doing justice to creative justifications: Creativity, Honesty-Humility, and (un) ethical justifications. *Journal of Research in Personality, 89*, 104033. https://doi.org/10.1016/j.jrp.2020.104033

Shalley, C. E., & Gilson, L. L. (2004). What leaders need to know: A review of social and contextual factors that can foster or hinder creativity. *The Leadership Quarterly, 15*(1), 33–53. https://doi.org/10.1016/j.leaqua.2003.12.004

Shalley, C., Hitt, M. A., Zhou, J., Van Knippenberg, D., & Hirst, G. (2015). A cross-level perspective on creativity at work: Person-in-situation interactions. In C. E. Shalley, M. A. Hitt, & J. Zhou (Eds.). *The Oxford handbook of creativity, innovation, and entrepreneurship* (pp. 225–244). Oxford University Press, USA. https://doi.org/10.1093/oxfordhb/9780199927678.013.0013

Sia, S. K., & Appu, A. V. (2015). Work autonomy and workplace creativity: Moderating role of task complexity. *Global Business Review, 16*(5), 772–784. https://doi.org/10.1177/0972150915591435

Silvia, P. J. (2006). Artistic training and interest in visual art: Applying the appraisal model of aesthetic emotions. *Empirical Studies of the Arts, 24*(2), 139–161. https://doi.org/10.2190/DX8K-6WEA-6WPA-FM84

Silvia, P. J., Kaufman, J. C., & Pretz, J. E. (2009a). Is creativity domain-specific? Latent class models of creative accomplishments and creative self-descriptions. *Psychology of Aesthetics, Creativity, and the Arts, 3*(3), 139–148. https://doi.org/10.1037/a0014940

Silvia, P. J., Nusbaum, E. C., Berg, C., Martin, C., & O'Connor, A. (2009b). Openness to experience, plasticity, and creativity: Exploring lower-order, high-order, and interactive effects. *Journal of Research in Personality, 43*(6), 1087–1090. https://doi.org/10.1016/j.jrp.2009.04.015

Silvia, P. J., Kaufman, J. C., Reiter-Palmon, R., & Wigert, B. (2011). Cantankerous creativity: Honesty–humility, agreeableness, and the HEXACO structure of creative achievement. *Personality and Individual Differences, 51*(5), 687–689. https://doi.org/10.1016/j.paid.2011.06.011

Silvia, P. J., Rodriguez, R. M., Beaty, R. E., Frith, E., Kaufman, J. C., Loprinzi, P., & Reiter-Palmon, R. (2021). Measuring everyday creativity: A Rasch model analysis of the Biographical Inventory of Creative Behaviors (BICB) scale. *Thinking Skills and Creativity, 39*, 100797. https://doi.org/10.1016/j.tsc.2021.100797

Stoycheva, K. (2010). Tolerance for ambiguity, creativity, and personality. *Bulgarian Journal of Psychology, 1–4*, 178–188.

Stoycheva, K. (2025). Tolerance of ambiguity and the creative action: To engage and endure. *The Journal of Creative Behavior*. 59(3), e1506. https://doi.org/10.1002/jocb.1506

Tromp, C., & Sternberg, R. J. (2022). Dynamic creativity: A person× task× situation interaction framework. *The Journal of Creative Behavior, 56*(4), 553–565. https://doi.org/10.1002/jocb.551

Tyagi, V., Hanoch, Y., Hall, S. D., Runco, M., & Denham, S. L. (2017). The risky side of creativity: Domain specific risk taking in creative individuals. *Frontiers in Psychology, 8*, 145. https://doi.org/10.3389/fpsyg.2017.00145

Wang, X., Li, H., & Yin, H. (2020). Antecedents and consequences of creativity in teams: When and how leader humility promotes performance via team creativity. *The Journal of Creative Behavior, 54*(4), 843–856. https://doi.org/10.1002/jocb.410

Widiger, T. A. (2009). Neuroticism. In M. R. Leary & R. H. Hoyle (Eds.), *Handbook of individual differences in social behavior* (pp. 129–146). The Guilford Press.

Wolfradt, U., & Pretz, J. E. (2001). Individual differences in creativity: Personality, story writing, and hobbies. *European Journal of Personality, 15*(4), 297–310. https://doi.org/10.1002/per.409

Zare, M., & Flinchbaugh, C. (2019). Voice, creativity, and big five personality traits: A meta-analysis. *Human Performance, 32*(1), 30–51. https://doi.org/10.1080/08959285.2018.1550782

Zenasni, F., Besançon, M., & Lubart, T. (2008). Creativity and tolerance of ambiguity: An empirical study. *The Journal of Creative Behavior, 42*(1), 61–73. https://doi.org/10.1002/j.2162-6057.2008.tb01080.x

CHAPTER 4

Am I Creative? Challenges to Accurate Assessment of Creative Self

Jean E. Pretz

Am I Creative? Challenges to Accurate Assessment of Creative Self

How do you know if you are creative? Do you trust your own judgment? The self-concept is based on observations of our own behavior and feedback provided by others, whether directly or indirectly. When it comes to creativity, however, people have fewer opportunities to receive feedback on the creativity of their work, and fewer chances to compare themselves to others. Even those who regularly engage in creative hobbies such as painting, crafting, or singing infrequently seek or receive critical feedback on the creativity of their work. A hobbyist may be extremely talented but not realize the uniqueness of their gift.

So what is the basis for creative self-perceptions? Self-assessments may be rooted in general stable personality traits or a general sense of self-efficacy and self esteem, or even values that contribute to a sense of personal identity. For some, there may be behavioral evidence of success or struggle that defines their self-beliefs. These may or may not accurately

J. E. Pretz (✉)
Professor of Psychology, Elizabethtown College, Elizabethtown, PA, USA
e-mail: pretzj@etown.edu

Z. Ivcevic (ed.), *Creators*, The Seven C's of Creativity,
https://doi.org/10.1007/978-3-032-09225-0_4

and objectively reflect a person's abilities. For others, they may have experiences that provided some objective feedback about their work, perhaps from a teacher or mentor.

If a person has a sense of self as creative, is it accurate? Is it fair to assume that those with a strong creative self-concept actually produce more creative ideas? Does the sense of self as creative generalize to all areas of life, or is it rooted in a specific domain? The validity of self-perceived creativity may depend on the basis for the self-evaluation. To the extent that it is based on specific behaviors or feedback, it is more likely to be domain specific. Some individuals who are highly creative in non-artistic domains may not even recognize their skill as creativity *per se*. Regardless of domain, if the individual lacks information about their ability, it is more likely to be a domain-general evaluation based on personality, general self-efficacy, self-esteem, or personal values. Psychological research on self-perceptions of creativity has explored these possibilities.

What Is the Creative Self?

In the psychological literature on the self, research has focused on constructs such as self-esteem and self-efficacy. Self-esteem is a general sense of self-worth (Coopersmith, 1967), whereas self-efficacy is the sense that one is capable of having an effect on the environment (Bandura, 1997). Accordingly, creative self-efficacy is "the belief that one has the ability to produce creative outcomes" (Tierney & Farmer, 2002, p. 1138).

Self-Esteem and Creativity

When it comes to beliefs about the self, current theory proposes that some self-beliefs are more central than others. These "core" beliefs are "basic, generalized, and relatively stable cognitions that reflect what individuals think about themselves within their social context" (Mussel, 2025, p. 2), and they are primarily a reflection of personality traits (McCrae & Costa, 1999). Core beliefs are rooted in personality and in response to life experiences. Self-esteem is considered a core belief, reflecting a sense of pride or self-worth (Mussel, 2025).

Self-esteem can also contribute to one's sense of self as creative. Though research on the relationship between self-esteem and creativity has been limited, evidence suggests a reliable but relatively weak relationship (Barbot, 2020; Deng & Zhang, 2011). Unfortunately, the literature contains many inconsistencies in the approach to the measurement of creativity and of self-esteem. Both constructs can be measured globally or more specifically to domains. For example, self-esteem has been assessed in domains such as physical, social, emotional, and academic (Barbot, 2020). The lack of literature combined with varying approaches to measurement makes it challenging to draw firm conclusions about this relationship.

One empirical investigation used a range of measures of self, including self-esteem as well as several measures of creative performance (Pretz & Nelson, 2017). Results showed significant positive relationships between general self-efficacy, self-esteem, and creative self-efficacy with performance on a divergent thinking task. In regression analyses, self-esteem was more strongly related to fluency scores than originality scores. Researchers concluded that "this pattern of results suggests that self-esteem is associated with higher levels of productivity, but higher-quality creative work is associated with creative self-efficacy" (Pretz & Nelson, 2017, p. 167). Self-esteem may fuel motivation in a global sense, but it may not necessarily be geared toward creative outcomes.

Barbot (2020) took a nuanced approach to the study of creativity and self-esteem by examining domain-relevant aspects of the constructs. In his work, he engaged adolescents in a music composition task, a story-writing task, and a drawing task. Results showed a correspondence between domain relevant aspects of self-esteem and domain-specific creativity. Global self-esteem was most strongly related to creativity on the music composition task. Academic and future self-esteem were significantly correlated with creativity on the story-writing task. Just as there was no domain-relevant measure of self-esteem related to visual arts, there were no significant relationships between self-esteem and performance on the drawing composition task beyond creative self-esteem, which was related to all three domains of creative performance. The relationships between self-esteem and creativity were much stronger than previously observed, confirming the value of this domain-specific approach.

Although minimal research has been conducted on creativity and self-esteem, a great deal of attention has been given to creative self-efficacy. A meta-analysis by Haase et al. (2018) revealed a medium effect size for the relationship between creative self efficacy and other measures of creativity. Creative self-beliefs were moderately related to creative performance, though this relationship was weaker for more objective performance measures such as divergent thinking tasks (Haase et al., 2018). It is not surprising that reflections on one's creative self-concept over a long period of time have a limited relationship with responses to a momentary brainstorming task. Yet stronger and substantial relationships were found between creative self-efficacy and self-reported creativity as measured in a variety of ways through the studies sampled in the meta-analysis. Most of the studies discussed in this chapter assess self-perceived creativity via measures of creative self-efficacy rather than self-esteem.

Creative Self-Efficacy

Creative self-efficacy is the belief that one has the capacity to be creative on a particular task. Research on creative self-efficacy has proliferated in recent years, in part because it has been shown to lead to higher levels of creativity on various tasks. Creative self-efficacy has been found to be relatively more dynamic than a person's overall creative self-concept (Karwowski et al., 2019). Specifically, research has shown that self-ratings of one's creative self-efficacy are influenced by the nature of the creativity task itself. Karwowski et al. (2019) found that pre-task creative self-efficacy was more strongly informed by general self-beliefs than was post-task creative self-efficacy, which was influenced more by familiarity with the task. This work shows that creative self-efficacy will vary based on context, including a person's experience with and confidence in their ability to perform the specific creative task.

One reason that researchers have focused on creative self-efficacy in recent years is because it has been shown to positively influence creative behavior. In Tierney and Farmer (2011)'s work on creativity in the workplace, they observed a longitudinal effect of creative self-efficacy on creative performance at work. Creative self-efficacy changed over time, and increases in creative self-efficacy predicted actual creative behavior in a real-world environment. This has important implications for enhancing creativity, showing that supervisors can foster creative performance by building creative self-efficacy.

Creative self-efficacy has also been found to mediate the influence of other variables on creative performance. In a study of college students in Mexico and Germany, Puente-Diaz et al. (2020) found that multicultural experiences were associated with higher levels of originality on a divergent thinking task. The mechanism through which these experiences had this beneficial relationship with creative behavior was scores on a measure of creative self-efficacy. Those with multicultural experiences experienced increased confidence in their creative ability which explained the relationship with increased originality. This supports Tierney and Farmer's (2011) earlier work, again showing that creative self-efficacy influenced actual creative behavior.

Li et al. (2021) provided an explanation for this relationship between creative self-efficacy and creative outcomes: effort. They reasoned that individuals with more confidence in their creative ability would also respond to a creative challenge with more effort. Their research confirmed this prediction, showing that supervisor ratings of creativity among engineers in an R&D company were higher among employees with high creative self-efficacy who took a prevention focus, an indicator of greater investment in their creative work. One reason that creative self-efficacy has consequences for actual creative performance is because it facilitates hard work.

Challenges to Accurate Assessment of Creative Capacity

When studying the sense of self as creative, it is not sufficient to consider only aspects of a person's personality or core self-beliefs. Creativity researchers recognize that a person's creative ability also depends on the environment in which a creative idea is developed as well as the social context in which it is received (Zandi et al., 2025). Creativity is not only ability to come up with ideas that are original (novel) and effective (useful or appropriate) (Runco & Jaeger, 2012), but also the ability to do so in a particular context. Plucker et al. (2004) elaborate on the definition of creativity as "the interaction among aptitude, process, and environment by which an individual or group produces a perceptible product that is both novel and useful as defined within a social context" (p. 90). That context influences the environment in which a person creates as well as the nature of the audience that receives and evaluates that work. According to the Creative Behavior as Agentic Action theory (Karwowski & Beghetto, 2019), creative behavior depends on both one's confidence in the ability to be creative and the perceived value of creativity in a given context. Even if an individual has high regard for their creative ability, they are unlikely to engage in creative behavior if they think it is not valued or could even be frowned upon in a given context. When evaluating creative sense of self, it is important to consider the self in context.

In this chapter, I will argue that the sense of self as creative is based on beliefs about creativity and contextual factors such as past experiences with creative work and that creative ability itself differs by domain. Beliefs, past experience, and domain all influence the individuals' understanding of themselves as creative. As a consequence, some people to have more accurate beliefs than others depending on beliefs about creativity, past experience with creative work, and the reference domain.

Misleading Beliefs About Creativity

Accurate self-understanding of one's creative ability and the creativity of one's work is dependent on an accurate understanding of what creativity is. Popular misconceptions about the nature of creativity are unfortunately common (Benedek et al., 2021; Sawyer, 2006). Researchers view creativity as a phenomenon that can occur in any domain, however many people view it as occurring strictly in the artistic domains. Creativity researchers recognize that creativity occurs at many levels of expertise, from amateur creative insights to professional creative work, yet many individuals view creativity as only the most eminent and transformational contributions. Finally, psychological research views creative ability as a function of both nature and nurture, yet a popular mindset frequently views creativity from a fixed mindset, an ability that is possessed without potential for growth. Any and all of these misconceptions limit the accuracy of self-perceptions of creativity.

Art Bias

The general understanding of the nature of creativity within the population tends to be quite narrow. Many individuals perceive creativity to be restricted to performance in the arts, for example, visual art, music, and drama. This "art bias" has been documented in many samples (Glăveanu, 2011; Kapoor et al., 2024; Wieth & Francis, 2018). College students are more likely to expect creative people to be artists, musicians, or designers as compared to other occupations requiring creative problem-solving (e.g., engineering, science) (Wieth & Francis, 2018). Similarly, when asked to estimate how important creativity is to various occupations, college students rated occupations in the arts and music as much higher than medicine or vocational fields (Wieth & Francis, 2018). Kapoor et al. (2024) extended these findings to a large sample of individuals, primarily from the US and India. Their results showed that laypeople view artistic occupations as significantly more creative than occupations in business or science, based on both implicit and explicit measures. These biases also related to self-perceived creativity in those domains. Results showed that "individuals who view themselves as creative in a particular occupation also tend to think of that occupation as creative" (Kapoor et al., 2024, p. 7).

Contributions in the arts are frequently original and effective, but these are not the only domains in which original ideas occur. Some of the most rapidly changing fields in the twenty-first century are those involving science and technology. Engineers frequently engage in creative problem-solving. Employees use creative thinking when navigating interpersonal conflicts. Everyday citizens employ creative thinking every time they must cook a meal with limited time and ingredients. To the extent that individuals are creative in domains outside of the arts, they are more likely to underestimate their sense of self as creative.

One study supported the influence of stereotypes on self-perceptions of creativity. In a study by Pretz (2017), gender differences were observed for self-rated creativity on the Kaufman Domains of Creativity Scale (KDOCS; Kaufman, 2012) in a sample of 933 college applicants. These mean differences in self-perceived creativity were aligned with gender stereotypes, with participants who identified as female gender rating themselves as more creative in interpersonal domains and artistic domains. Participants identifying as male rated themselves significantly more creative in math/science domains than female-identifying participants. Gender differences were not observed for scores on the KDOCS scale for scholarly creativity or performance creativity. Correlations between KDOCS scores and global creative self-efficacy scores showed that artistic creativity was more highly correlated to creative self-efficacy among female-identifying applicants than among male-identifying applicants. Regression analyses using all KDOCS scores to predict global creative self-efficacy for female- and male-identifying applicants showed that artistic creativity was the strongest predictor of CSE for women but was non-significant for men.

Eminence Bias

Another tendency to limit the understanding of creativity is a bias toward eminent creative contributions. When asked to report examples of creative individuals or ideas, people tend to emphasize examples with historic significance and those that had a lasting, transformative impact on their field. According to the 4C model of creativity, this assumption is very limited.

Kaufman and Beghetto (2009) dispel this biased view of creativity by describing creativity at four levels of expertise from mini-c to little-c to Pro-C to Big-C. Big-C creative contributions are those at the stereotypically eminent level, ideas that had a historically transformative impact on their field. Pro-C creative contributions are professional-level ideas that have a smaller, perhaps more incremental, impact. Little-c creativity is the everyday creativity that people engage in their own lives. Kaufman and Beghetto (2009) even consider ideas that many would not consider actually original to be creative even though they are personally novel. The ideas themselves may not be new to an entire field, yet a child or novice who discovers them for the first time is nevertheless engaging in creativity. To the extent that people limit creativity only to the Big-C contributions, their self-perceptions will be very limited.

Mindset Bias

One misconception about creativity is related to nature vs. nurture. Many people view creative ability as innate and unchangeable. The consequences of holding a fixed mindset about one's ability have been described extensively by Dweck (2017). Creativity researchers have described fixed and growth mindsets with regard to creative ability. Karwowski (2014) developed a measure of these mindsets and showed that growth mindset was more strongly related to creative self-efficacy than was a fixed mindset. He also showed that fixed mindset was negatively related to creative problem-solving, and among those with low fixed mindset, endorsement of a growth mindset was positively predictive of creative problem-solving success.

Other researchers who have explored the impact of creativity mindset have helped clarify its relationship to creative confidence and creative performance. Additional work has confirmed the positive relationship between growth mindset and creative self-efficacy (Hass et al., 2019), though this work showed that the negative impact of fixed mindset on creativity was stronger than the relationship between growth mindset and creative performance measures. Royston and Reiter-Palmon (2019) further explore the relationship between mindset, creative self-efficacy, and creative performance. Their research revealed that growth mindset was related to originality and quality of ideas on a creative problem-solving task but only for those of high creative self-efficacy.

Individuals who possess a fixed mindset are unlikely to seek out opportunities to grow in their ability. Yet evidence has shown that creativity can be fostered through instruction and practice (Scott et al., 2004). In one study, students in grades 5–12 endorsed conflicting statements about the nature of creativity (Stone & Hess, 2020). Many agreed that creativity is innate while simultaneously agreeing with a statement that creativity can be learned. This suggests that evidence about mindsets should be regarded with caution as more research is needed to understand the basis for participant viewpoints.

Personal Experience with Creativity

Where do participants get information about creativity and their own creative ability? If they hold misconceptions about creativity, where do those ideas come from? If they view themselves as lacking creativity, what is the basis for that judgment? Self-perceptions of creativity can still be limited, even among individuals who recognize creativity that can occur outside of the arts and without recognized eminence. Research suggests that self-beliefs about creativity are based on feedback on one's own creative work and the perceived value of creativity in a given context (Karwowski & Beghetto, 2019), including the environment in which people engage in creative work and the audiences that receive and evaluate it.

Self-Perceptions Based on Feedback

An important source of information on their creative abilities comes from feedback from others. In a school setting, many people gain frequent and detailed feedback on their academic work, leading to a well-developed academic self-concept (Trautwein & Möller, 2016, as cited in Zandi et al., 2025). Feedback is important because it helps people calibrate their understanding of their own ability. In the context of creativity, this can lead them to engage more in creative activities, encourage them to work toward improvement, or avoid taking on creative tasks. However, few people get substantive feedback on the creativity of their work, especially in school. In fact, many psychologists have criticized the educational system as devaluing creativity (Sternberg, 2010; Wieth & Francis, 2018).

Even when feedback is provided, it can have a harmful effect on creative confidence. Beghetto (2014) describes a phenomenon he calls "creative mortification" which is "the loss of one's willingness to pursue a particular creative aspiration following a negative performance outcome" (p. 266). In his research, Beghetto experimentally manipulated feedback on creative work to examine the causal impact of negative feedback on participants' reactions. Results showed that the experience of creative mortification was predicted by higher levels of shame and higher levels of attributing the negative feedback to a fixed creative ability. In a follow-up study, he found that mortifying experiences were more likely when negative feedback was provided at an earlier age and among those who experienced self-conscious emotions, in particular, shame. In some participants, the negative feedback had a motivating effect, especially among those who were older and those who believed they could improve their abilities. This work showed that feedback on creative work has a substantial impact on the creative self-perceptions and the likelihood of pursuing more creative work. Notably, having a fixed mindset was especially detrimental, whereas having a growth mindset was related to motivating rather than mortifying responses.

In cases where feedback on creative work is positive, it may not be sufficient to form accurate self-perceptions. Research has shown that creative self-perceptions are often inaccurate (Pretz & McCollum, 2014). In this study, researchers examined the relationship between specific ratings of performance on a recent task, scores on a global measure of creative self-efficacy, self-reported past creative achievement, and personality. Results showed that self-ratings of creativity on the specific task predicted rated creativity on that task. However, creative self-efficacy was unrelated to performance on the task. Creative self-efficacy was significantly correlated to past creative achievement, but creative self-efficacy scores did not predict achievement better than personality did. Researchers concluded that creative self-efficacy is based on personality more than on performance unless the self-ratings are tied to a very specific task. When limited information is available, only general sense of self can inform one's judgments of creative self-efficacy. This confirms prior work that showed that openness to experience (one of the Big Five personality traits) was consistently the strongest predictor of creative self-beliefs, especially for domain-general beliefs (Karwowski & Lebuda, 2016).

Feedback on one's creative work is the basis for creative metacognition, one's thoughts about their ability to be creative. Even metacognitive feelings such as the perceived ease of recalling past experiences of being creative can influence a person's self-perceived creativity. Puente-Diaz and Cavazos-Arroyo (2020) used a clever instructional manipulation to influence participants' metacognitive feelings about their creative ability, asking participants to either recall two or five times they have been creative in the past. Those who only needed to recall two instances of past creativity had the impression (metacognitive feeling) that they were more creative—it was easier to recall fewer instances. Puente-Diaz and Cavazos-Arroyo (2020) found that higher levels of metacognitive feelings predicted higher levels of creative self-efficacy, and creative self-efficacy was related to originality on a divergent thinking task. Their analyses showed that metacognitive feelings had an indirect effect on originality through their influence on creative self-efficacy. Metacognitive feelings and creative self-efficacy scores had a similar effect on task enjoyment. This study showed how subtle shifts in self-concept can have a substantial impact on actual creative behavior as well as enjoyment of creative tasks.

One reason that individuals may have difficulty with creative metacognition can be because creative metacognition is based on limited information (Puente-Diaz & Cavazos-Arroyo, 2022). By their nature, creative tasks have multiple "right" solutions. When attempting to assess one's success on such a task, this introduces a level of uncertainty which makes it more difficult to draw a conclusion about whether one's performance was of high quality. This allows room for self-beliefs to play a larger role. This line of reasoning aligns with the findings of Pretz and McCollum (2014) who showed that personality had a stronger influence on global ratings of creative self-efficacy than did actual creative performance.

Perceived Value of Creativity

As proposed by the theory of Creative Behavior as Agentic Action (Karwowski & Beghetto, 2019), creative behavior depends not only on self-confidence but also the perceived value of creativity. In one study, Karwowski (2015) showed that being surrounded by peers who are highly creative did not reduce creative confidence in others as social comparison theory might predict, but rather increased self-confidence in one's ability to be creative. Karwowski argued that this effect occurred because it conveyed that the social context valued and expected creative behavior, thus fostering it among all members of the group.

This work suggests that creative behavior will be more likely for some individuals in certain contexts. Even those who have a strong sense of self as creative will only engage in creative behavior when they think it is appropriate and valued. Kaufman and Beghetto (2013) explained that creative metacognition includes the understanding of not only one's ability to be creative, but also a sense of when to use that creative ability. For example, performing a routine surgery is probably not an appropriate time to be creative and try something new. Another example is School settings, which are well known for being focused on rules, structure, and right answers. This stereotype may not apply to all educational settings, but students still expect it.

Most people think creativity is valued more in some fields and less in others. There is a general perception that creativity is more highly valued in artistic fields as compared to business or science (Kapoor et al., 2024). Research on college students has shown that the relationship between creativity and academic achievement differs by field of study. Cotter et al. (2015) showed that self-beliefs about creativity predicted academic achievement positively for some majors and negatively for others. Specifically, among Arts, Humanities, and Social Science majors, those who reported higher levels of creative self-efficacy were more successful academically than those who considered themselves less creative. In contrast, there was no relationship between creative self-efficacy and academic performance among those majoring in professional studies fields (e.g., business, education). These patterns provide some evidence that success in some fields is more strongly related to creativity than others. A concerning finding was that among science majors, ratings of creativity in the sciences predicted lower grades, though this finding was only marginally significant. A study of undergraduate engineering majors confirmed this trend (Atwood & Pretz, 2016). Engineering majors who considered themselves highly creative were significantly less likely to persist and graduate in the major. Clearly, the value of creativity is perceived differently in different contexts, and this affects the likelihood that individuals will engage in creative behavior and value their own creative potential in that context.

Domain Specificity of the Creative Self

Creativity has long been conceptualized as an individual difference variable similar to intelligence or personality traits. However, over the years, it has become clear that a person's creative behavior varies by domain. According to the Amusement Park Theory of Creativity (Baer & Kaufman, 2005), in order to be creative, a person must meet some general requirements but also some requirements that are specific to the domain. For example, a baseline requirement that applies to all domains might be a certain level of intelligence and/or motivation, but a domain-specific requirement might be the ability to play a musical instrument. According to the theory, all domains of creativity require the general "initial requirements," but at the domain or micro-domain level, what is valuable in one domain may be irrelevant in another.

This domain-specific perspective has been validated in empirical studies of creative individuals. Silvia et al. (2009) used latent class analysis to identify groups of creative individuals based on their self-reported creative achievements. Results showed a class of participants with achievements in the visual arts which was distinct from a class of participants with achievements in music, writing, and theater arts. A third class of participants reported very low levels of creative achievement.

Just as creative performance or achievement is domain-specific, the sense of self is also known to vary by domain. Core self-beliefs are considered stable traits that influence behavior across time and place (Mussel, 2025), however some beliefs about the self are less stable and may change more substantially depending on the situation. These are considered "surface" beliefs (Asendorpf & van Aken, 2003). Researchers generally view self-beliefs about creativity in this category (Zandi et al., 2025).

To what extent these predictions from the broader psychology of the self apply to the creative self is still subject to some uncertainty. The work of Silvia et al. (2009) suggests that whereas creative achievements may be clearly differentiated by domain, the same may not be true for creative self-beliefs. When the individuals who reported achievements in the visual arts and performing arts were asked to provide ratings of creative self-efficacy, no distinction was detectable between the groups. Using domain-specific self-efficacy scores, participants simply fell into two classes—creative and not creative. This suggests that participants' sense of self as creative is not domain specific after all.

Yet other researchers have provided evidence for the domain specificity of self-perceptions of creativity. . In one study of a large sample of college students using numerous measures of self-perceived creativity, personality, and creative performance, results showed that participants rated their creative ability in work, school, and hobby differently (Reiter-Palmon et al., 2012).

More recent work has confirmed that domains are relevant to self-perceptions of creativity. In a large-scale study of American college students, Snyder et al. (2021) explored self-perceptions of creativity including creative self-efficacy, creative personal identity, and self-perceived creativity in various domains as measured by the KDOCS (Kaufman, 2012). Results showed that students did not differentiate between creative self-efficacy and creative personal identity, but rather differentiated between their self-perceived creativity in various domains. This was most pronounced in the difference between the domain of Math/Science and all other domains. Similar findings were obtained in a study by Boldt et al. (2024). In their work, participants also distinguished creativity in Math/Science as different from creativity in other domains. Further, these differences show different patterns of relationship to personality characteristics and self-esteem. Creativity in math and science was associated with lower agreeableness and conscientiousness, whereas creativity in other fields was associated with higher openness and extraversion (Boldt et al., 2024). These findings affirm that individuals have some insight into how their creative potential compares in some domains, specifically math and science vs. other domains.

Impact of Self-Perceptions on Creative Behavior

This domain distinction among self-perceptions of creativity has the potential to impact creative behavior, particularly in math and science. Given the fact that many people hold a misconception of creativity as applying primarily to artistic fields, individuals may underestimate their levels of self-perceived creativity in the sciences. The sciences tend to emphasize critical thinking with regard to the interpretation of evidence. However, the design of research studies and the problem-solving process involved in any discovery process is inherently creative. Research has shown that the disposition to rely on critical thinking only predicted creativity in the sciences among those with a high creative self-efficacy (Qiang et al., 2020). These results show that self-perceptions have real consequences, at least in the sciences.

One intervention study provided some encouraging evidence regarding increasing self-perceived creativity in various domains. Lee and Portillo (2022) provided a domain-general creativity training course to college students and documented the change in creative self-efficacy. Their results showed that the general intervention increased self-perceived creativity in general and for specific domains as assessed with the KDOCS. The researchers categorized participants based on the amount of pre- to post-test change in creative personal identity scores, a measure of how central creativity was to their own identity. In the group of students who showed the largest change in creative personal identity from pre- to post-test, increases occurred for domain-general and -specific measures alike. However, another cluster of students was found to have significant increases in artistic, performance, and math/science creativity but not for everyday creativity or scholarly creativity. This supports the work of Snyder et al. (2021), showing that college students can make the distinction between their creative abilities in different domains. Lee and Portillo (2022) further this understanding by showing that self-perceptions of creativity can change as the result of a single semester-long course, and that a domain-general intervention can influence domain-specific self-beliefs about creativity.

Overall, the evidence for a domain-based perspective on the creative self is mixed. Whereas it is likely that individuals exhibit creative behavior and achievement in specific domains and not necessarily all domains, the evidence that they can accurately assess their ability domain by domain is limited. The strongest evidence affirms that people can tell whether they are creative in math and science as compared to other fields of study. Further work is needed to determine how nuanced those judgments can be, for example, comparing various domains within the arts.

Conclusions

When it comes to understanding one's own creative ability, there are many obstacles that block self-insight. The ability to perceive one's own creative ability is obscured by misconceptions about the nature of creativity, lack of personal feedback on one's own performance, and the domain-specific nature of creativity itself. Most individuals do not know how creative they are because they have a narrow view of what it means to be creative. Even when they know that creativity goes beyond eminent artistic contributions and can be nurtured in anyone, most people have few opportunities for feedback, and sometimes the feedback they get is harmful. Even when meaningful feedback is available, it does not necessarily translate into changing a person's sense of self. Among people who do see themselves as creative, it is not necessarily related to their creative behavior but may be based more strongly on their personality. Even among those individuals in stereotypically creative (artistic fields), research has shown that they rate themselves as creative in a general not domain-specific sense.

Research on the psychology of self-perceptions of creativity has numerous applications as well as implications for future research. Creativity is an essential skill in a rapidly changing world with growing challenges. If we hope to develop higher levels of creativity in society, it will be important to develop creative metacognition as well. Without valid self-insight, individuals may fail to recognize their own creative abilities or lack the motivation to strengthen their creative potential.

Education is needed to dispel common misconceptions of creativity including the art bias, eminence bias, and the mindset that creativity is fixed and cannot be developed. One way to attempt to overcome these biases could be direct instruction about the nature of creativity. Another approach is to provide opportunities to engage in creative work in an environment with psychological safety (Edmondson, 1999). Such an environment is one in which it is safe to fail, and creative risk-taking is tolerated. Opportunities to practice creativity can happen in the classroom or workplace. When individuals practice creativity, there is an opportunity for feedback, and when criticism is constructive, it can serve to increase creative outcomes. Through these experiences, individuals can begin to recognize their own improvement, refuting a bias toward fixed mindset. Research on peer influence on creativity is encouraging—being around others who are creative does not create a negative social comparison but instead builds up creative self-efficacy because creativity is valued (Karwowski, 2015).

Celebrating creative contributions, whether big or small, in the arts or sciences, is important for breaking down stereotypes. It is important for people to see how creativity is evident in any field. This will help them improve their understanding of their own creative ability. It will also help gatekeepers keep creative people in fields that actually require creativity, rather than letting them flounder or get frustrated and potentially leave the field before they can make their creative impact. This applies to stereotypes about domains in which creativity is more valued, but also other stereotypes such as those linked to gender or personality. Education should provide diverse examples of creative individuals, those who are extraverted as well as those who are introverted, those who are non-conforming and independent as well as those who are collaborative and agreeable.

There are several likely fruitful directions for this growing area of research on the creative self. More work is needed to clarify self-perceptions of creativity by domain, based on the mixed findings described here. Additional work is needed on self-esteem and creativity, as researchers have primarily focused on creative self-efficacy in recent years. More work is needed to see how self-perceptions of creativity evolve over the lifespan. If the creative self-concept is established early, then more priority must be placed on dispelling misconceptions and providing opportunities to develop creative abilities earlier in life. To the extent that a person's reflection on their sense of self as creative is more global and based on personality, it may be sufficient to develop creativity in any one domain in order to boost creative self-efficacy.

Psychological research on self-perceptions of creativity reveals numerous obstacles to the development of clear self-understanding. Yet evidence is clear that those who have a stronger sense of self as creative are more likely to produce creative work and develop innovative approaches to problems. It is essential that we can work to improve insights into the creative self so everyone can recognize the role they can play in adapting to novel challenges and developing creative solutions that will benefit all of society.

References

Asendorpf, J. B., & Van Aken, M. A. G. (2003). Personality–relationship transaction in adolescence: Core versus surface personality characteristics. *Journal of Personality, 71*(4), 629–666. https://doi.org/10.1111/1467-6494.7104005

Atwood, S. A., & Pretz, J. E. (2016). Creativity as a factor in persistence and academic achievement of engineering undergraduates. *Journal of Engineering Education, 105*(4), 540–559. https://doi.org/10.1002/jee.20130

Baer, J., & Kaufman, J. C. (2005). Bridging generality and specificity: The amusement park theoretical (Apt) model of creativity. *Roeper Review, 27*(3), 158–163. https://doi.org/10.1080/02783190509554310

Bandura, A. (1997). *Self-efficacy: The exercise of control.* W H Freeman/Times Books/ Henry Holt & Co.

Barbot, B. (2020). Creativity and self-esteem in adolescence: A study of their domain-specific, multivariate relationships. *The Journal of Creative Behavior, 54*(2), 279–292. https://doi.org/10.1002/jocb.365

Beghetto, R. A. (2014). Creative mortification: An initial exploration. *Psychology of Aesthetics, Creativity, and the Arts, 8*(3), 266–276. https://doi.org/10.1037/a0036618

Benedek, M., Karstendiek, M., Ceh, S. M., Grabner, R. H., Krammer, G., Lebuda, I., et al. (2021). Creativity myths: Prevalence and correlates of misconceptions on creativity. *Personality and Individual Differences, 182*, 111068. https://doi-org.proxy-etown.klnpa.org/10.1016/j.paid.2021.111068

Boldt, G. T., Ivcevic, Z., & Kaufman, J. C. (2024). Do you think you are creative? Patterns of self-perceived creativity in adolescents and young adults. *Creativity Research Journal*, 1–16. https://doi.org/10.1080/10400419.2024.2371261

Coopersmith, S. (1967). *The antecedents of self-esteem.* W H Freeman and Company.

Cotter, K., Pretz, J., & Kaufman, J. (2015). *Self-reported creativity predicts college GPA beyond high school grades.* Poster presented at the annual meeting of the American Psychological Association, Toronto, ON.

Deng, X.-P., & Zhang, X.-K. (2011). Understanding the relationship between self-esteem and creativity: A meta-analysis. *Advances in Psychological Science, 19*, 645–651. https://doi.org/10.3724/SP.J.1042.2011.00645

Dweck, C. (2017). *Mindset: Changing the way you think to fulfil your potential* (Revised edition). Robinson.

Edmondson, A. (1999). Psychological safety and learning behavior in work teams. *Administrative Science Quarterly, 44*(2), 350–383. https://doi.org/10.2307/2666999

Glăveanu, V. P. (2011). Is the lightbulb still on?: Social representations of creativity in a Western context. *International Journal of Creativity and Problem Solving, 21*(1), 53–72.

Haase, J., Hoff, E. V., Hanel, P. H. P., & Innes-Ker, Å. (2018). A meta-analysis of the relation between creative self-efficacy and different creativity measurements. *Creativity Research Journal, 30*(1), 1–16. https://doi.org/10.1080/10400419.2018.1411436

Hass, R. W., Katz-Buonincontro, J., & Reiter-Palmon, R. (2019). The creative self and creative thinking: An exploration of predictive effects using Bayes factor analyses. *Psychology of Aesthetics, Creativity, and the Arts, 13*(4), 375–387. https://doi.org/10.1037/aca0000169

Kapoor, H., Gurjar, S., Mahadeshwar, H., Rezaei, S., & Kaufman, J. C. (2024). Who is the most creative of them all?: Art bias in laypersons' explicit and implicit beliefs. *Psychology of Aesthetics, Creativity, and the Arts.* https://doi.org/10.1037/aca0000663

Karwowski, M. (2014). Creative mindsets: Measurement, correlates, consequences. *Psychology of Aesthetics, Creativity, and the Arts, 8*(1), 62–70. https://doi.org/10.1037/a0034898

Karwowski, M. (2015). Peer effect on students' creative self-concept. *The Journal of Creative Behavior, 49*(3), 211–225. https://doi.org/10.1002/jocb.102

Karwowski, M., & Beghetto, R. A. (2019). Creative behavior as agentic action. *Psychology of Aesthetics, Creativity, and the Arts, 13*(4), 402–415. https://doi.org/10.1037/aca0000190

Karwowski, M., & Lebuda, I. (2016). The big five, the huge two, and creative self-beliefs: A meta-analysis. *Psychology of Aesthetics, Creativity, and the Arts, 10*(2), 214–232. https://doi.org/10.1037/aca0000035

Karwowski, M., Han, M.-H., & Beghetto, R. A. (2019). Toward dynamizing the measurement of creative confidence beliefs. *Psychology of Aesthetics, Creativity, and the Arts, 13*(2), 193–202. https://doi.org/10.1037/aca0000229

Kaufman, J. C. (2012). Counting the muses: Development of the Kaufman Domains of Creativity Scale (K-DOCS). *Psychology of Aesthetics, Creativity, and the Arts, 6*(4), 298–308. https://doi.org/10.1037/a0029751

Kaufman, J. C., & Beghetto, R. A. (2009). Beyond big and little: The four C model of creativity. *Review of General Psychology, 13*(1), 1–12. https://doi.org/10.1037/a0013688

Kaufman, J. C., & Beghetto, R. A. (2013). In praise of Clark Kent: Creative metacognition and the importance of teaching kids when (not) to be creative. *Roeper Review, 35*(3), 155–165. https://doi.org/10.1080/02783193.2013.799413

Lee, J. H., & Portillo, M. (2022). Transferability of creative self-belief across domains: The differential effects of a creativity course for university students. *Thinking Skills and Creativity, 43*, 100996. https://doi.org/10.1016/j.tsc.2021.100996

Li, C.-R., Yang, Y., Lin, C.-J., & Xu, Y. (2021). Within-person relationship between creative self-efficacy and individual creativity: The mediator of creative process engagement and the moderator of regulatory focus. *The Journal of Creative Behavior, 55*(1), 63–78. https://doi.org/10.1002/jocb.435

McCrae, R. M., & Costa, P. T. (1999). A five-factor theory of personality. In L. A. Pervin & O. P. John (Eds.), *Handbook of personality: Theory and research* (2nd ed., pp. 139–153). Guilford.

Mussel, P. (2025). The structure of self-related core beliefs. *Journal of Personality and Social Psychology*. https://doi.org/10.1037/pspp0000553

Plucker, J. A., Beghetto, R. A., & Dow, G. T. (2004). Why isn't creativity more important to educational psychologists? Potentials, pitfalls, and future directions in creativity research. *Educational Psychologist, 39*(2), 83–96. https://doi.org/10.1207/s15326985ep3902_1

Pretz, J. (2017). *Gender differences in self-perceived and actual creativity*. Talk presented at the annual meeting of the American Psychological Association.

Pretz, J. E., & McCollum, V. A. (2014). Self-perceptions of creativity do not always reflect actual creative performance. *Psychology of Aesthetics, Creativity, and the Arts, 8*(2), 227–236. https://doi.org/10.1037/a0035597

Pretz, J. E., & Nelson, D. (2017). Creativity is influenced by domain, creative self-efficacy, mindset, self-efficacy, and self-esteem. In M. Karwowski & J. C. Kaufman (Eds.), *The creative self* (pp. 155–170). Elsevier. https://doi.org/10.1016/B978-0-12-809790-8.00009-1

Puente-Diaz, R., & Cavazos-Arroyo, J. (2020). Creative metacognitive feelings as a source of information for creative self-efficacy, creativity potential, intrapersonal idea selection, and task enjoyment. *The Journal of Creative Behavior, 54*(3), 499–507. https://doi.org/10.1002/jocb.384

Puente-Díaz, R., & Cavazos-Arroyo, J. (2022). Creative self-efficacy and metacognitive feelings as sources of information when generating, evaluating, and selecting creative ideas: A metacognitive perspective. *The Journal of Creative Behavior, 56*(4), 647–658. https://doi.org/10.1002/jocb.557

Puente-Diaz, R., Toptas, S. D., Cavazos-Arroyo, J., Wimschneider, C., & Brem, A. (2020). Creative potential and multicultural experiences: The mediating role of creative self-efficacy. *The Journal of Creative Behavior, 54*(4), 815–823. https://doi.org/10.1002/jocb.408

Qiang, R., Han, Q., Guo, Y., Bai, J., & Karwowski, M. (2020). Critical thinking disposition and scientific creativity: The mediating role of creative self-efficacy. *The Journal of Creative Behavior, 54*(1), 90–99. https://doi.org/10.1002/jocb.347

Reiter-Palmon, R., Robinson-Morral, E. J., Kaufman, J. C., & Santo, J. B. (2012). Evaluation of self-perceptions of creativity: Is it a useful criterion? *Creativity Research Journal, 24*(2–3), 107–114. https://doi.org/10.1080/10400419.2012.676980

Royston, R., & Reiter-Palmon, R. (2019). Creative self-efficacy as mediator between creative mindsets and creative problem-solving. *The Journal of Creative Behavior, 53*(4), 472–481. https://doi.org/10.1002/jocb.226

Runco, M. A., & Jaeger, G. J. (2012). The standard definition of creativity. *Creativity Research Journal, 24*(1), 92–96. https://doi.org/10.1080/10400419.2012.650092

Sawyer, R. K. (2006). *Explaining creativity: The science of human innovation*. Oxford University Press.

Scott, G., Leritz, L. E., & Mumford, M. D. (2004). The effectiveness of creativity training: A quantitative review. *Creativity Research Journal, 16*(4), 361–388. https://doi.org/10.1080/10400410409534549

Silvia, P. J., Kaufman, J. C., & Pretz, J. E. (2009). Is creativity domain-specific? Latent class models of creative accomplishments and creative self-descriptions. *Psychology of Aesthetics, Creativity, and the Arts, 3*(3), 139–148. https://doi.org/10.1037/a0014940

Snyder, H. T., Sowden, P. T., Silvia, P. J., & Kaufman, J. C. (2021). The creative self: Do people distinguish creative self-perceptions, efficacy, and personal identity? *Psychology of Aesthetics, Creativity, and the Arts, 15*(4), 627–636. https://doi.org/10.1037/aca0000317

Sternberg, R. J. (2010). *College admissions for the 21st century*. Harvard University Press. https://doi.org/10.4159/9780674058590

Stone, D. L., & Hess, J. (2020). School students' implicit theories of creativity and their self-perceptions as artists. *Creativity Research Journal, 32*(4), 369–377. https://doi.org/10.1080/10400419.2020.1821555

Tierney, P., & Farmer, S. M. (2002). Creative self-efficacy: Its potential antecedents and relationship to creative performance. *Academy of Management Journal, 45*(6), 1137–1148. https://doi.org/10.2307/3069429

Tierney, P., & Farmer, S. M. (2011). Creative self-efficacy development and creative performance over time. *Journal of Applied Psychology, 96*(2), 277–293. https://doi.org/10.1037/a0020952

Wieth, M. B., & Francis, A. P. (2018). Conflicts and consistencies in creativity research and teaching. *Teaching of Psychology, 45*(4), 363–370. https://doi.org/10.1177/0098628318796924

Zandi, N., Karwowski, M., Forthmann, B., & Holling, H. (2025). How stable is the creative self-concept? A latent state-trait analysis. *Psychology of Aesthetics, Creativity, and the Arts, 19*(1), 101–111. https://doi.org/10.1037/aca0000521

CHAPTER 5

What Motivates Creative People?

Shengjie Lin

What Motivates Creative People?

The fundamental question about what motivates creative people has long intrigued psychologists. Creativity, by its very nature, involves uncertainty, risk-taking, and the willingness to venture beyond the familiar (Beghetto, 2021; Glaveanu et al., 2013; Kashdan & Fincham, 2002), making motivation a critical ingredient in the creative process. Motivation offers a complementary and increasingly vital lens for understanding why individuals engage in creative activities and persist through challenges. This chapter explores the intersection of motivation and creativity by reviewing two major streams of research: the application of general motivational theories to creativity, and the development of creativity-specific motivational constructs.

S. Lin (✉)
Department of Individual, Family, and Community Education,
The University of New Mexico, Albuquerque, NM, USA
e-mail: shengjielin@unm.edu

Z. Ivcevic (ed.), *Creators*, The Seven C's of Creativity,
https://doi.org/10.1007/978-3-032-09225-0_5

Motivation as a Lens to Understand Creative Individuals

Motivation refers to the energy behind actions (Elliot & Dweck, 2013; Wigfield et al., 2021). Over the past 50 years, different theoretical perspectives have been developed to explain and guide human behavior and achievement (Elliot & Dweck, 2013; Latham, 2011; Renninger & Hidi, 2019; Ryan, 2012). Thanks to the richness of these motivational theories, creativity researchers have drawn on their nuances to better understand what motivates or demotivates individual creativity (including but not limited to creative thinking, personality, behavior, performance, and achievement). In the following section, I first review how major motivational theories have been applied to the field of creativity.

Intrinsic and Extrinsic Motivation

Intrinsic motivation refers to the extent to which individuals engage in an activity because they find it inherently interesting or enjoyable (Amabile & Pillemer, 2012). In Amabile's componential theory of creativity (1983, 1996), intrinsic motivation was posited as the fundamental motivation enhancing creativity. Researchers have suggested that the primary mechanism through which intrinsic motivation fosters creativity is its control of attention (Liu et al., 2016; Zhang & Bartol, 2010). The greater the intrinsic motivation, the more individuals' attention will be directed toward creative pursuits. When individuals are intrinsically motivated for an activity, they invest more time and effort in seeking new information, solving problems, and developing original solutions (Deci & Ryan, 2000). In contrast, when intrinsic motivation is low, individuals are more likely to exhibit reduced cognitive flexibility and rely on existing routines and conventional approaches (Amabile et al., 2005).

Numerous empirical studies have examined the relationships between intrinsic motivation and various aspects for creativity, predominantly identifying positive associations. In a meta-analysis involving employees and students, de Jesus et al. (2013) identified positive relationships between intrinsic motivation and creative products (creative ideas, solutions, or objects). Focusing on the workplace context, Liu et al.'s (2016) meta-analysis found that employee intrinsic motivation is positively associated with their generation of creative ideas (e.g., suggestions for incremental adaptations or radical breakthroughs).

Other studies have found that intrinsic motivation serves as a mediator underlying the relationships between personal (e.g., conscientiousness,

Furnham et al., 2005; openness to experience, Furnham, 1999) and contextual (e.g., job complexity, Oldham & Cummings, 1996; supportive leadership, Shalley & Gilson, 2004) factors and creativity in various contexts. For example, in a study among researchers in an agricultural research institute, Yesuf et al. (2023) found that intrinsic motivation mediated the relationship between individual domain-relevant skills and creative behavior. This suggests that the translation of creative potential into enacted behavior depends on whether people are intrinsically interested in the domain. Another study found that a safe ethical climate characterized by shared ethically appropriate norms and values lays the groundwork for employee intrinsic motivation, which in turn enhances their creative behavior (Santiago-Torner et al., 2023).

While the positive role of intrinsic motivation in creativity has long been recognized, fostering intrinsic motivation may be challenging. Comparatively, extrinsic motivation is often easier to elicit through external stimuli such as evaluations and rewards. However, the majority of early literature suggests that extrinsic motivation can be detrimental to creativity, indicating reduced creativity when rewards (Amabile, 1983; Hennessey et al., 1989) or evaluation (Amabile, 1979; White & Owen, 1970) are provided. Extrinsic motivation has consistently been found to improve performance on tasks that require rote memorization, precise execution under time pressure, or the completion of familiar routines (Hennessey, 2019). In contrast, creative goals are typically open-ended and ill-defined (Lubart, 1994; Reiter-Palmon & Illies, 2004). Scholars have also argued that extrinsic motivation may shift attention toward external goals rather than the activity itself, thus undermining both intrinsic motivation and hindering creative performance (Lepper et al., 1973; Xue et al., 2020).

Some other studies have noted that extrinsic motivation does not necessarily reduce creativity (Al-Dhamit & Kreishan, 2016; Gerhart et al., 2015; Gong et al., 2017; Yoon et al., 2015). One line of research focuses on the type of external stimuli, arguing that extrinsic motivation is not detrimental if rewards or evaluations are supportive (e.g., constructive feedback) or confirm individual competence (e.g., acknowledging the value of contributions). For instance, Shalley and Perry-Smith (2001) found that when informational evaluation is expected, participants solved management-related problems more creatively compared to groups expecting controlling evaluation.

Another line of research examines how extrinsic motivation can interact with intrinsic motivation, jointly enhancing creativity. In a study conducted at an international consulting company in Germany, Fischer et al. (2019) found that relational rewards (a type of extrinsic motivation involving recognition and appreciation from colleagues) moderate the relationship between intrinsic motivation and creative behavior. When individuals perceive high relational rewards and experience strong intrinsic motivation, the positive impact on creativity and innovation is strengthened. Similarly, a study in a Chinese company found that intrinsic and extrinsic motivation synergistically amplify personal creativity goals (Gong et al., 2017).

Achievement Goal Orientation

Achievement goal models make a basic distinction between two orientations: mastery (also called learning orientation) and performance orientation (VandeWalle, 1997). Achievement goal orientation refers to individual differences in self-developmental beliefs that shape how people identify, interpret, and respond to task performance situations (Dweck, 1986; Dweck & Leggett, 1988; Elliot & McGregor, 2001; Nicholls, 1984).

A mastery orientation directs individuals toward acquiring new knowledge and developing competence in order to master challenging tasks (Elliot & McGregor, 2001). Its emphasis on skill development suggests that individuals with this orientation are task-focused. This typically results in deeper and more sustained engagement, which often leads to greater creativity (Hirst et al., 2009). Moreover, those who are mastery orientated often prefer challenging tasks (VandeWalle, 1997), making them more likely to engage in creative activities that involve uncertainty and some risk of error or failure.

Last, creative individuals may benefit from a mastery orientation because of its influence on development of both domain-relevant and creativity-relevant skills. These skills form the foundational knowledge base necessary for creative work in a particular domain (Amabile, 1996). Reflecting these theoretical links, empirical studies have reported a positive association between mastery orientation and creativity in both workplace and educational contexts (Du et al., 2020; Hirst et al., 2009; Kumar et al., 2022; Liu et al., 2019; Mao et al., 2020). A recent meta-analysis on achievement goal orientation and employee creativity found a moderate effect size ($r = .32$) between mastery goal orientation and various aspects of creativity, including creative thinking and creative performance (Nandi & Watts, 2025).

In contrast, performance orientation involves the goal of outperforming others, seeking favorable evaluations, and demonstrating superior competence (VandeWalle & Cummings, 1997). Researchers have further differentiated this into performance-approach orientation, which involves striving to demonstrate competence, and performance-avoidance orientation, which focuses on avoiding failure or negative evaluations (Elliot & McGregor, 2001). Individuals with a performance-approach orientation may be driven by extrinsic motivation, such as the desire to demonstrate competence or gain external recognition (e.g., winning an art competition). While this can positively influence creativity in the short term, the effect may be difficult to sustain or translate into long-term creative achievement. Conversely, individuals with a strong performance-avoidance orientation tend to avoid situations that might involve mistakes, failure, or negative feedback (Brett & VandeWalle, 1999). As a result, they are less likely to take risks, experiment with novel approaches, or engage in cognitive flexibility, which are all essential for creative performance (Hirst et al., 2009).

Findings on the relationship between performance orientation and creativity have been mixed, possibly due to the relatively small number of relevant studies compared to those focused on mastery orientation. In their meta-analysis, Nandi and Watts (2025) found that performance-approach orientation was positively related to creativity, while performance-avoidance orientation was negatively related to creativity outcomes in workplace contexts. However, these associations were weak (r = .18 for performance-approach orientation and r = -.10 for performance-avoidance orientation).

Autonomy

Self-determination theory is a comprehensive theory of motivation that emphasizes the satisfaction of individuals' basic needs (Ryan & Deci, 2000). At its core, autonomy refers to the need to feel psychologically free and to have a sense of ownership over one's actions (Ryan & Deci, 2000). This theory proposes that individual motivation lies on a continuum, from fully autonomous (acting with a sense of volition and choice) to fully controlled (acting under external pressures or demands, where people feel compelled by forces perceived as external to the self; Deci & Ryan, 2008; Ryan & Deci, 2000). When individuals feel free to explore ideas without excessive external pressure, they are more likely to take intellectual risks, persist through challenges, and experiment with unconventional approaches, thereby supporting their creative ideas, goals, and actions.

Individual autonomy needs are enabled by contextual autonomy supports. To date, the positive role of contextual autonomy support in individuals' creativity (e.g., job autonomy, flexible scheduling, choice in assignments; Li et al., 2018; Liu et al., 2011; Yang & Ok Choi, 2009) has been well established in creativity research. It contributes to a sense of self-determination by allowing people to act with volition and experience freedom from external controls, such as pressures or punishments that dictate how they should think or behave (Ryan & Deci, 2000). These supports engender a sense of psychological safety that is necessary for creativity to flourish. For example, autonomy-supportive supervisory style (e.g., absence of close monitoring, offering choices and options) contributes to employee cognitive flexibility and persistence in generating creative ideas and solutions (Nili & Tasavori, 2022; Ye et al., 2025; Zhou, 1998). Moreover, Sia and Appu (2015) examined three aspects of contextual autonomy support, autonomy in work methods, work schedules, and work criteria, and found that all three were related to creative ideas and behavior at work. Similarly, autonomy support from teachers and parents enhances children's creative thinking and behavior (Han et al., 2024; Huang, 2025; Sheldon, 1995).

In addition to positive role of contextual autonomy support, researchers have found that individuals who perceive having more autonomy need satisfaction tend to display higher creative thinking and behavior (Çekmecelioğlu & Günsel, 2011; Kirsch et al., 2015; Liu et al., 2011; Yu et al., 2021). Kirsch et al. (2015) showed that social scientists with higher autonomy need satisfaction tended to display greater creative thinking. In the school context, Baum and Baumann (2018) also found that students' autonomy need satisfaction positively predicted not only their performance on a creative figural drawing task but also their daily creative behavior in class, as rated by teachers.

Values

Values are personally endorsed core beliefs, which often drive one's priorities in action (Feather, 1995; Schwartz, 1992). The examination of the relationship between values and creativity can be traced back to studies conducted by UC Berkeley's Institute of Personality Assessment and Research (IPAR). Among architects, mathematicians, and writers, researchers found that valuing independence and cognitive engagement was positively related to creative behavior, whereas favoring conservative values was negatively related to creative behavior (Barron, 1968; Helson, 1971; Helson et al., 1995).

Kasof et al. (2007) also found that different values relate to creativity differently. Using Schwartz's (1992) framework of ten core values, they found that self-direction (independent thought and action), stimulation (seeking novelty and challenge), and universalism (concern for others) were positively linked to creative behavior. In contrast, tradition (commitment to established customs and ideas), conformity (restraint of impulses to violate social norms), and security (life stability) were negatively associated with creative behavior. Furthermore, reflecting a domain-specific view of creativity, Taylor and Kaufman (2020) examined Schwartz's ten values in relation to visual and verbal creative task performance. They found that self-direction and stimulation were positively associated with both creativity criteria, whereas stimulation was only associated with visual creativity. These studies suggest that certain values may serve as motivational drivers for creativity in specific contexts, highlighting the importance of considering the specificity of both values and creativity domains.

In addition to these general life values, motivation researchers also focus on task value. Situated expectancy-value theory (Eccles & Wigfield, 2020, 2023) is a motivational framework that focuses on types of task values, examining how one's expectancy for success and perceived task values influence choice and persistence. Expectancies for success address the question "Can I do this?", which closely aligns with the concept of self-efficacy (Bandura, 1982). As creative self-efficacy will be discussed in the following section, my emphasis here is on task value. Task value concerns the question "Do I want to do this?", reflecting the reasons individuals choose to engage in particular tasks.

Task value consists of four components: intrinsic value (often used interchangeably with intrinsic motivation; the enjoyment derived from a task), attainment value (the importance of doing well on a task as it relates to one's identity), utility value (the perceived usefulness of the task for achieving current or future goals), and perceived cost (what one must sacrifice to succeed in the task; Eccles & Wigfield, 2020, 2023). Perceived cost can be further divided into effort cost (the task requires too much effort), opportunity cost (having to give up other valued opportunities), and emotional cost (experiencing negative emotions when engaging in an activity; Eccles & Wigfield, 2023).

Aside from intrinsic value, which has been discussed earlier, task values have been a less commonly used motivational variable in understanding creativity. However, a few studies suggest their potential relevance. Pukkeeree et al. (2020) found that employee attainment value was positively related to innovative work behavior. This indicates that individuals who place high importance on their job tasks are more likely to engage in creative behavior, as they perceive these tasks to be personally meaningful and aligned with their identity.

Utility value is traditionally considered an extrinsic form of task value; therefore, its relationship to creativity may be complex. Among secondary school students, a recent study did not find a significant relationship between utility value in STEM (Science, Technology, Engineering, and Mathematics) and creative thinking competency (Saw et al., 2025). Usefulness can be also examined not in relation to self, but in terms of usefulness of creativity in helping others. In this case, researchers refer to prosocial motivation (Bolino & Grant, 2016; Forgeard, 2024; Grant & Berg, 2011; Liu et al., 2016). They found that prosocial motivation drives individuals to consider others' perspectives, thereby generating more potentially useful novel ideas. For instance, in organizational contexts, when employees adopt others' viewpoints with the aim of understanding their preferences, needs, and values, they develop more innovative ideas (Grant & Berg, 2011). Among professional artists and scientists, Forgeard (2024) also found that prosocial motivation was one of the four main categories mentioned when they were asked what drives their creative behavior.

Perceived cost is a relatively newer construct in situated expectancy-value theory (Eccles & Wigfield, 2020), referring to the perceived negative aspects of engaging in a task. Accordingly, the link between perceived task cost and creativity remains unclear. While the creative process requires individuals to take intellectual risks and persist through challenges, high perceived task cost can interfere with this process. For instance, if an engineering student views a class project to design a control motor for a robot as too time-consuming or high in opportunity cost (e.g., having to give up other activities they are more interested in, such as social activities), they may approach it with a minimal, compliance-driven orientation, limiting original thinking or creative engagement. By contrast, moderate levels of perceived cost may not necessarily be detrimental to creativity. It is possible that recognizing such costs may motivate individuals to think creatively in order to make the process more efficient and less burdensome. Of note,

Kapoor and Kaufman (2022) have proposed that conditions of pressure or constraint can give rise to dark creativity, such as engaging in creative behaviors to achieve malicious goals. For example, when students perceive that preparing for a math exam requires too much effort and time, they may devise a creative way to cheat. Thus, whether and how perceived task cost is related to creativity remains an open question for future research.

Creativity-Specific Motivational Constructs

The previous section highlighted how researchers have applied motivational theories to explore what motivates creative individuals. Building on this foundation, creativity scholars over the past two decades have increasingly integrated motivational constructs into creativity research, proposing creativity-specific motivation constructs (e.g., creative self-efficacy).

Creative Self-Efficacy

Based on social cognitive theory (Bandura, 1989), creative self-efficacy refers to an individual's belief in their ability to generate creative ideas and engage in creative actions (Tierney & Farmer, 2002; Karwowski, 2016). This theory suggests that people are less likely to invest substantial time and effort in their work unless they are confident that their actions will lead to positive outcomes and help avoid negative ones (Bandura, 2001). Accordingly, creative self-efficacy is an attribute to creative individuals that fosters both engagement and sustained involvement in creative processes by reinforcing the belief that one can successfully carry out these tasks, serving as a "can-do" motivational force (Bandura, 2001; Guo et al., 2024; Liu et al., 2016; Tierney & Farmer, 2002). Karwowski and Beghetto (2019) have formulated a model of creativity as agentic action which defines creative self-efficacy as a central motivational attribute at the intersection of potential and its enactment. This model emphasizes that creative self-efficacy is not merely a byproduct of creative potential but can indeed predict creative behavior above and beyond previously shown creative ability.

Multiple research syntheses have showed a positive relationship between creative self-efficacy and different aspects of creativity (Haase et al., 2018; Karwowski & Lebuda, 2016; Liu et al., 2016; Unal et al., 2021). Haase et al.'s (2018) meta-analysis showed an overall moderate correlation between creative self-efficacy and creativity ($r = .39$). It was more strongly associated with self-rated creativity (e.g., self-reported creative personality, creative activities; $r = .53$) than with other-rated creativity (e.g., performance on divergent thinking tasks; $r = .23$). This is consistent with the idea that creative self-efficacy, as a self-perception, aligns more closely with self-evaluated creativity than with externally assessed performance. In workplace settings, another meta-analysis found a positive relationship between creative self-efficacy and creative idea generation (Liu et al., 2016). Such finding suggests that employees with low creative self-efficacy may be more hesitant to explore and generate innovative ideas and solutions.

Researchers have also explored its antecedents; that is, the factors that make individuals feel more confident in their creative abilities (McKay et al., 2018; Puente-Diaz, 2016; Puente-Diaz & Cavazos-Arroyo, 2018). These studies have shown that both personal factors (e.g., personality traits such as openness to experience and extraversion; Puente-Diaz, 2016) and contextual factors (e.g., leader creativity expectations; Adil et al., 2018) are related to individual creative self-efficacy. In addition, Lin et al. (2018) applied Bandura's (1982) framework of four sources of self-efficacy to examine college students' responses to the open-ended question, "What made you feel more confident in your creativity?" Responses from students in both the United States and China indicated that previous experiences in creative tasks were the most frequently cited source of creative self-efficacy. However, Chinese students reported more instances of social persuasion (encouragement or positive feedback from others on their creative performance or potential) compared to their U.S. counterparts. This may be attributed to the collectivist orientation of Chinese culture, which places greater emphasis on social validation and interpersonal influence in shaping self-beliefs.

These findings not only shed light on the antecedents of creative self-efficacy but also inform the design of targeted interventions intended to strengthen creative self-efficacy (Mathisen & Bronnick, 2009; Meinel et al., 2019; Vally et al., 2019). For example, Mathisen and Bronnick (2009) designed a one-week course for college students that embedded mastery experiences, whereby participants engaged in creative tasks to build their creative efficacy beliefs, and verbal persuasion, in which participants were encouraged and reassured that they possessed the capabilities needed to act creatively. Participants' creative self-efficacy increased after the one-week course and remained stable at a two-month follow-up. Another 13-week training program enhanced college students' creative self-efficacy by providing them repeated mastery experiences (Vally et al.,

2019). The program offered multiple opportunities for participants to engage in the practical application of various techniques to creatively solve real-world problems, thereby reinforcing their confidence through successful creative task performance.

Creative Values and Attitudes

Different from earlier section that discussed how general life values (e.g., valuing self-direction and stimulation) and specific task values (e.g., attainment value of an engineering task) drive creative individuals, the focus here is to focus on values specifically toward creativity (creative values). In a unidimensional measure of creativity attitudes and values developed by Acar and Runco (2014), they included statements addressing both the importance of creative thinking (e.g., "There is clear benefit to thinking about ideas that other people will not consider") and the usefulness of approaches to creative thinking (e.g., "When solving problems, it is often beneficial to postpone judgment about possible solutions"). They found that creativity attitudes and values predicted the extent to which individuals provided remote responses on divergent thinking tasks (Acar & Runco, 2014). Furthermore, creativity attitudes and values are positively related to college students' creative activities engagement out of school, even after controlling for the personality traits that are central to creativity (Runco et al., 2017).

Another emerging line of research has explored the multidimensional aspects of creative attitudes and values and examined their roles in predicting creativity-related outcomes among students. Ivcevic and Hoffmann (2022) developed a measure and identified three aspects of attitudes toward creativity: (1) valuing creativity, the perception that creativity is important and worthwhile (e.g., "It is important to me to have an opportunity to work on creative projects"), (2) anxious risk aversion, self-conscious emotional reaction and the belief that the potential costs of being creative outweigh the benefits (e.g., "It would be embarrassing to suggest an idea that my teachers or mentors did not like"), and (3) anticipating negative social consequences, expecting critical evaluation of one's creative ideas from relevant others (e.g., "If I suggested an original or unique ideas, other people may get angry at me"). To some degree, valuing creativity can be seen as an expression of attainment value (the personal importance placed on engaging in creativity). Anxious risk aversion and anticipating negative social consequences may represent emotion cost and social cost, respectively, marking the first time the cost concept from the situated expectancy-value theory has been applied to motivation for creativity. Among high school students in the United States, Ivcevic and Hoffmann (2022) found that valuing creativity positively predicted creativity at school, whereas anxious risk aversion negatively predicted it, even after controlling for openness to experience, a core personality trait that is central to creativity. In another study with high school students in Mexico, valuing creativity positively predicted students' everyday creative behavior in school, whereas anticipating negative social consequences negatively predicted it (Hoffmann et al., 2025).

Future Directions

This chapter reviewed two streams of research related to motivation and creativity. First, it discussed how motivational theories have been used as lenses to understand what motivates or demotivates creative individuals. Second, it focused on specific creative motivation constructs developed within the creativity literature and examined their relationships to creativity outcomes. The field of research on the motivational processes underlying creativity is growing rapidly, and the directions highlighted below may offer insights for future investigation.

First, most studies examining the relationship between motivation and creativity have adopted a single motivational theory as their theoretical lens. Future research would benefit from integrating constructs from multiple motivational theories, as each theory can illuminate distinct aspects of the motivational processes underlying creativity. For example, combining autonomy from self-determination theory with task value from situated expectancy-value theory can provide a more comprehensive view of motivation underlying creativity. While autonomy addresses the quality of motivation (whether it is self-driven or externally controlled), task value addresses the reasons why one might be motivated. Integrating these two perspectives could allow researchers to better understand both the source and strength of motivation, offering a more nuanced account than either theory could provide alone. Moreover, this integrative approach may also enhance predictive power, and ultimately inform more targeted programs designed to foster specific types of creativity.

Second, future research should expand the methodological breadth of studies. For example, qualitative methods, such as interviews or case studies (Benedek et al., 2020; Forgeard, 2024), can offer in-depth insights into subjective motivational experiences, uncovering nuanced motivational dynamics often overlooked by purely quantitative approaches. Additionally, longitudinal methods can be employed to track the trajectory of motivation over time. The selection of a specific longitudinal design should depend on the particular type of motivation being studied. When examining trait-like aspect of motivation (e.g., creative confidence), traditional longitudinal designs using repeated-measures surveys conducted over months or years are suitable, as these designs allow researchers to understand how relatively stable motivational characteristics predict creative development and action over time. On the other hand, capturing fluctuations in state-like aspects of motivation (e.g., momentary interest, perceived cost of a current task) may require more temporally focused methods such as experience sampling methodology (e.g., Martin et al., 2020; Lee & Bong, 2022; Oschwald et al., 2025), which can track moment-to-moment changes within a day or a week.

Third, future studies should specify aspects of creativity being examined and, based on that, propose motivational constructs that correspond in breadth to the creativity outcome of interest. Creativity is an umbrella term encompassing multiple distinct aspects, such as creative behavior, creative thinking, and creative achievement (Ivcevic, 2022; Reiter-Palmon & Schoenbeck, 2020). Thus, it can be misleading to generalize findings using the broad term "creativity" without clearly identifying its specific form. Moreover, motivational processes beneficial for one aspect of creativity might not necessarily generalize to another. For example, mastery orientation from goal orientation theory may be highly relevant for predicting creative achievement, where sustained effort toward specific goals is essential. However, mastery orientation may be less relevant to one's performance on divergent thinking tasks, as such time-bound tasks often require spontaneous idea generation or cognitive flexibility rather than persistent goal-directed long-term effort. Therefore, researchers should carefully align motivational constructs with specific creativity outcomes to ensure conceptual clarity and accurate interpretation of results.

Fourth, future research should aim to develop more creative motivation constructs that are grounded in the context of creativity itself. Although classical motivational theories have shed light on creativity, many were originally developed with fixed-endpoint achievements in mind, such as academic success or job performance, which may not fully account for the ill-defined characteristics of creativity. Developing motivation constructs rooted specifically in the creativity context may contribute to a more accurate theoretical understanding and support the design of programs that more effectively foster creative engagement. For example, adopting the approach- and avoidance-orientation from the classical achievement goal framework (Elliot & McGregor, 2001), Denis Dumas and colleagues (personal communication, March 12) developed the construct and measure of creativity goals. In this new creative motivation construct, they incorporated the two essential aspects of creativity, originality and usefulness/impact, and proposed four types of creativity goals: originality-approach, originality-avoidance, impact-approach, and impact-avoidance creativity goals.

Another direction concerns the domains of creativity and their associated motivations. Benedek and colleagues (2020) found that creativity in literature, music, and visual arts were more strongly motivated by expression and coping motives, whereas handicrafts and creative cooking were more strongly motivated by prosocial motives. Comparing creativity in the arts and sciences, researchers have also found that they are driven by different motives. Forgeard (2024) reported that creative achievement in the arts was positively associated with prosocial behavior, whereas no such association was found in the sciences. Lin et al. (2024) noted that stress tolerance—one dimension of curiosity, often viewed as the motivation to pursue knowledge or experience (Kashdan et al., 2018)—was negatively related to creative achievement in the arts but unrelated in the sciences. This emerging evidence suggests that creative individuals in different domains might have different motivations. Given that creativity in different domains has its own nature and challenges, future studies should further investigate the corresponding motivation for each.

In addition, the links between motivation and creativity should be examined in cross-cultural contexts due to different values and norms across cultures. For example, there has long been recognition that expressions of autonomy can differ across cultures (Ryan & Deci, 2017). In individualistic cultures, autonomy may be associated with personal choice and self-expression, whereas in collectivistic cultures, autonomy may be expressed through fulfilling group goals or aligning with social expectations (Ryan & Deci, 2017). Accordingly, the operationalization of autonomy's role in creativity may also vary depending on the cultural context (Guo et al., 2021; Guo et al., 2025). This suggests that motivational constructs cannot be assumed to function uniformly across cultures, and their relationships to creativity should be studied with cultural sensitivity and contextual relevance.

What motivates creative people? Based on the above review, the answer is complex. Different theories of motivation have their own origins and emphases: self-determination theory focuses on need satisfaction, situated expectancy-value theory emphasizes perceived value, and self-efficacy theory highlights the role of prior experiences. One promising approach is continuing development of creativity-native constructs rather than relying solely on those from broader motivation theories. Such constructs could offer a more grounded understanding of creative individuals and inform the design of targeted training or interventions to foster creativity-relevant motivation.

References

Acar, S., & Runco, M. A. (2014). Assessing associative distance among ideas elicited by tests of divergent thinking. *Creativity Research Journal, 26*(2), 229–238. https://doi.org/10.1080/10400419.2014.901095

Adil, M. S., Khan, M. N., Khan, I., & Qureshi, M. A. (2018). Impact of leader creativity expectations on employee creativity: Assessing the mediating and moderating role of creative self-efficacy. *International Journal of Management Practice, 11*(2), 171–189.

Al-Dhamit, Y., & Kreishan, L. (2016). Gifted students' intrinsic and extrinsic motivations and parental influence on their motivation: From the self-determination theory perspective. *Journal of Research in Special Educational Needs, 16*(1), 13–23. https://doi.org/10.1111/1471-3802.12048

Amabile, T. M. (1979). Effects of external evaluation on artistic creativity. *Journal of Personality and Social Psychology, 37*(2), 221–233. https://doi.org/10.1037/0022-3514.37.2.221

Amabile, T. M. (1983). The social psychology of creativity: A componential conceptualization. *Journal of Personality and Social Psychology, 45*, 357–376. https://doi.org/10.1037/0022-3514.45.2.357

Amabile, T. M. (1996). *Creativity in context*. Westview Press

Amabile, T. M., & Pillemer, J. (2012). Perspectives on the social psychology of creativity. *Journal of Creative Behavior, 46*, 3–15. https://doi.org/10.1002/jocb.001

Amabile, T. M., Barsade, S. G., Mueller, J. S., & Staw, B. M. (2005). Affect and creativity at work. *Administrative Science Quarterly, 50*, 367–403. https://doi.org/10.2189/asqu.2005.50.3.367

Bandura, A. (1982). Self efficacy mechanism in human agency. *American Psychologist, 37*(2), 122–147. https://doi.org/10.1037/0003-066X.37.2.122

Bandura, A. (1989). Human agency in social cognitive theory. *American Psychologist, 44*(9), 1175–1184. https://doi.org/10.1037/0003-066X.44.9.1175

Bandura, A. (2001). Social cognitive theory: An agentic perspective. *Annual Review of Psychology, 52*(1), 1–26. https://doi.org/10.1146/annurev.psych.52.1.1

Barron, F. (1968). *Creativity and personal freedom.* VanNostrand.

Baum, I. R., & Baumann, N. (2018). Autonomous creativity: The implicit autonomy motive fosters creative production and innovative behavior at school. *Gifted and Talented International, 33*(1-2), 15–25. https://doi.org/10.1080/15332276.2019.1608136

Beghetto, R. A. (2021). There is no creativity without uncertainty: Dubito Ergo Creo. *Journal of Creativity, 31*, 100005. https://doi.org/10.1016/j.yjoc.2021.100005

Benedek, M., Bruckdorfer, R., & Jauk, E. (2020). Motives for creativity: Exploring the what and why of everyday creativity. *The Journal of Creative Behavior, 54*(3), 610–625. https://doi.org/10.1002/jocb.396

Bolino, M. C., & Grant, A. M. (2016). The bright side of being prosocial at work, and the dark side, too: A review and agenda for research on other-oriented motives, behavior, and impact in organizations. *Academy of Management Annals, 10*(1), 599–670. https://doi.org/10.1080/19416520.2016.1153260

Brett, J. F., & Vandewalle, D. (1999). Goal orientation and goal content as predictors of performance in a training program. *Journal of Applied Psychology, 84*(6), 863–873. https://doi.org/10.1037/0021-9010.84.6.863

Çekmecelioğlu, H. G., & Günsel, A. (2011). Promoting creativity among employees of mature industries: The effects of autonomy and role stress on creative behaviors and job performance. *Procedia-Social and Behavioral Sciences, 24*, 889–895. https://doi.org/10.1016/j.sbspro.2011.09.020

De Jesus, S. N., Rus, C. L., Lens, W., & Imaginário, S. (2013). Intrinsic motivation and creativity related to product: A meta-analysis of the studies published between 1990–2010. *Creativity Research Journal, 25*(1), 80–84. https://doi.org/10.1080/10400419.2013.752235

Deci, E. L., & Ryan, R. M. (2000). The "what" and "why" of goal pursuits: Human needs and the self-determination of behavior. *Psychological Inquiry, 11*, 227–268. https://doi.org/10.1207/S15327965PLI1104_01

Deci, E. L., & Ryan, R. M. (2008). Self-determination theory: A macrotheory of human motivation, development, and health. *Canadian Psychology/Psychologie Canadienne, 49*(3), 182–185. https://doi.org/10.1037/a0012801

Du, K., Wang, Y., Ma, X., Luo, Z., Wang, L., & Shi, B. (2020). Achievement goals and creativity: the mediating role of creative self-efficacy. *Educational Psychology, 40*(10), 1249–1269. https://doi.org/10.1080/01443410.2020.1806210

Dweck, C. S. (1986). Motivational processes affecting learning. *American Psychologist, 41*(10), 1040–1048. https://doi.org/10.1037/0003-066x.41.10.1040

Dweck, C. S., & Leggett, E. L. (1988). A social-cognitive approach to motivation and personality. *Psychological Review*, 95(2), 256–273. https://doi.org/10.1037/0033-295X.95.2.256

Eccles, J. S., & Wigfield, A. (2020). From expectancy-value theory to situated expectancy-value theory: A developmental, social cognitive, and sociocultural perspective on motivation. *Contemporary Educational Psychology, 61*, 101859. https://doi.org/10.1016/j.cedpsych.2020.101859

Eccles, J. S., & Wigfield, A. (2023). Expectancy-value theory to situated expectancy-value theory: Reflections on the legacy of 40+ years of working together. *Motivation Science, 9*(1), 1–12. https://doi.org/10.1037/mot0000275

Elliot, A. J., & Dweck, C. S. (Eds.). (2013). *Handbook of competence and motivation*. Guilford Publications.

Elliot, A. J., & McGregor, H. A. (2001). A 2× 2 achievement goal framework. *Journal of Personality and Social Psychology*, 80(3), 501–519. https://doi.org/10.1037/0022-3514.80.3.501

Feather, N. T. (1995). Values, valences, and choice: The influences of values on the perceived attractiveness and choice of alternatives. *Journal of Personality and Social Psychology, 68*(6), 1135–1151. https://doi.org/10.1037/0022-3514.68.6.1135

Fischer, C., Malycha, C. P., & Schafmann, E. (2019). The influence of intrinsic motivation and synergistic extrinsic motivators on creativity and innovation. *Frontiers in Psychology, 10*, 137. https://doi.org/10.3389/fpsyg.2019.00137

Forgeard, M. (2024). Prosocial motivation and creativity in the arts and sciences: Qualitative and quantitative evidence. *Psychology of Aesthetics, Creativity, and the Arts, 18*(2), 222–244. https://doi.org/10.1037/aca0000435

Furnham, A. (1999). Personality and creativity. *Perceptual and Motor Skills, 88*, 407–408. https://doi.org/10.2466/pms.1999.88.2.407

Furnham, A., Zhang, J., & Chamorro-Premuzic, T. (2005). The relationship between psychometric and self-estimated intelligence, creativity, personality and academic achievement. *Imagination, Cognition and Personality, 25*, 119–145. https://doi.org/10.2190/530V-3M9U-7UQ8-FMBG

Gerhart, B., & Fang, M. (2015). Pay, intrinsic motivation, extrinsic motivation, performance, and creativity in the workplace: Revisiting long-held beliefs. *Annual Review of Organizational Psychology and Organizational Behavior.*, 2(1), 489 521. https://doi.org/10.1146/annurev-orgpsych-032414-111418

Glaveanu, V., Lubart, T., Bonnardel, N., Botella, M., De Biaisi, P. M., Desainte-Catherine, M., et al. (2013). Creativity as action: Findings from five creative domains. *Frontiers in Psychology, 4*, 1–14. https://doi.org/10.3389/fpsyg.2013.00176

Gong, Y., Wu, J., Song, L. J., & Zhang, Z. (2017). Dual tuning in creative processes: Joint contributions of intrinsic and extrinsic motivational orientations. *Journal of Applied Psychology, 102*(5), 829–844. https://doi.org/10.1037/apl0000185

Grant, A. M., & Berg, J. M. (2011). *Prosocial motivation at work: When, why, and how making a difference makes a difference.* In K. Cameron & G. Spreitzer (Eds.), *Handbook of positive organizational scholarship.* Oxford University Press.

Guo, Y., Lin, S., Guo, J., Lu, Z. L., & Shangguan, C. (2021). Cross-cultural measurement invariance of divergent thinking measures. *Thinking Skills and Creativity, 41*, 100852. https://doi.org/10.1002/jocb.643

Guo, Y., Lin, S., Williams, Z. J., Grantham, T. C., Guo, J., Cole Clark, L. Q., & Zou, W. (2024). Creative potential and creative self-belief: Measurement invariance in cross-cultural contexts. *The Journal of Creative Behavior, 58*(2), 209–226. https://doi.org/10.1002/jocb.643

Guo, J., Jiang, Y., Lin, S., & Pang, W. (2025). Individualism and collectivism as predictors of creative potentials and real-life creativity in China and US. *Creativity Research Journal, 37*(1), 120–131. https://doi.org/10.1080/10400419.2023.2217028

Haase, J., Hoff, E. V., Hanel, P. H., & Innes-Ker, Å. (2018). A meta-analysis of the relation between creative self-efficacy and different creativity measurements. *Creativity Research Journal, 30*(1), 1–16. https://doi.org/10.1080/10400419.2018.1411436

Han, X., Shi, Y., Miao, H., & Wang, L. (2024). Parenting behaviors and creativity: The roles of autonomous and controlled motivation. *Journal of Child and Family Studies, 33*(4), 1148–1157. https://doi.org/10.1007/s10826-023-02781-z

Helson, R. (1971). Women mathematicians and the creative personality. *Journal of Consulting and Clinical Psychology, 36*, 210–220. https://doi.org/10.1037/h0030728

Helson, R., Roberts, B., & Agronick, G. (1995). Enduringness and change in creative personality and the prediction of occupational creativity. *Journal of Personality and Social Psychology, 69*, 1173–1183. https://doi.org/10.1037/0022-3514.69.6.1173

Hennessey, B. A. (2019). Motivation and creativity. In J. C. Kaufman & R. J. Sternberg (Eds.), *The Cambridge handbook of creativity* (2nd ed., pp. 374–395). Cambridge University Press. https://doi.org/10.1017/9781316979839.020

Hennessey, B. A., Amabile, T. M., & Martinage, M. (1989). Immunizing children against the negative effects of reward. *Contemporary Educational Psychology, 14*(3), 212–227. https://doi.org/10.1016/0361-476X(89)90011-8

Hirst, G., Van Knippenberg, D., & Zhou, J. (2009). A cross-level perspective on employee creativity: Goal orientation, team learning behavior, and individual creativity. *Academy of Management Journal, 52*(2), 280–293. https://doi.org/10.5465/amj.2009.37308035

Hoffmann, J. D., Ivcevic, Z., & Castillo-Gualda, R. (2025). School climate and students' attitudes toward creativity. *Thinking Skills and Creativity, 101880*. https://doi.org/10.1016/j.tsc.2025.101880

Huang, X. (2025). Can students' perceived teacher autonomy support promote creativity? A moderated chain mediation model. *Current Psychology*, 1–11. https://doi.org/10.1007/s12144-025-07927-4

Ivcevic, Z. (2022). Conceptual and measurement specificity are key: The case of creativity and emotions. *Creativity Research Journal, 34*(4), 391–400. https://doi.org/10.1080/10400419.2022.2122373

Ivcevic, Z., & Hoffmann, J. D. (2022). The creativity dare: Attitudes toward creativity and prediction of creative behavior in school. *The Journal of Creative Behavior, 56*(2), 239–257. https://doi.org/10.1002/jocb.527

Kapoor, H., & Kaufman, J. C. (2022). The evil within: The AMORAL model of dark creativity. *Theory & Psychology, 32*(3), 467–490. https://doi.org/10.1177/09593543221074326

Karwowski, M. (2016). The dynamics of creative self-concept: Changes and reciprocal relations between creative self-efficacy and creative personal identity. *Creativity Research Journal, 28*(1), 99–104. https://doi.org/10.1080/10400419.2016.1125254

Karwowski, M., & Beghetto, R. A. (2019). Creative behavior as agentic action. *Psychology of Aesthetics, Creativity, and the Arts, 13*(4), 402–415. https://doi.org/10.1037/aca0000190

Karwowski, M., & Lebuda, I. (2016). The big five, the huge two, and creative self-beliefs: a meta-analysis. *Psychology of Aesthetics, Creativity, and the Arts, 10*(2), 214–232. https://doi.org/10.1037/aca0000035

Kashdan, T. B., & Fincham, F. D. (2002). "Facilitating creativity by regulating curiosity": Comment. *American Psychologist, 57*, 373–374. https://doi.org/10.1037/0003-066X.57.5.373

Kashdan, T. B., Stiksma, M. C., Disabato, D. J., McKnight, P. E., Bekier, J., Kaji, J., & Lazarus, R. (2018). The five-dimensional curiosity scale: Capturing the bandwidth of curiosity and identifying four unique subgroups of curious people. *Journal of Research in Personality, 73*, 130–149. https://doi.org/10.1016/j.jrp.2017.11.011

Kasof, J., Chen, C., Himsel, A., & Greenberger, E. (2007). Values and creativity. *Creativity Research Journal, 19*(2-3), 105–122. https://doi.org/10.1080/10400410701397164

Kirsch, C., Lubart, T., & Houssemand, C. (2015). Creative personality profile in social sciences: The leading role of autonomy. *Creativity. Theories–Research-Applications, 2*(2), 180–211. https://doi.org/10.1515/ctra-2015-0020

Kumar, D., Upadhyay, Y., Yadav, R., & Goyal, A. K. (2022). Psychological capital and innovative work behaviour: The role of mastery orientation and creative self-efficacy. *International Journal of Hospitality Management, 102*, 103157. https://doi.org/10.1016/j.ijhm.2022.103157

Latham, G. P. (2011). *Work motivation: History, theory, research, and practice.* Sage Publications.

Lee, M., & Bong, M. (2022). Patterns of motivation and learning during test-preparation of Korean adolescents: An experience sampling approach. *Educational Psychology, 42*(2), 200–221. https://doi.org/10.1080/01443410.2021.2016634

Lepper, M. R., Greene, D., & Nisbett, R. E. (1973). Undermining children's intrinsic interest with extrinsic reward: A test of the "overjustification" hypothesis. *Journal of Personality and Social Psychology, 28*(1), 129–137. https://doi.org/10.1037/h0035519

Li, H., Li, F., & Chen, T. (2018). A motivational–cognitive model of creativity and the role of autonomy. *Journal of Business Research, 92*, 179–188. https://doi.org/10.1016/j.jbusres.2018.07.025

Lin, S., Guo, J., & Wang, B. (2018, August). *Creativity self-efficacy in Chinese college students: Sources, SNS use, and loneliness.* Poster presented at the Annual Meeting of the American Psychological Association (APA), San Francisco, CA.

Lin, S., Ivcevic, Z., Kashdan, T. B., & Kaufman, S. B. (2024). Curious and persistent, but not consistent: Self-regulation traits and creativity. *The Journal of Creative Behavior, 59*(1), e638. https://doi.org/10.1002/jocb.638

Liu, D., Chen, X. P., & Yao, X. (2011). From autonomy to creativity: a multilevel investigation of the mediating role of harmonious passion. *Journal of Applied Psychology, 96*(2), 294–309. https://doi.org/10.1037/a0021294

Liu, D., Jiang, K., Shalley, C. E., Keem, S., & Zhou, J. (2016). Motivational mechanisms of employee creativity: A meta-analytic examination and theoretical extension of the creativity literature. *Organizational Behavior and Human Decision Processes, 137*, 236–263. https://doi.org/10.1016/j.obhdp.2016.08.001

Liu, Y., Wang, S., & Yao, X. (2019). Individual goal orientations, team empowerment, and employee creative performance: A case of cross-level interactions. *The Journal of Creative Behavior, 53*(4), 443–456. https://doi.org/10.1002/jocb.220

Lubart, T. I. (1994). *Product-centered self-evaluation and the creative process.* Unpublished doctoral dissertation, Yale University, New Haven, CT.

Mao, J., Chen, J., Ling, Y., & Huebner, E. S. (2020). Impact of teachers' leadership on the creative tendencies of students: The mediating role of goal-orientation. *Creativity Research Journal, 32*(3), 228–236. https://doi.org/10.1080/10400419.2020.1821569

Martin, A. J., Mansour, M., & Malmberg, L. E. (2020). What factors influence students' real-time motivation and engagement? An experience sampling study of high school students using mobile technology. *Educational Psychology, 40*(9), 1113–1135. https://doi.org/10.1080/01443410.2018.1545997

Mathisen, G. E., & Bronnick, K. S. (2009). Creative self-efficacy: An intervention study. *International Journal of Educational Research, 48*(1), 21–29. https://doi.org/10.1016/j.ijer.2009.02.009

McKay, A. S., Lovelace, J. B., & Howard, M. C. (2018). The heart of innovation: Antecedents and consequences of creative self-efficacy in organizations. In *Individual creativity in the workplace* (pp. 223–244). Academic Presss

Meinel, M., Wagner, T. F., Baccarella, C. V., & Voigt, K. I. (2019). Exploring the effects of creativity training on creative performance and creative self-efficacy: Evidence from a longitudinal study. *The Journal of Creative Behavior, 53*(4), 546–558. https://doi.org/10.1002/jocb.234

Nandi, S., & Watts, L. L. (2025). Achievement goal orientation and employee creativity: A meta-analysis. *Psychology of Aesthetics, Creativity, and the Arts.* Advance online publication. https://doi.org/10.1037/aca0000749

Nicholls, J. G. (1984). Achievement motivation: Conceptions of ability, subjective experience, task choice, and performance. *Psychological Review, 91*(3), 328–346.

Nili, F., & Tasavori, M. (2022). Linking an autonomy-supportive climate and employee creativity: the influence of intrinsic motivation and company support for creativity. *European Business Review, 34*(5), 666–688. https://doi.org/10.1108/EBR-06-2021-0146

Oldham, G. R., & Cummings, A. (1996). Employee creativity: Personal and contextual factors at work. *Academy of Management Journal, 39*, 607–634. https://doi.org/10.2307/256657

Oschwald, A., Moeller, J., Kracke, B., Viljaranta, J., & Dietrich, J. (2025). Student motivation and instructional clarity: Linking experience sampling method data to objective behavioural observations. *British Journal of Educational Psychology.* Advance online publication. https://doi.org/10.1111/bjep.12775

Puente-Díaz, R. (2016). Creative self-efficacy: An exploration of its antecedents, consequences, and applied implications. *The Journal of Psychology, 150*(2), 175–195. https://doi.org/10.1080/00223980.2015.1051498

Puente-Diaz, R., & Cavazos-Arroyo, J. (2018). An exploration of some antecedents and consequences of creative self-efficacy among college students. *The Journal of Creative Behavior, 52*(3), 256–266. https://doi.org/10.1002/jocb.149

Pukkeeree, P., Na-Nan, K., & Wongsuwan, N. (2020). Effect of attainment value and positive thinking as moderators of employee engagement and innovative work behaviour. *Journal of Open Innovation: Technology, Market, and Complexity, 6*(3), 69. https://doi.org/10.3390/joitmc6030069

Reiter-Palmon, R., & Illies, J. J. (2004). Leadership and creativity: Understanding leadership from a creative problem-solving perspective. *The Leadership Quarterly, 15*, 55–77. https://doi.org/10.1016/j.leaqua.2003.12.005

Reiter-Palmon, R., & Schoenbeck, M. (2020). *Creativity equals creativity—or does it? How creativity is measured influences our understanding of creativity.* In V. Dörfler & M. Stierand (Eds.), *Handbook of research methods on creativity* (pp. 290–300). Edward Elgar Publishing.

Renninger, K. A., & Hidi, S. E. (2019). *The Cambridge handbook of motivation and learning*. Cambridge University Press.

Runco, M. A., Acar, S., & Cayirdag, N. (2017). A closer look at the creativity gap and why students are less creative at school than outside of school. *Thinking Skills and Creativity, 24*, 242–249. https://doi.org/10.1016/j.tsc.2017.04.003

Ryan, R. M. (Ed.). (2012). *The Oxford handbook of human motivation.* Oxford University Press.

Ryan, R. M., & Deci, E. L. (2017). *Self-determination theory: Basic psychological needs in motivation, development, and wellness.* Guilford Publications.

Ryan, R. M., & Deci, E. L. (2000). Self-determination theory and the facilitation of intrinsic motivation, social development, and well-being. *American Psychologist, 55*(1), 68–78. https://doi.org/10.1037/0003-066X.55.1.68

Santiago-Torner, C., Tarrats-Pons, E., & Corral-Marfil, J. A. (2023). Effects of intensity of teleworking and creative demands on the cynicism dimension of job burnout. *Employee Responsibilities and Rights Journal*, 1–23. https://doi.org/10.1007/s10672-023-09464-3

Saw, G. K., Kunisaki, L. T., Lin, S., Culbertson, R., & Megyesi-Brem, K. A. (2025). Opportunities for deeper learning and adolescents' creative thinking competency in STEM: The mediating role of situated expectancy-value beliefs. *International Journal of Science and Mathematics Education*, 1–24. https://doi.org/10.1007/s10763-025-10567-6

Schwartz, S. H. (1992). Universals in the content and structure of values: Theory and empirical tests in 20 countries. In M. Zanna (Ed.), *Advances in experimental social psychology* (Vol. 25, pp. 1–65). Academic Press. https://doi.org/10.1016/S0065-2601(08)60281-6

Shalley, C. E., & Gilson, L. L. (2004). What leaders need to know: A review of social and contextual factors that can foster or hinder creativity. *The Leadership Quarterly, 15*, 33–53. https://doi.org/10.1016/j.leaqua.2003.12.004

Shalley, C. E., & Perry-Smith, J. E. (2001). Effects of social-psychological factors on creative performance: The role of informational and controlling expected evaluation and modeling experience. *Organizational Behavior and Human Decision Processes, 84*, 1–22. https://doi.org/10.1006/obhd.2000.2918

Sheldon, K. M. (1995). Creativity and self-determination in personality. *Creativity Research Journal, 8*(1), 25–36. https://doi.org/10.1207/s15326934crj0801_3

Sia, S. K., & Appu, A. V. (2015). Work autonomy and workplace creativity: Moderating role of task complexity. *Global Business Review, 16*(5), 772–784. https://doi.org/10.1177/0972150915591435

Tierney, P., & Farmer, S. M. (2002). Creative self-efficacy: Its potential antecedents and relationship to creative performance. *Academy of Management journal, 45*(6), 1137–1148. https://doi.org/10.5465/3069429

Unal, A., & Tasar, M. (2021). A systematic review of creative self-efficacy literature in education. *EURASIA Journal of Mathematics, Science and Technology. Education, 17*(12). https://doi.org/10.29333/ejmste/11404

Vally, Z., Salloum, L., AlQedra, D., El Shazly, S., Albloshi, M., Alsheraifi, S., & Alkaabi, A. (2019). Examining the effects of creativity training on creative production, creative self-efficacy, and neuro-executive functioning. *Thinking Skills and Creativity, 31*, 70–78. https://doi.org/10.1016/j.tsc.2018.11.003

Vandewalle, D. (1997). Development and validation of a work domain goal orientation instrument. *Educational and Psychological Measurement, 57*(6), 995–1015. https://doi.org/10.1177/0013164497057006009

Vandewalle, D., & Cummings, L. L. (1997). A test of the influence of goal orientation on the feedback-seeking process. *Journal of Applied Psychology, 82*(3), 390–400. https://doi.org/10.1037/0021-9010.82.3.390

White, K., & Owen, D. (1970). Locus of evaluation for classroom work and the development of creative potential. *Psychology in the Schools, 7*(3), 292–295. https://doi.org/10.1002/1520-6807(197007)7

Wigfield, A., Muenks, K., & Eccles, J. S. (2021). Achievement motivation: What we know and where we are going. *Annual Review of Developmental Psychology, 3*(1), 87–111. https://doi.org/10.1146/annurev-devpsych-050720-103500

Xue, Y., Gu, C., Wu, J., Dai, D. Y., Mu, X., & Zhou, Z. (2020). The effects of extrinsic motivation on scientific and artistic creativity among middle school students. *The Journal of Creative Behavior, 54*(1), 37–50. https://doi.org/10.1002/jocb.239

Yang, S. B., & Ok Choi, S. (2009). Employee empowerment and team performance: Autonomy, responsibility, information, and creativity. *Team Performance Management: An International Journal, 15*(5/6), 289–301. https://doi.org/10.1108/13527590910983549

Ye, L., Li, Y., & Zhang, N. (2025). The impact of autonomy-supportive organizational environments on employees' emotions and creative performance: A self-determination theory perspective. *PLoS One, 20*(5), e0322184. https://doi.org/10.1371/journal.pone.0322184

Yesuf, Y. M., Getahun, D. A., & Debas, A. T. (2023). Factors affecting "employees' creativity": the mediating role of intrinsic motivation. *Journal of Innovation and Entrepreneurship, 12*(1), 31. https://doi.org/10.1186/s13731-023-00299-8

Yoon, H. J., Sung, S. Y., Choi, J. N., Lee, K., & Kim, S. (2015). Tangible and intangible rewards and employee creativity: The mediating role of situational extrinsic motivation. *Creativity Research Journal, 27*(4), 383–393. https://doi.org/10.1080/10400419.2015.1088283

Yu, H., Zuo, S., Liu, Y., & Niemiec, C. P. (2021). Toward a personality integration perspective on creativity: Between-and within-persons associations among autonomy, vitality, and everyday creativity. *The Journal of Positive Psychology, 16*(6), 789–801. https://doi.org/10.1080/17439760.2020.1818810

Zhang, X., & Bartol, K. M. (2010). Linking empowering leadership and employee creativity: The influence of psychological empowerment, intrinsic motivation, and creative process engagement. *Academy of Management Journal, 53*, 107–128. https://doi.org/10.5465/amj.2010.48037118

Zhou, J. (1998). Feedback valence, feedback style, task autonomy, and achievement orientation: Interactive effects on creative performance. *Journal of Applied Psychology, 83*(2), 261–276. https://doi.org/10.1037/0021-9010.83.2.261

CHAPTER 6

Five Key Cognitive Attributes of Highly Creative Individuals

Denis Dumas and Sofiia Kagan

Five Key Cognitive Attributes of Highly Creative Individuals

Highly creative individuals are those people who consistently produce, refine, and articulate ideas that are particularly original and task-appropriate within their context (Guilford, 1962; Plucker et al., 2004; Torrance, 1993). Although the construct of creativity encompasses the generation of ideas that are original and task-appropriate only to the creator themselves (generally referred to as: personal creativity, Runco, 2007; mini-c, Beghetto & Kaufman, 2007; primary creativity; Runco & Beghetto, 2019;

Author Note
Correspondence concerning this paper should be addressed to Denis Dumas, Department of Educational Psychology, University of Georgia: 624 Aderhold Hall, 110 Carlton St., Athens, GA, 30602. Email: denis.dumas@uga.edu. This work follows all ethical guidelines of the American Psychological Association, and the authors declare they have no conflict of interest.

D. Dumas (✉) • S. Kagan
Department of Educational Psychology, University of Georgia, Athens, GA, USA
e-mail: denis.dumas@uga.edu; sofiia.kagan@uga.edu

Z. Ivcevic (ed.), *Creators*, The Seven C's of Creativity,
https://doi.org/10.1007/978-3-032-09225-0_6

or self-referenced creativity, Dumas et al., 2024b), an individual would likely not be considered *highly* creative unless their ideas are also judged to be creative by others (referred to as: little, Pro, or Big-C, Kaufman & Beghetto, 2009; secondary creativity, Runco & Beghetto, 2019; socially referenced creativity, Dumas & Kaufman, 2024). To put it another way, a highly creative individual contributes to the evolution of human culture by generating and sharing ideas that are worth imitating by others, at least within their local community (Dietrich, 2019; Gabora, 2019; Gabora & Tseng, 2017; Ivcevic & Kaufman, 2024).

In order to support their creativity, highly creative people have also developed several additional cognitive attributes, whose functions underlie their capacity to be creative. Indeed, one reason why creativity is a fascinating psychological construct to study is that the creative process is highly complex, and it requires an array of cognitive and metacognitive abilities for it to occur successfully (Lebuda & Benedek, 2023; Mumford et al., 1988; Ward & Kolomyts, 2010). If you consider the entirety of the creative process, from generating a novel idea that also fits the circumstances, developing that idea into something mature and ready to share with others, and then communicating that idea to others, you might be hard-pressed to find a cognitive attribute that is *not* relevant. Depending on the domain of creativity, even non-cognitive attributes such as motor planning (e.g., in the domain of dance; Biasutti & Habe, 2021), empathy (e.g., in the domain of acting; Goldstein, 2024), and curiosity (e.g., in the sciences; Peterson, 2020) clearly play a role. And of course, personality attributes (e.g., openness, volatility) have perennially been shown to either support or undermine creativity across domains (Barron, 1957; Dumas et al., 2024; Eysenck, 1993; Feist, 2010). So, what psychological attributes and processes are relevant to creativity? Perhaps all of them.

Despite this very wide-ranging diversity of psychological antecedents of creativity, in this chapter, we narrow the aperture to focus on and highlight five key cognitive attributes that play an especially strong role in the psychological make-up of creative individuals. These five cognitive attributes were chosen based on their demonstrated importance to creators across domains, contexts, and tasks, as well as for their relative under-appreciation within the creativity research literature. In this chapter, although we draw our conclusions from existing literature, we also strive to highlight what we see as very important cognitive attributes that are also as-yet under-studied within creativity science. This choice is visible not just in the cognitive attributes we have chosen to foreground, but also in those that we have chosen to background.

For instance, one cognitive attribute that we have explicitly chosen to place in the background of the current discussion is divergent thinking. Divergent thinking is a mental ability to generate a wide set of ideas that differ (i.e., "diverge") from the prompt that elicited them, or from one another (Runco & Acar, 2019; Wilson et al., 1954), and it is certainly the most-studied mental attribute in the psychology of creativity (e.g., Forthmann et al., 2020; Dumas et al., 2021b; Weiss et al., 2021). In fact, regular readers of creativity research will know that there is hardly an issue of any of our journals that is released without at least one paper on divergent thinking being featured. Perhaps this emphasis on divergent thinking makes sense for our community, because divergent thinking is clearly relevant to the creative process as it occurs in vivo. Especially during the ideation phase of the creative process, in which generating a large quantity of original ideas is of high importance, divergent thinking must play a role, although it is far from the whole story of creativity (e.g., Benedek et al., 2023). It may be that our field's heavy emphasis on divergent thinking, while teaching us much, has also contributed to certain blind-spots in our understanding of the phenomena of human creativity (Glăveanu & Kaufman, 2020). This might be especially true in regard to the use of domain-general divergent thinking tasks, such as the Alternate Uses Task (Guilford, 1956) that require only basic world knowledge to respond to. Although such domain-general tasks have been especially useful in studying children's creativity because children typically do not possess the necessary knowledge to innovate within an established domain (Acar et al., 2024), divergent thinking is fundamentally divorced from the more complex requirements of the real-world creativity of adults, which tends to be nested within domains (Dumas et al., 2022; Simonton, 2009; Zabelina et al., 2022).

For these reasons, our intention in this chapter is to table the ongoing scholarly discussions on divergent thinking and focus on five additional cognitive attributes that we contend are crucial for the creative process, but as-yet under-studied within our field. Our hope in making this choice is that this chapter provides insights about creativity as it occurs in contexts outside of the laboratory (e.g., schools; businesses) that go beyond what is most often found in the creativity journals. If you are a cognitively oriented creativity researcher who has mainly focused on divergent thinking in your past work, and you are seeking additional cognitive attributes to include in future studies, then this chapter is intended to be for you. In order to accomplish our goal, we draw strongly on applied psychological literature, especially educational psychology, to conceptualize how a highly creative individual might interact with what is normative or habitual (i.e., accepted as useful, but not original) in their field, and then go beyond that normative behavior to posit something novel and creative. Throughout, we make the supposition that, in order to be *highly* creative (as the title of this chapter dictates), the individual must generate ideas that are not solely judged to be creative by themselves, but are also seen as novel and meaningful by others, at least within their immediate context or local community.

The five key cognitive attributes that we highlight as important for high levels of creativity are: (1) knowledge in the domain within which the creativity is taking place; (2) epistemic cognition that supports the critical appraisal of that existing knowledge; (3) relational reasoning to make new connections and associations among ideas; (4) problem-finding to identify open areas of the domain that are ripe for innovation; and (5) the ability to self-evaluate ideas, in order to select those that are most worth investing in. As already mentioned, these are far from the only five cognitive attributes that support high levels of creativity, but we offer them here as five that are necessary for creative impact, and that are worth deeper consideration in our field.

Domain Knowledge

In order to generate an idea that is original and task-appropriate, creative individuals fundamentally must go beyond what is already known. For this reason, it has often been argued that learning is itself a creative act wherein the learner generates novel and meaningful insights into the phenomenon they are learning about (Karwowski et al., 2020; Piaget, 1973; Runco, 2007). Interestingly, this conceptualization implies a kind of paradox vis-à-vis knowledge and creativity: when an individual has very low levels of prior knowledge (e.g., in early childhood) the opportunities for learning, and therefore creativity, abound; but as an individual learns more, fewer and fewer concepts are novel to them, and therefore the opportunities for learning and creativity are necessarily fewer (Dumas et al., 2024a). This knowledge paradox is one reason why young children are widely seen as so creative: their low level of prior knowledge means that they are continually generating novel and useful insights about their world, enacting not-yet-habituated behaviors for the first time, and expressing themselves in idiosyncratic and unique ways (Berthiaume et al., 2024; Celume et al., 2019; Russ, 2016). Of course, the ideas that are generated by low-knowledge individuals such as children, or novices that are acclimating to a new domain of learning, are necessarily only creative to themselves or to other learners at their level, and are not likely to be seen as creative by those individuals who are more knowledgeable (Dumas & Kaufman, 2024). For this reason, novice learners typically need to learn more, and grow their knowledge, in order to make a socially referenced creative impact. Therefore, we do not consider novices engaged in this kind of self-referenced or mini-c creativity to be highly creative, as defined here.

In order to make the kind of social impact that is required for an individual to be highly creative, they must possess a requisite amount of knowledge within their domain of innovation. Importantly, this domain knowledge includes both declarative knowledge, which can be represented verbally in straightforward way, and procedural knowledge, which is represented as a sequence of steps of behaviors for the individual to enact (Alexander, 1992). Without such knowledge, it would not be possible for an individual to know the established norms of their field, in order to strategically break them, or move beyond them. To use a colloquial phrase: highly creative individuals choose to zag while others zig. So, they need to understand what it means to zig (i.e., the typical practices) in their domain, in order to find an appropriate way to zag (i.e., contribute something new and useful).

As individuals learn in their domain, their knowledge is growing and also organizing around the key tenets of the domain, allowing them to prioritize more important aspects of the domain, while also identifying those aspects that are more peripheral (Zeitz & Spoehr, 1989). This increasingly effective organization of both declarative and procedural knowledge means that individuals with a high level of expertise in a domain are not only able to accomplish domain-specific tasks very rapidly and effectively, but they are also able to process and assimilate new information with a high degree of efficiency, by relating it to what they already know (Ericsson, 2005). In this way, domain knowledge, especially the procedural knowledge that constitutes domain-specific strategies and skills, supports the performance of domain experts in real time, in every instance that the individual is working within the domain. For this reason, domain experts can appear to others to possess a facility of thinking and capability of memory and problem-solving that could be mistaken for innate mental capacity, when actually the domain-specific processes that allow for their high performance were learned and practiced (Ericsson & Staszewski, 1989; Sternberg, 1995). In addition, because of its reliance on domain-specific procedural and declarative knowledge, expert performance is unlikely to transfer across domains (e.g., Kalyuga. 2013), meaning that just because an individual is impressively capable of creativity in one domain (e.g., music) does not imply that they will be in another (e.g., biology).

What this means more practically is that individuals are not capable of developing a high level of socially referenced creativity in any given domain without requisite training to develop the knowledge they need. In cases of very high precocity, individuals might develop much earlier in their lifespan than others typically do in their domain, but nonetheless the training period must take place. In support of this pattern, existing historiometric studies of highly creative and impactful individuals have continually demonstrated that some knowledge development and training period is necessary for even a very precocious and promising student to develop their capacity to make a creative impact (e.g., Kopiez, 2011; Simonton, 2024a; Yi et al., 2023). Although important differences in domains do exist—for instance, Simonton (1986) classically demonstrated, using data from Goertzel (1978), that eminent poets needed much less formal education than did eminent scientists—all domains require some formal or informal knowledge development to support later creative accomplishment. Even in the case of poets, who may need little or no formal education or credentialing to support highly creative poetry, clearly, highly creative poets have read (or listened to) a huge amount of poetry; a process that can be thought of as informal education in the domain.

In fact, we might hypothesize that, because of their high levels of intrinsic motivation and curiosity, individuals who are on track to be highly creative are likely to rely more heavily on informal and individual learning experiences than are other learners who might need more formal instructor-led educational experiences. This pattern might serve to obscure the role of education in the life of the eminent creative, who may be seen as prodigies who miraculously appear to not have needed to be taught. Of course, we would contend that it is impossible to truly avoid the need for learning and knowledge development: no baby is born knowing what they need to know in order to make a creative contribution to any domain, and therefore learning must take place. For this reason, it would be impossible for a young person to even know about the existence of a domain without the influence, however indirect, of a more knowledgeable individual at some point in their lives: otherwise, they would need to completely re-invent the wheel in their domain, rather than making a novel and cutting-edge contribution. So, if an individual wishes to be highly creative and impactful, what should they do? In our view, the first and most important thing would be learning within their chosen domain.

One pragmatic implication of this argument for the field of creativity research is the need to include more domain-specific measures in our research. Although domain-general creative tasks are suitable for children who, by necessity of their youth, are very unlikely to possess the domain knowledge needed to be creative within a domain, participants who are older should be challenged to be creative in a more ecologically valid, and therefore domain-specific, way. Concomitant with the need for additional domain-specific tasks and measures in our field is a need for domain knowledge to be measured as a covariate, as a way to determine (or at least control for) how knowledge in the domain influenced participants' capacity to be creative. Another research strategy associated with this focus on domain-specific knowledge is the purposeful recruitment of participants with established expertise in a given domain, or students who are working toward expertise, as a way to cross-sectionally infer how the development of knowledge within the domain might change creative thinking processes (e.g., Dumas et al., 2020). In any case, in order to meaningfully understand the role of domain knowledge in creativity, future work will need a greater emphasis on this issue as research studies are designed and executed.

Epistemic Cognition

In order to be creative, a creator must go beyond what they have been taught to do. But how does a person know what existing practices in their domain stand on firmly justified ground, and therefore should not be changed, versus identifying other practices that might be more tenuously justified, and therefore changeable? Epistemic cognition is thinking about the nature of and justification for knowledge (Hofer, 2016; Chinn et al., 2011), and it is through this process that individuals consider whether what they know can be generalized, trusted, or applied with confidence (Alexander, 2016b; Kitchner, 2009). Without a capacity for epistemic cognition, thinking critically about what has been taught, and potentially evaluating claims to be false, misleading, or non-dogmatic, would not be possible (Kuhn, 1999). Indeed, the consideration of the development of epistemic cognition, and even how to help students improve their epistemic thinking, lies deep at the heart of educational psychology.

One of the earliest still-surviving, and most influential, texts of western thinking about education is Plato's *Theaetatus* (369 BCE). This is the text from which the often-discussed "Socratic method" of teaching—which features principally one-on-one conversation between teacher and student, where the teacher mainly asks probing questions of the student—is derived. The piece is written as dialogue, in which Socrates teaches a promising and gifted adolescent (i.e., Theaetatus) about the nature of knowledge and knowing. As such, Plato provided the reader simultaneously with an example of how to teach using the Socratic method (via Socrates' dialogue), as well as an epistemic justification for why that teaching method is preferable to others. The definition of knowledge to which Socrates and Theaetatus eventually arrive is *justified true belief*, a definition still discussed among epistemologists today (de Grefte, 2023). So, while the previous section of this chapter focused on the need to know *what* and *how* (i.e., declarative and procedural knowledge in a domain), it is also necessary to know *why* by justifying and evaluating the trustworthiness of what is known.

Epistemic cognition is currently known to develop as an individual grows and matures, and in conjunction with their learning in a domain (Greene & Yu, 2016; Hofer & Pintrich, 1997; Schommer, 1998). Young children begin in a *realist* phase of epistemic cognition development, where they believe what they are told by their caretakers are perfect copies of an objective, knowable reality (Felton & Kuhn, 2007). If a realist wants to know something, their process will simply involve asking an adult and trusting what they say. But as children grow, they will enter an *absolutist* phase, where they now understand that individual people can be incorrect (Mason & Boscolo, 2004). However, as the name implies, absolutists maintain an absolute trust of certain authorities, such as teachers, experts, or other leaders, and therefore coming to know something for an absolutist is a process of identifying an authoritative source and then believing it absolutely. While it is rare to find typically developing students in formal schooling who retain realist epistemic beliefs from young childhood, absolutist beliefs are unfortunately more common, especially in the K-12 setting, and lead to a host of negative academic outcomes, especially vis-à-vis the interpretation and integration of multiple sources (e.g., Barzilai & Zohar, 2012).

With maturation and learning, an individual will enter the *multiplist* phase of epistemic cognition development, where they now understand that knowledge is a mental construction of reality, which can change over time (Kuhn et al., 2000). However, they have not yet developed the capacity and motivation to evaluate claims on their own, and therefore are overwhelmed by conflicting viewpoints, and believe that determining which viewpoint is most trustworthy is not possible. For a multiplist, the genuine justification and evaluation of competing claims is not possible, so they simply stop, throw up their proverbial hands, and believe that nothing can really be known. Although this multiplist phase is also associated with poor performance when individuals are required to integrate multiple competing viewpoints (Thomm et al., 2017), it nonetheless appears to be a necessary step in the development toward mature epistemic cognition, which occurs in the final *evaluativist* phase. Those individuals who reach the evaluativist phase have now developed relatively mature capacity for epistemic cognition, and recognize the need to reconcile a subjective viewpoint with a more objective reality through critical evaluation and the weighing of specific evidence (Bendixen, 2016; Kuhn & Wienstock, 2002). Evaluativists typically accept that complete knowledge of the universe is likely impossible for a human, but they also believe in the process of learning and improvement of knowledge through reflective thinking about experience and evidence. Evaluativist epistemic beliefs are consistently associated with better academic outcomes, and interventions to support the development of these beliefs have repeatedly shown significant positive effects on academic achievement (see Cartiff et al., 2021, for a recent meta analysis).

We would hypothesize that, without a developed evaluativist capacity for epistemic cognition—at least within the domain where an individual is working—it would likely be very difficult for them to make a creative contribution in that domain. If an individual is content to firmly trust the attestations of authoritative experts, or if they believe that all perspectives are equally true regardless of justification, the process of creativity in a domain is unlikely to even begin. This is because creativity is fundamentally about contributing original ideas that are somehow better suited to a particular context than previous ideas. But for those who hold absolutist or multiplist epistemic understandings, improving on or contributing to a domain is not actually possible, either because authoritative experts have already achieved absolute understanding, or because knowledge is so subjective that no contribution can be better than any other. In accordance with this hypothesis, a clear argument has been posited, recently from Beghetto (e.g., 2021, 2022) and stemming from classic work from Torrance (1975), that teaching students to deal meaningfully with uncertainty and competing viewpoints, even as early as elementary school, is a key part of creative education.

Given the already rich argument concerning the necessity of incorporating uncertainty into a creative curriculum, we would add that providing learners with the domain-specific knowledge they need to effectively weigh evidence, and therefore begin to alleviate that uncertainty, is needed lest learners become stuck in the multiplist phase. Perhaps the application and explanation of uncertainty might be enough to help learners move from the absolutist to the multiplist phase, but we do not want learners to believe that accepting uncertainty, and believing that uncertainty to be immutable, is the goal in and of itself. Of course, uncertainty cannot be avoided in creative work, but—assuming that creativity is happening intentionally and not accidentally—the eventual goal of a creator would be to provide a novel insight or idea that makes new meaning, and contributes a new understanding to the domain, rather than simply adding to the uncertainty. The key here may be identifying how an individual learner thinks epistemically (e.g., absolutist, multiplist), and providing the particular experience they need in order to move to the next stage. When learners have reached an evaluativist stage of epistemic cognition in a domain, and have developed a capacity for reflective thought about the evidence for or against differing perspectives in their discipline, they are then likely to be ready for more specific and targeted thinking about novel and original ideas in their domain.

Relational Reasoning

Alexander Bain's highly influential phrase "stream of consciousness" (1864) describes human mental experience as a continuous unbroken flow of thoughts that (at least during waking hours) is constantly occurring. In order to produce this cohesive experience of consciousness, the mind must be continually relating information from the present moment to information stored in memory (Baird, 2013; Hofstadter, 2007). That said, not all associations made by the mind represent the same amount of conceptual distance (i.e., associations can be more proximal or more distant; Kenett et al., 2017), and different people, even encountering the same stimuli, will draw different associations from one another (i.e., associates can differ among individuals; Gray et al., 2019). While most individuals might identify a proximal associate to a given piece of information, individuals who map very distal relations are rarer, and therefore likely to be more unique and original. For these reasons, the capacity to intentionally map more distant—and therefore probably more original—associations among ideas has long been considered to be a core cognitive process associated with high levels of creativity (e.g., Beaty & Kenett, 2023; Benedek et al., 2012; Mednick, 1962).

The process through which individuals effortfully and reflectively identify such patterns among pieces of information is often referred to as relational reasoning (Dumas et al., 2013; Holyoak & Lu, 2021). Relational reasoning is an umbrella construct that includes the mapping of many different types of relations, including relations of similarity (i.e., analogies; Green et al., 2012), relations of discrepancy (i.e., anomalies; Mason, 2001), relations of incompatibility (i.e., antinomies; Alexander, 2016a), and relations of opposition (i.e., antitheses; Capitani et al., 2020). Often described as a domain-general construct, relational reasoning can be measured in multiple modalities including verbally (Alexander et al., 2016; Krumnack et al., 2011) and figurally (Dumas & Alexander, 2016; Gentner & Maravilla, 2017), and can be observed in individuals engaged in creative work across domains, including producing novel designs in engineering (Chan & Schunn, 2015), diagnosing patients' conditions in medicine (Dumas et al., 2014), and developing hypotheses in the life sciences (Dunbar, 2000). In general, observational studies of scientists, engineers, and medical doctors, which attempt to identify the psychological processes that support thinking in these STEM professions, have consistently underscored the importance of relational reasoning (Dunbar & Blanchette, 2001; Schunn, 2017).

The relational reasoning of many eminent creative individuals has also been studied, using primary historical documents such as notebooks, revealing its importance for expert-level, impactful, Big-C creativity. For example, close studies of the relational reasoning of Johannes Kepler (Gentner et al., 1997), the Wright Brothers (Johnson-Laird, 2005), and Leonardo Da Vinci (Güss et al., 2021), among others, have shown how the mapping of relations between familiar concepts and the novel phenomena being studied or worked on is quintessentially a part of the creative process. For instance, while the Wright brothers were far from the best funded, or even the most educated, individuals to be working on the invention of a heavier-than-air flying vehicle, they benefited from the mapping of an analogy between their expertise area of bicycles to the airplane. Specifically, both the bicycle and the airplane need to be able to tip along their central axis in order to be able to turn (this can be disconcerting to airplane passengers!), which is a design element that the Wright brothers' competitors failed to identify and incorporate. For those inventors who were attempting to create a version of the airplane that would turn without tipping to the side, maintaining the lift from the wings to keep the plane in the air while it turned was impossible.

Evidence also exists that individuals with domain-specific creative expertise may map relations differently than non-experts, even on a domain-general task. In one relatively recently designed task—the Analogy Finding Task (AFT; Weinberger et al., 2016)—the participant is shown a matrix of word pairs that can be mapped analogically onto one another (or not). For example, the word pair *Helmet:Head* can be defined by the functional relation "protects," as in the helmet protects the head. As such, this word pair can be analogically mapped onto *Kneepad:Knee*, because a kneepad also protects the knee. On the AFT, it is the participants' job to determine which available analogies are valid and which are non-valid. As such, participant responses can be scored for both sensitivity, or the amount of valid analogies that participants correctly identified as valid, and selectivity, or the amount of non-valid analogies that participants correctly identified as non-valid. In one empirical study, our group (Dumas et al., 2021a) observed that professional actors showed significantly greater sensitivity to valid analogies than did non-actors. Further, when the AFT was administered with the additional instruction to "think creatively" about the analogies, the actors shifted their behavior more than the non-actors, becoming significantly less selective, and casting a much wider net around the analogical relations.

As a follow-up to this study, our team (Dumas et al., 2022) interviewed a subsample of the professional actors who participated in the first study and who were in the bottom 50% of analogical selectivity, meaning they mapped more non-valid analogies than the median professional actor. In an interview setting, we posed both valid and non-valid word pairings from the AFT to the professional actors and asked them to try and map the analogy between them and explain it. What we found was that, while the AFT had been written so that all the valid analogies relied on a functional relation between the word pairs, which focused on how the object described is designed to work, the professional actors were capable of connecting even very semantically distant word pairs using other kind of relations. Namely, the actors went beyond the planned-for functional relations and mapped analogies using visual, temporal, and symbolic relations. For example, one analogy that was meant to be non-valid on the AFT that many actors mapped was *Helmet is to Head as Eraser is to Pencil.* Because the psychologists who designed the AFT were focused on functional relations, this analogy was meant to be non-valid (i.e., the eraser does not protect the pencil the way a helmet protects the head). However, by using a visualization strategy, the actors readily mapped this analogy by explaining that the helmet sits atop a person, in a similar way that an eraser often sits atop a pencil.

Our interpretation of these studies is that, for those individuals who have been trained to generate original ideas (as is commonly the case in actors' training programs), their aperture within which they are capable of connecting ideas may be wider than the typical person. While most individuals might focus on relatively concrete and widely known functional relations among ideas, the creatively expert individual appears to intentionally broaden that set of relations, leading them to ideas that most other people would not think of. In this way, those who are highly creative would be expected to generate a greater quantity of novel connections among ideas, and those connections would be more distal, and therefore more original, than the connections made by a more typical individual. Of course, this scenario leaves open the issue of how highly creative individuals select or hone the subset of their ideas that are more likely to be socially impactful within their domain. If all relations among all ideas were equally likely to be attended to and followed-up on, the creator would certainly have difficulty making an impact. In the next two sections, we discuss some processes by which highly creative individuals select among the ideas they come up with, or guide their thinking processes toward those ideas that they believe will be most socially impactful.

Problem-Finding

In the behaviorist psychological thinking of the mid- and early-twentieth century, it was believed that problems did not need to be found. Perhaps because of the trauma imparted on Western culture from the two world wars during that time period, the prevailing belief was that problems arose regardless of whether or not someone was looking for them, and that individuals were chiefly motivated to return to a state of peaceful equilibrium by solving the problems that they could not avoid (Symonds, 1934). However, in the period of abundance and affluence following the second world war, humans' innate tendencies toward exploration, curiosity, and creativity began to receive more attention both from the public and from psychologists (e.g., White, 1959; Harlow, 1954). It was during this period that Getzels and colleagues (e.g., 1964) introduced the idea of problem-finding to the psychological literature and pointed out its high importance to the creative process. Getzels' breakthrough came by two routes: the first was the observation that intelligence (which can be thought of as a problem-solving ability) alone was insufficient to explain creative performance and achievement in adolescents (Getzels & Jackson, 1962), and the second was the conceptualization of a visual artists' picture as a solution to a problem that was personally meaningful to the artist (Getzels & Csikszentmihalyi, 1966).

At the heart of the conceptualization of problem-finding is the age-old point that it is not necessarily your capabilities or capacities that matter for achievement, instead it is what you do with them that matters. For instance, even the most cognitively capable and knowledgeable individual cannot be creative unless they point their capabilities in an original and useful direction. In contrast, an individual of comparatively weaker problem-solving or intellectual ability, if that ability is directed toward a novel and contextually appropriate goal, can make an important creative impact. In search of empirical observations of this problem-finding process, Getzels and Csikszentmihalyi (1969) observed visual artists while they selected objects for inclusion in a still life and while they painted. Then, they had an expert jury rate the aesthetic value, originality, and craftsmanship of each resulting painting. The artists who engaged in behaviors that indicated problem-finding processes—such as searching for interesting objects to paint by picking up and manipulating them, choosing objects that were less commonly chosen, and finalizing the structure of their painting later in their total painting time—also produced paintings with higher ratings on all outcome variables.

Much more recently, Abdulla et al. (2020) conducted a meta-analysis of empirical research on problem-finding that was published between 1960 and 2015. Across the 40 included studies, the overall correlation between problem-finding on creative outcomes was estimated to be r = .22, indicating a positive, albeit modest, relation. However, this finding was highly heterogeneous across contexts, with correlations as high as .36 being estimated in the domain of creative writing, and as small as .09 being estimated in the domain of the social sciences. The correlation was also found to be substantially different across samples with greater than 75% males (r = .18), as compared to samples with greater than 75% females

($r = .29$). The reasons why problem-finding might be relevant to a greater or lesser extent across domains, or for individuals of different sexes, remain less-than-fully understood in the field, but it may be that certain contexts reward problem-finding more than others, perhaps because those contexts present more open-ended and ill-defined tasks. In addition, differences among scholars in the ways in which problem-finding has been defined and measured in extant research could also be contributing to the heterogeneity of this effect, implying a possible need for more cohesion among researchers in this area.

Another aspect of the relation between problem-finding and creativity, which continues to be fertile ground for debate and empirical work in the field, is the possible explanatory role that problem-finding may play in the connection between high creativity and certain mental health challenges. For instance, Mraz and Runco (1994) demonstrated that problem-finding ability might be related to the frequency of suicidal thoughts in some creative individuals. Although this process is different in important ways than the original conceptualization of problem-finding from Getzels and Csikszentmihalyi (1969), the connection makes theoretical sense, because if an individual is particularly adept at identifying unsolved problems in their own lives and the world around them, it could feasibly lead to a sense of overwhelm and gloominess about the world, wherein life seems like an endless stretch of new problems. In this way, an underlying sensitivity to problems might underlie both creativity and some forms of mental health challenge, such as depression or suicidality: a pattern that appears to be supported, or at least not ruled-out, by existing accounts of eminent highly creative individuals' mental health (e.g., Kaufman, 2001). This possibility is intriguing, but it also called into question by Chen et al.' (2016) study that found that problem-solving ability in middle school students, measured specifically within the domain of science, was related to positive, rather than negative, mood. Perhaps, the problem-finding task used in this study (i.e., listing as many scientific questions as the students could think of) relied more on the participants' crystalized domain knowledge, functioning more like a memory test of past scientific problems they had been exposed to, and less of a measure of their sensitivity to new problems they may encounter. That said, the inter-relations among problem-finding, creative outcomes, and mood-related variables (including susceptibility to mood disorders like depression) remains an open question in the field that may have promised to yield important and interesting results.

Idea Evaluation and Selection

During the creative process, individuals typically generate many more ideas than they could feasibly pursue, or develop into fully fleshed-out, finished creative products (e.g., Puente-Díaz et al., 2021). So, critical to being highly creative is the evaluation and selection of the subset of ideas, among those that were generated, that are worthy of investment and pursuit. Probably the most highly formalized theory of creativity is the Blind-Variation-Selective-Retention (BVSR) perspective (Campbell, 1960; Simonton, 2024b), which, right in the name of the theory, highlights the high importance of evaluating and selecting among ideas that have been generated. Further, the influential metaphor between the creative process and the process of investing—in which the creator identifies ideas before their time has come, and therefore "buys low and sells high"—is another theoretical account of creativity that emphasizes the importance of weighing the relative merits of various previously generated ideas, in order to determine which is the most likely to gain value in the future (Sternberg & Lubart, 1991).

In order to evaluate and select among their own ideas, highly creative individuals must hold a set of criteria for judging the originality and utility, and potential impact, of their ideas. In order to do this, they must use their domain knowledge to predict what others in their domain would see as novel and meaningful, triangulate those expected judgments with their own goals, and then make informed decisions about how to spend their energy and effort. A highly creative individual might be aware that choosing to pursue a particular creative project might result in conflict with others working in their discipline, or open them up to criticism or even rejection, but if they truly believe that the idea is a potentially impactful one that will gain value and traction in the future, they can pursue the idea, and persist through setbacks, failure, and rejection. That said, lifelong persistence through rejection (e.g., as Vincent Van Gogh continued to paint despite rejection for his entire life) is expected to be very difficult and rare; creators would therefore need some positive evaluations from others in their domain, and some degree of impact to their ideas (however small and local) in order to be motivated to create for their whole life.

As part of this process of idea evaluation and selection, a creator may seek (or receive unsolicited) feedback and evaluations of their ideas from others who work in their domain. Recently, Dumas and Kaufman (2024) worked to identify from what sources this kind of feedback would be most helpful to the creator. To do this, they identified four general sets of judges: the creator themselves, their local community, consumers of work in their domain, and critics or gatekeepers in their domain. As creators gain knowledge and expertise in their domain, and the intended impact of their ideas widens, they need feedback from a more and more stringent set of judges. A young learner, for example, whose personal creative insight in the classroom supports their learning, might only need to themselves judge the novelty and utility of their mini-c idea. However, as learners progress and begin to work toward increasing larger levels of creative impact (e.g., little-, Pro-, or even Big-C), they need feedback from others. The creator who intends to make little-c impact (e.g., a hobbyist musician who forms a band to play at a local venue) needs feedback about the creativity of their work from their local community who might attend, or book, their shows. The creator who intends to make a Pro-C level of creative impact, making their living through their creative work in a domain (e.g., a professional architect starting a new firm), needs feedback from consumers in their domain, as to which of their creative products are most desirable and worth paying for, lest they risk losing their customers. The creator who desires to make a Big-C level of creative impact (e.g., a novelist who aspires to win accolades and be influential among other novelists for a long time to come) further needs feedback from domain gatekeepers and critics, whose judgments of their work can influence the longevity of an idea and its status in the field going into the future.

As creators become more expert in their domain, they may be able to preempt or predict what these evaluators would say about an idea, without actually having to receive the feedback explicitly. In this way, they might achieve a degree of sightedness to their creative process (cf. blind versus sighted variation; Sternberg, 1998), or put another way, they might positively correlate their own self-judgments of their ideas with the judgments of others, referred to as socially referenced creativity (Dumas et al., 2024). In this situation, highly expert individuals might no longer need to explicitly consider the perspective of their critics, consumers, or others in their domain, they may simply be able to judge on their own whether an idea has merit: they have internalized the "taste" (and sometimes choose to run counter to the established taste; Ivcevic, 2025) of their domain within their own mind, and cognitively automated the process of idea evaluation and selection. But despite the possibility of this process being rapid, automatic, and even beneath conscious awareness for experts, we would contend that it would necessarily need to be more conscious and effortful for those with less expertise and experience, as with other cognitive procedures (e.g., reading; Samuels & Flor, 1997) that begin effortful and slow, and eventually develop into a rapid and automatic process. In this way, the five cognitive attributes we have presented and reviewed here come full circle, back to the knowledge that the individual possesses within their domain of creativity. With increased domain knowledge, idea evaluation and selection become increasingly rapid, automatic, and socially referenced, and therefore more likely to serve the goals of the creator to produce the kind of impact they are intending to make.

Conclusion

In this chapter, we have presented and reviewed five key attributes that support high levels of creativity. We began with knowledge in the domain a creator is working within, an attribute that is an absolute necessity for creative work that has impact beyond the creator themselves. While novices with low levels of knowledge (including young children) are certainly capable of personally meaningful self-referenced creativity, they cannot produce ideas that are worth imitating by others without knowing what other ideas already exist in their area. We then moved to a discussion of epistemic cognition, which supports dynamism and change within a domain by allowing creators to critically evaluate the existing knowledge in their domain and identify areas of their domain that are in need of further improvement. Next, we discussed relational reasoning, which facilitates distal connections and associations among ideas, whether those relations are characterized by structural similarity or dissimilarity and incompatibility. By allowing for the mapping of structural patterns among ideas, relational reasoning supports creativity by connecting concepts that, previously within a domain, had not been connected before, thereby producing novel insights and combinations. The fourth cognitive attribute we reviewed was the ability to identify new problems (rather than solve them) in a domain. Highly adept problem-solvers who nonetheless struggle to identify new problems to solve will inherently struggle to be creative, because they will necessarily be engaged in the solving of problems identified by others, rather than breaking new ground that they themselves have discovered. Finally, we discussed the need for idea evaluation and selection for highly creative individuals. Given the continuous nature of the stream of consciousness, most creators are expected to generate quite a bit more ideas than they can feasibly pursue given their time and resources. Effectively choosing to pursue the ideas that are most likely to meet their creative goals and produce the kind of creative impact they are aspiring to would be required for an individual to be highly creative.

Taken together, these five cognitive attributes support high levels of creativity among individuals. Importantly, all five are also malleable in response to experience and instruction: an observation that may allow for the beginning of a fuller psychological conceptualization of how high levels of creativity emerge and develop. Overall, the picture that has emerged of highly creative individuals throughout this chapter is one of highly knowledgeable and expert individuals who think critically about the veracity of commonly held beliefs in their domain, connect and recombine distal concepts, and identify new open problems that remain unsolved. Using their knowledge in conjunction with their goals to make a creative impact, these individuals then evaluate and judge their ideas using a socially referenced process, in order to expend their energy and time judiciously, and move their domain forward in ways that may have a lasting influence.

References

Abdulla, A. M., Paek, S. H., Cramond, B., & Runco, M. A. (2020). Problem finding and creativity: A meta-analytic review. *Psychology of Aesthetics, Creativity, and the Arts, 14*(1), 3–14. https://doi.org/10.1037/aca0000194

Acar, S., Dumas, D., Organisciak, P., & Berthiaume, K. (2024). Measuring original thinking in elementary school: Development and validation of a computational psychometric approach. *Journal of Educational Psychology, 116*(6), 953–981. https://doi.org/10.1037/edu0000844

Alexander, P. A. (1992). Domain knowledge: Evolving themes and emerging concerns. *Educational Psychologist, 27*(1), 33–51. https://doi.org/10.1207/s15326985ep2701_4

Alexander, P. A. (2016a). The arguments for and the reasoning about epistemic cognition. In J. Greene, W. Sanodoval, & I. Bråten (Eds.), *Handbook of epistemic cognition*. Routledge.

Alexander, P. A. (2016b). Relational thinking and relational reasoning: Harnessing the power of patterning. *Npj Science of Learning, 1*(1), 1–7. https://doi.org/10.1038/npjscilearn.2016.4

Alexander, P. A., Singer, L. M., Jablansky, S., & Hattan, C. (2016). Relational reasoning in word and in figure. *Journal of Educational Psychology, 108*(8), 1140–1152. https://doi.org/10.1037/edu0000110

Bain, A. (1861). *The Senses and the Intellect*. Longman, Green, Longman, Roberts, and Green.

Baird, P. (2013). Information, universality, and consciousness: A relational perspective. *Mind and Matter, 11*(1), 21–43.

Barron, F. (1957). Originality in relation to personality and intellect. *Journal of Personality, 25*(6), 730–742. https://doi.org/10.1111/j.1467-6494.1957.tb01561.x

Barzilai, S., & Zohar, A. (2012). Epistemic thinking in action: Evaluating and integrating online sources. *Cognition and Instruction, 30*(1), 39–85. https://doi.org/10.1080/07370008.2011.636495

Beaty, R. E., & Kenett, Y. N. (2023). Associative thinking at the core of creativity. *Trends in Cognitive Sciences, 27*(7), 671–683. https://doi.org/10.1016/j.tics.2023.04.004

Beghetto, R. A. (2021). There is no creativity without uncertainty: Dubito Ergo Creo. *Journal of Creativity, 31*, 100005. https://doi.org/10.1016/j.yjoc.2021.100005

Beghetto, R. A. (2022). Engaging uncertainty: Principles and provocations for promoting creative learning futures. In D. Henriksen & P. Mishra (Eds.), *Creative provocations: Speculations on the future of creativity, technology & learning* (pp. 195–212). Springer International Publishing. https://doi.org/10.1007/978-3-031-14549-0_14

Beghetto, R. A., & Kaufman, J. C. (2007). Toward a broader conception of creativity: A case for "mini-c" creativity. *Psychology of Aesthetics, Creativity, and the Arts, 1*(2), 73–79. https://doi.org/10.1037/1931-3896.1.2.73

Bendixen, L. D. (2016). Teaching for epistemic change in elementary classrooms. In J. Greene, W. Sanodoval, & I. Bråten (Eds.), *Handbook of epistemic cognition*. Routledge.

Benedek, M., Könen, T., & Neubauer, A. C. (2012). Associative abilities underlying creativity. *Psychology of Aesthetics, Creativity, and the Arts, 6*(3), 273–281. https://doi.org/10.1037/a0027059

Benedek, M., Beaty, R. E., Schacter, D. L., & Kenett, Y. N. (2023). The role of memory in creative ideation. *Nature Reviews Psychology, 2*(4), 246–257. https://doi.org/10.1038/s44159-023-00158-z

Berthiaume, K. C., Acar, S., & Dumas, D. (2024). "My brain said that … ": A qualitative study of sources of children's creative ideas. *Creativity Research Journal*, 1–25. https://doi.org/10.1080/10400419.2024.2336739

Biasutti, M., & Habe, K. (2021). Dance improvisation and motor creativity in children: Teachers' conceptions. *Creativity Research Journal, 33*(1), 47–62. https://doi.org/10.1080/10400419.2020.1833576

Campbell, D. T. (1960). Blind variation and selective retentions in creative thought as in other knowledge processes. *Psychological Review, 67*(6), 380–400. https://doi.org/10.1037/h0040373

Capitani, E., Branchini, E., Burro, R., Savardi, U., & Bianchi, I. (2020). The opposite of a transformation process. An exploration based on diagrams.

Journal of Cognitive Psychology, 32(7), 698–714. https://doi.org/10.1080/20445911.2020.1814307

Cartiff, B. M., Duke, R. F., & Greene, J. A. (2021). The effect of epistemic cognition interventions on academic achievement: A meta-analysis. *Journal of Educational Psychology, 113*(3), 477–498. https://doi.org/10.1037/edu0000490

Celume, M. P., Besançon, M., & Zenasni, F. (2019). Fostering children and adolescents' creative thinking in education. Theoretical model of drama pedagogy training. *Frontiers in Psychology, 9*. https://doi.org/10.3389/fpsyg.2018.02611

Chan, J., & Schunn, C. (2015). The impact of analogies on creative concept generation: Lessons from an in vivo study in engineering design. *Cognitive Science, 39*(1), 126–155. https://doi.org/10.1111/cogs.12127

Chen, B., Hu, W., & Plucker, J. A. (2016). The effect of mood on problem finding in scientific creativity. *The Journal of Creative Behavior, 50*(4), 308–320. https://doi.org/10.1002/jocb.79

Chinn, C. A., Buckland, L. A., & Samarapungavan, A. (2011). Expanding the dimensions of epistemic cognition: Arguments from philosophy and psychology. *Educational Psychologist, 46*(3), 141–167. https://doi.org/10.1080/00461520.2011.587722

de Grefte, J. (2023). Knowledge as justified true belief. *Erkenntnis, 88*(2), 531–549. https://doi.org/10.1007/s10670-020-00365-7

Dietrich, A. (2019). Types of creativity. *Psychonomic Bulletin & Review, 26*(1), 1–12. https://doi.org/10.3758/s13423-018-1517-7

Dumas, D., & Alexander, P. A. (2016). Calibration of the test of relational reasoning. *Psychological Assessment, 28*(10), 1303–1318. https://doi.org/10.1037/pas0000267

Dumas, D., & Kaufman, J. C. (2024). Evaluation is creation: Self and social judgments of creativity across the four-c model. *Educational Psychology Review, 36*(3), 107. https://doi.org/10.1007/s10648-024-09947-1

Dumas, D., Alexander, P. A., & Grossnickle, E. M. (2013). Relational reasoning and its manifestations in the educational context: A systematic review of the literature. *Educational Psychology Review, 25*(3), 391–427. https://doi.org/10.1007/s10648-013-9224-4

Dumas, D., Alexander, P. A., Baker, L. M., Jablansky, S., & Dunbar, K. N. (2014). Relational reasoning in medical education: Patterns in discourse and diagnosis. *Journal of Educational Psychology, 106*(4), 1021–1035. https://doi.org/10.1037/a0036777

Dumas, D., Doherty, M., & Organisciak, P. (2020). The psychology of professional and student actors: Creativity, personality, and motivation. *PLOS ONE, 15*(10), e0240728. https://doi.org/10.1371/journal.pone.0240728

Dumas, D., Dong, Y., & Doherty, M. (2021a). The influence of creative expertise on the sensitivity and selectivity of analogical reasoning. *Mind, Brain, and Education, 15*(3), 239–249. https://doi.org/10.1111/mbe.12287

Dumas, D., Organisciak, P., & Doherty, M. (2021b). Measuring divergent thinking originality with human raters and text-mining models: A psychometric comparison of methods. *Psychology of Aesthetics, Creativity, and the Arts, 15*(4), 645–663. https://doi.org/10.1037/aca0000319

Dumas, D., Doherty, M., & Dong, Y. (2022). To map or not to map: Professional actors are capable of validly connecting extremely distant verbal analogues. *Psychology of Aesthetics, Creativity, and the Arts*. https://doi.org/10.1037/aca0000502

Dumas, D., Dong, Y., Kagan, S., & Campbell, W. K. (2024a). Exploring the creative personality: Using machine learning to predict fluency and originality in divergent thinking. *Creativity Research Journal, 1–10*. https://doi.org/10.1080/10400419.2024.2371725

Dumas, D., Forthmann, B., & Alexander, P. (2024b). Using a model of domain learning to understand the development of creativity. *Educational Psychologist, 59*(3), 143–158. https://doi.org/10.1080/00461520.2023.2291577

Dunbar, K. (2000). How scientists think in the real world: Implications for science education. *Journal of Applied Developmental Psychology, 21*(1), 49–58. https://doi.org/10.1016/S0193-3973(99)00050-7

Dunbar, K., & Blanchette, I. (2001). The in vivo/in vitro approach to cognition: The case of analogy. *Trends in Cognitive Sciences, 5*(8), 334–339. https://doi.org/10.1016/S1364-6613(00)01698-3

Ericsson, K. A. (2005). Recent advances in expertise research: A commentary on the contributions to the special issue. *Applied Cognitive Psychology, 19*(2), 233–241. https://doi.org/10.1002/acp.1111

Ericsson, K. A., & Staszewski, J. J. (1989). Skilled memory and expertise: Mechanisms of exceptional performance. In D. Klahr & K. Kotovsky (Eds.), *Complex information processing* (pp. 255–288). Psychology Press.

Eysenck, H. J. (1993). Creativity and personality: Suggestions for a theory. *Psychological Inquiry, 4*(3), 147–178. https://doi.org/10.1207/s15327965pli0403_1

Feist, G. J. (2010). The function of personality in creativity. In J. C. Kaufman & R. J. Sternberg (Eds.), *The Cambridge handbook of creativity* (pp. 113–130). Cambridge University Press.

Felton, M. K., & Kuhn, D. (2007). "How do i know?" The epistemological roots of critical thinking. *Journal of Museum Education, 32*(2), 101–110. https://doi.org/10.1080/10598650.2007.11510562

Forthmann, B., Paek, S. H., Dumas, D., Barbot, B., & Holling, H. (2020). Scrutinizing the basis of originality in divergent thinking tests: On the measurement precision of response propensity estimates. *British Journal of Educational Psychology, 90*(3), e12325. https://doi.org/10.1111/bjep.12325

Gabora, L. (2019). Creativity: Linchpin in the quest for a viable theory of cultural evolution. *Current Opinion in Behavioral Sciences, 27*, 77–83. https://doi.org/10.1016/j.cobeha.2018.09.013

Gabora, L., & Tseng, S. (2017). The social benefits of balancing creativity and imitation: Evidence from an agent-based model. *Psychology of Aesthetics, Creativity, and the Arts, 11*(4), 403–419. https://doi.org/10.1037/aca0000132

Gentner, D., & Maravilla, F. (2017). Analogical reasoning. In L. Ball & V. A. Thompson (Eds.), *International handbook of thinking and reasoning*. Routledge.

Gentner, D., Brem, S., Ferguson, R. W., Markman, A. B., Levidow, B. B., Wolff, P., & Forbus, K. D. (1997). Analogical reasoning and conceptual change: A case study of Johannes Kepler. *Journal of the Learning Sciences, 6*(1), 3–40. https://doi.org/10.1207/s15327809jls0601_2

Getzels, J. W. (1964). Creative thinking, problem-solving, and instruction. *Teachers College Record, 65*(9), 240–267. https://doi.org/10.1177/016146816406500910

Getzels, J. W., & Csikszentmihalyi, M. (1966). The study of creativity in future artists: The criterion problem. In O. J. Harvey (Ed.), *Experience structure & adaptability* (pp. 349–368). Springer. https://doi.org/10.1007/978-3-662-40230-6_15

Getzels, J. W., & Csikszentmihalyi, M. (1969). Aesthetic opinion: An empirical study. *Public Opinion Quarterly, 33*(1), 34–45. https://doi.org/10.1086/267665

Getzels, J. W., & Jackson, P. W. (1962). *Creativity and intelligence: Explorations with gifted students*. Wiley.

Glăveanu, V. P., & Kaufman, J. C. (2020). The creativity matrix: Spotlights and blind spots in our understanding of the phenomenon. *The Journal of Creative Behavior, 54*(4), 884–896. https://doi.org/10.1002/jocb.417

Goertzel, M. G. (1978). *Three hundred eminent personalities: A psychological analysis of the famous*. Jossey-Bass Publishers.

Goldstein, T. R. (2024). *Why theatre education matters: Understanding its cognitive, social, and emotional benefits*. Teachers College Press.

Gray, K., Anderson, S., Chen, E. E., Kelly, J. M., Christian, M. S., Patrick, J., Huang, L., Kenett, Y. N., & Lewis, K. (2019). "Forward flow": A new measure to quantify free thought and predict creativity. *American Psychologist, 74*(5), 539–554. https://doi.org/10.1037/amp0000391

Green, A. E., Kraemer, D. J. M., Fugelsang, J. A., Gray, J. R., & Dunbar, K. N. (2012). Neural correlates of creativity in analogical reasoning. *Journal of Experimental*

Psychology: Learning, Memory, and Cognition, 38(2), 264–272. https://doi.org/10.1037/a0025764

Greene, J. A., & Yu, S. B. (2016). Educating critical thinkers: The role of epistemic Cognition. *Policy Insights from the Behavioral and Brain Sciences, 3*(1), 45–53. https://doi.org/10.1177/2372732215622223

Guilford, J. P. (1956). The structure of intellect. *Psychological Bulletin, 53*(4), 267.

Guilford, J. P. (1962). Potentiality for creativity. *Gifted Child Quarterly, 6*(3), 87–90. https://doi.org/10.1177/001698626200600307

Güss, C. D., Ahmed, S., & Dörner, D. (2021). From da Vinci's flying machines to a theory of the creative process. *Perspectives on Psychological Science, 16*(6), 1184–1197. https://doi.org/10.1177/1745691620966790

Harlow, H. F. (1954). Motivational forces underlying learning. In *Learning theory, personality theory, and clinical research: The Kentucky symposium* (pp. 36–53). John Wiley & Sons. https://doi.org/10.1037/11280-003

Hofer, B. K. (2016). Epistemic cognition as a psychological construct: Advancements and challenges. In J. Greene, W. Sanodoval, & I. Bråten (Eds.), *Handbook of epistemic cognition*. Routledge.

Hofer, B. K., & Pintrich, P. R. (1997). The development of epistemological theories: Beliefs about knowledge and knowing and their relation to learning. *Review of Educational Research, 67*(1), 88–140. https://doi.org/10.3102/00346543067001088

Hofstadter, D. R. (2007). *I Am a Strange Loop*. Basic Books.

Holyoak, K. J., & Lu, H. (2021). Emergence of relational reasoning. *Current Opinion in Behavioral Sciences, 37*, 118–124. https://doi.org/10.1016/j.cobeha.2020.11.012

Ivcevic, Z. (2025). *The creativity choice: The science of making decisions to turn ideas into action*. PublicAffairs.

Ivcevic, Z., & Kaufman, J. C. (2024). Inside the box: Considering the role of appropriateness for creativity. *Psychology of Aesthetics, Creativity, and the Arts*. https://doi.org/10.1037/aca0000703

Johnson-Laird, P. N. (2005). Flying bicycles: How the Wright brothers invented the airplane. *Mind & Society, 4*(1), 27–48. https://doi.org/10.1007/s11299-005-0005-8

Kalyuga, S. (2013). Enhancing transfer by learning generalized domain knowledge structures. *European Journal of Psychology of Education, 28*(4), 1477–1493. https://doi.org/10.1007/s10212-013-0176-3

Karwowski, M., Jankowska, D. M., Brzeski, A., Czerwonka, M., Gajda, A., Lebuda, I., & Beghetto, R. A. (2020). Delving into creativity and learning. In V. P. Glăveanu, I. J. Ness, & C. de Saint Laurent (Eds.), *Creative learning in digital and virtual environments: Opportunities and challenges of technology-enabled learning and creativity* (pp. 7–29). Routledge. https://doi.org/10.4324/9781003094630-2

Kaufman, J. C. (2001). The Sylvia Plath effect: Mental illness in eminent creative writers. *The Journal of Creative Behavior, 35*(1), 37–50. https://doi.org/10.1002/j.2162-6057.2001.tb01220.x

Kaufman, J. C., & Beghetto, R. A. (2009). Beyond big and little: The four c model of creativity. *Review of General Psychology, 13*(1), 1–12. https://doi.org/10.1037/a0013688

Kenett, Y. N., Levi, E., Anaki, D., & Faust, M. (2017). The semantic distance task: Quantifying semantic distance with semantic network path length. *Journal of Experimental Psychology: Learning, Memory, and Cognition, 43*(9), 1470–1489. https://doi.org/10.1037/xlm0000391

Kitchner, K. S. (2009). Cognition, metacognition, and epistemic cognition: A three-level model of cognitive processing. *Human Development, 26*(4), 222–232. https://doi.org/10.1159/000272885

Kopiez, R. (2011). The musical child prodigy (wunderkind) in music history: A historiometric analysis. In *Music and the Mind. Essays in Honour of John Sloboda* (pp. 225–236). Oxford University Press.

Krumnack, A., Bucher, L., Nejasmic, J., Nebel, B., & Knauff, M. (2011). A model for relational reasoning as verbal reasoning. *Cognitive Systems Research, 12*(3), 377–392. https://doi.org/10.1016/j.cogsys.2010.11.001

Kuhn, D. (1999). A developmental model of critical thinking. *Educational Researcher, 28*(2), 16–46. https://doi.org/10.3102/0013189X028002016

Kuhn, D., & Weinstock, M. (2002). What is epistemological thinking and why does it matter? In B. Hofer & P. Pintrich (Eds.), *Personal epistemology*. Routledge.

Kuhn, D., Cheney, R., & Weinstock, M. (2000). The development of epistemological understanding. *Cognitive Development, 15*(3), 309–328. https://doi.org/10.1016/S0885-2014(00)00030-7

Lebuda, I., & Benedek, M. (2023). A systematic framework of creative metacognition. *Physics of Life Reviews*.. https://www.sciencedirect.com/science/article/pii/S1571064523000787

Mason, L. (2001). Responses to anomalous data on controversial topics and theory change. *Learning and Instruction, 11*(6), 453–483. https://doi.org/10.1016/S0959-4752(00)00042-6

Mason, L., & Boscolo, P. (2004). Role of epistemological understanding and interest in interpreting a controversy and in topic-specific belief change. *Contemporary Educational Psychology, 29*(2), 103–128. https://doi.org/10.1016/j.cedpsych.2004.01.001

Mednick, S. (1962). The associative basis of the creative process. *Psychological Review, 69*, 220–232. https://doi.org/10.1037/h0048850

Mraz, W., & Runco, M. A. (1994). Suicide ideation and creative problem solving. *Suicide and Life-Threatening Behavior, 24*(1), 38–47. https://doi.org/10.1111/j.1943-278X.1994.tb00661.x

Mumford, M. D., & Gustafson, S. B. (1988). Creativity syndrome: Integration, application, and innovation. *Psychological Bulletin, 103*(1), 27–43. https://doi.org/10.1037/0033-2909.103.1.27

Peterson, E. G. (2020). Supporting curiosity in schools and classrooms. *Current Opinion in Behavioral Sciences, 35*, 7–13. https://doi.org/10.1016/j.cobeha.2020.05.006

Piaget, J. (1973). *To understand is to invent: The future of education* (G. Roberts, Trans). Grossman Publishers.

Plato. (369 BCE/2004). *Theaetetus*. Penguin.

Plucker, J. A., Beghetto, R. A., & Dow, G. T. (2004). Why isn't creativity more important to educational psychologists? Potentials, pitfalls, and future directions in creativity research. *Educational Psychologist, 39*(2), 83–96. https://doi.org/10.1207/s15326985ep3902_1

Puente-Díaz, R., Cavazos-Arroyo, J., & Puerta-Sierra, L. (2021). Idea generation, selection, and evaluation: A metacognitive approach. *The Journal of Creative Behavior, 55*(4), 1015–1027. https://doi.org/10.1002/jocb.505

Runco, M. A. (2007). To understand is to create: An epistemological perspective on human nature and personal creativity. In *Everyday creativity and new views of human nature: Psychological, social, and spiritual perspectives* (pp. 91–107). American Psychological Association. https://doi.org/10.1037/11595-004

Runco, M. A., & Acar, S. (2019). Divergent thinking. In J. C. Kaufman & R. J. Sternberg (Eds.), *The Cambridge handbook of creativity* (2nd ed., pp. 224–254). Cambridge University Press. https://doi.org/10.1017/9781316979839.013

Runco, M. A., & Beghetto, R. A. (2019). Primary and secondary creativity. *Current Opinion in Behavioral Sciences, 27*, 7–10. https://doi.org/10.1016/j.cobeha.2018.08.011

Russ, S. W. (2016). Pretend play: Antecedent of adult creativity. *New Directions for Child and Adolescent Development, 2016*(151), 21–32. https://doi.org/10.1002/cad.20154

Samuels, S. J., & Flor, R. F. (1997). The importance of automaticity for developing expertise in reading. *Reading & Writing Quarterly, 13*(2), 107–121. https://doi.org/10.1080/1057356970130202

Schommer, M. (1998). The influence of age and education on epistemological beliefs. *British Journal of Educational Psychology, 68*(4), 551–562. https://doi.org/10.1111/j.2044-8279.1998.tb01311.x

Schunn, C. D. (2017). Building from in vivo research to the future of research on relational thinking and learning. *Educational Psychology Review, 29*(1), 97–104. https://doi.org/10.1007/s10648-016-9384-0

Simonton, D. K. (1986). Biographical typicality, eminence and achievement styles. *The Journal of Creative Behavior*.. https://psycnet.apa.org/record/1987-28219-001

Simonton, D. K. (2009). Varieties of (scientific) creativity: A hierarchical model of domain-specific disposition, development, and achievement. *Perspectives on Psychological Science, 4*(5), 441–452. https://doi.org/10.1111/j.1745-6924.2009.01152.x

Simonton, D. K. (2024a). Combinatorial creativity as blind-variation and selective-retention: A definitional update. *Physics of Life Reviews, 51*, 27–30. https://doi.org/10.1016/j.plrev.2024.09.008

Simonton, D. K. (2024b). Historiometric approaches to assessment: Products, persons, and periods and places. In M. Runco & S. Acar (Eds.), *Handbook of creativity assessment* (pp. 270–285). Edward Elgar Publishing.

Sternberg, R. J. (1995). Expertise in complex problem solving: A comparison of alternative conceptions. In *Complex problem solving*. Psychology Press.

Sternberg, R. J. (1998). Cognitive mechanisms in human creativity: Is variation blind or sighted? *The Journal of Creative Behavior, 32*(3), 159–176. https://doi.org/10.1002/j.2162-6057.1998.tb00813.x

Sternberg, R. J., & Lubart, T. I. (1991). An investment theory of creativity and its development. *Human Development, 34*(1), 1–31. https://doi.org/10.1159/000277029

Symonds, P. M. (1934). Human drives. *Journal of Educational Psychology, 25*(9), 681–694. https://doi.org/10.1037/h0075041

Thomm, E., Barzilai, S., & Bromme, R. (2017). Why do experts disagree? The role of conflict topics and epistemic perspectives in conflict explanations. *Learning and Instruction, 52*, 15–26. https://doi.org/10.1016/j.learninstruc.2017.03.008

Torrance, E. P. (1975). Sociodrama as a creative problem-solving approach to studying the future. *The Journal of Creative Behavior, 9*(3), 182–195. https://doi.org/10.1002/j.2162-6057.1975.tb00998.x

Torrance, E. P. (1993). The beyonders in a thirty year longitudinal study of creative achievement. *Roeper Review, 15*(3), 131–135. https://doi.org/10.1080/02783199309553486

Ward, T. B., & Kolomyts, Y. (2010). Cognition and creativity. In J. C. Kaufman & R. J. Sternberg (Eds.), *The Cambridge handbook of creativity, 5* (pp. 93–112). Cambridge University Press.

Weinberger, A. B., Iyer, H., & Green, A. E. (2016). Conscious augmentation of creative state enhances "real" creativity in open-ended analogical reasoning. *PLOS ONE, 11*(3), e0150773. https://doi.org/10.1371/journal.pone.0150773

Weiss, S., Steger, D., Kaur, Y., Hildebrandt, A., Schroeders, U., & Wilhelm, O. (2021). On the trail of creativity: Dimensionality of divergent thinking and its relation with cognitive abilities, personality, and insight. *European Journal of Personality, 35*(3), 291–314. https://doi.org/10.1002/per.2288

White, R. W. (1959). Motivation reconsidered: The concept of competence. *Psychological Review, 66*(5), 297–333. https://doi.org/10.1037/h0040934

Wilson, R. C., Guilford, J. P., Christensen, P. R., & Lewis, D. J. (1954). A factor-analytic study of creative-thinking abilities. *Psychometrika, 19*, 297–311.

Yi, X., Hong, P., Chen, P., Bai, X., Li, S., Qi, S., & Runco, M. A. (2023). Creative achievement of eminent scientists in Tang and Song dynasties of China: A historiometric study. *The Journal of Creative Behavior, 57*(4), 650–660. https://doi.org/10.1002/jocb.607

Zabelina, D. L., Zaonegina, E., Revelle, W., & Condon, D. M. (2022). Creative achievement and individual differences: Associations across and within the domains of creativity. *Psychology of Aesthetics, Creativity, and the Arts, 16*(4), 618–636. https://doi.org/10.1037/aca0000439

Zeitz, C. M., & Spoehr, K. T. (1989). Knowledge organization and the acquisition of procedural expertise. *Applied Cognitive Psychology, 3*(4), 313–336. https://doi.org/10.1002/acp.2350030404

CHAPTER 7

Development of Creative Individuals

Jean Urbaniak and Baptiste Barbot

Introduction

Creativity is a phenomenon resulting from the complex interplay between cognitive abilities, personality traits, social influences, and educational experiences (e.g., the 7C model; Lubart & Thornhill-Miller, 2020). This highlights the dynamic nature of creativity development. By considering these multiple influences, we can better understand how creative individuals develop.

In this chapter, the development of creative individuals is discussed from two complementary and interconnected perspectives, providing a comprehensive understanding of how both the development of creativity and the uniqueness of individuals are shaped. On the one hand, we address the development of creative potential following an individual differences perspective that emphasizes how psychological and environmental factors influence creative skills development over time. On the other hand, we examine the interplay between creativity and identity development, in line with a socio-cognitive approach that highlights the dynamic relationship

J. Urbaniak (✉) • B. Barbot
Catholic University of Louvain, Psychological Sciences Research Institute, Louvain-la-Neuve, Belgium
e-mail: jean.urbaniak@uclouvain.be; baptiste.barbot@uclouvain.be

Z. Ivcevic (ed.), *Creators*, The Seven C's of Creativity,
https://doi.org/10.1007/978-3-032-09225-0_7

between the individual and their social environment. Specifically, we first explore the developmental trends in creativity and the various sources of individual differences in creativity development. A particular emphasis is placed on the effects of the school environment on creativity development and its underlying individual resources: cognitive, conative (i.e., referring to the preferred or habitual ways in which an individual behaves), and emotional. We also discuss the developmental asynchronicity of resources involved in creative potential, as well as the challenges in converting creative potential into creative achievements (enactment). Finally, we introduce early theories rooted in the humanistic approach that have addressed the development of creative individuals by linking creativity and self-actualization. We then discuss how identity develops as a creative process and can be interpreted as a creative product. The dynamic interplay between creativity and identity development is illustrated, highlighting critical aspects of creativity that influence identity formation. We punctuate this chapter with illustrations derived from the life of an eminent creator (i.e., Big C creativity): Charles Darwin. Not only no biologist had as much influence as Charles Darwin on his field ("Nothing makes sense in biology, except in the light of evolution"; Dobzhansky, 1973, p. 125), but his life is also remarkably well documented thanks to his book *The Voyage of the Beagle* (Darwin, 1845) and his autobiography (Darwin, 1887).

Individual Differences in Development

The individual differences perspective offers some keys to understanding creative people's development as both "creative" and "people". This perspective assumes that everyone has a creative potential resulting from a combination of a range of factors, many of which are pivotal in the development of self. For example, the multivariate approach to creativity posits that creative potential is the set of individual (cognitive, conative, emotional) and environmental resources that contribute to creative success (e.g., Lubart & Guignard, 2004; Sternberg & Lubart, 2004). Even if individual resources (e.g., divergent thinking) are not equivalent to creativity, they contribute to it, and their development impacts creative potential—and as discussed herein, identity development as well. Indeed, creativity resources are not static and evolve over the lifespan due to biological maturation or environmental factors (Barbot et al., 2013; Barbot & Eff, 2019).

Like any human attribute, creativity has a genetic ground, with environmental influences shaping its development throughout the lifespan (Barbot & Eff, 2019; Han et al., 2018). From an early age, when children engage in pretend play, they use cognitive and affective mechanisms similar to creativity, stimulating their imagination and fostering their divergent thinking (DT) skills, while simultaneously allowing the child to simulate possible selves. However, the impact of pretend play on other aspects of creative potential (e.g., perspective-taking) is not so well known (Russ, 2016). Besides, most studies about creativity development focus on DT abilities because they can be measured very early and are known to be a good predictor of future creative achievements (Ishiguro et al., 2022; Said-Metwaly et al., 2022). This is how we know DT skills globally increase in preschool age with already well-marked interindividual differences (Bijvoet-van den Berg & Hoicka, 2014).

During childhood, DT abilities continue to increase (Barbot & Rogh, 2020; Hui et al., 2019), but this growth is not linear. A developmental slowdown or "slump" is often observed around the age of 9–10 (fourth grade) followed by a more marked slump three years later (seventh grade) (Said-Metwaly et al., 2021). Several explanations for this nonlinear developmental trajectory have been proposed. Some refer to cognitive factors (e.g., changes in brain structure; Barbot & Tinio, 2015) or hormonal changes (Karwowski & Lebuda, 2014), while others attribute it to conative factors (e.g., effect of identity development, Barbot & Heuser, 2017). Moreover, it should be noted that the period of appearance of these discontinuities, their intensity, and duration varies from one context to another (Barbot et al., 2016), illustrating the impact of environmental factors, such as culture and country of origin, on creative potential.

During adolescence, individuals develop their areas of interest and have more agency on what they devote time. By doing so, they progressively get expertise in their chosen domain while often abandoning creative activities invested during childhood, whether due to a loss of interest in these activities or the impact of negative performance feedback (i.e., creative mortification; Beghetto, 2014). At the same time, important neurobiological changes occur, strengthening commonly used brain connections and pruning those not often used, which has the potential to "specialize" the adolescent brain into (domain-)specific skills (Barbot & Tinio, 2015). Consequently, creativity development may be marked by a transition from a "generalized" creative ability to a more domain-specific creative ability during adolescence (Barbot & Tinio, 2015), much akin to the key developmental process during that age band: identity formation. Indeed, identity formation is a process in which the individual both expands the range of possibilities (e.g., "who am I?", "what can I be?") and must converge toward articulated and well-rounded choices and commitments in important domains of life; a task particularly salient during adolescence.

Not much is known about the extent of Charles Darwin's creative skills during his childhood and adolescence. Worth noting though is his self-reported little-c creativity anecdote from his youth—a quote omitted from his original autobiography but restored in a later edition:

> *About this time, or as I hope at a somewhat earlier age, I sometimes stole fruit for the sake of eating it; and one of my schemes was ingenious. The kitchen garden was kept locked in the evening, and was surrounded by a high wall, but by the aid of neighbouring trees I could easily get on the coping. I then fixed a long stick into the hole at the bottom of a rather large flower-pot, and by dragging this upwards pulled off peaches and plums, which fell into the pot and the prizes were thus secured.* (Darwin, 1958, p. 24)

While illustrating Darwin's clever ingenuity that certainly indicates a good creative potential, this excerpt also highlights how experimentation, risk-taking, and limits testing contribute to youth development and the positioning of the individual in society.

During adulthood, expertise deriving from earlier interests develops, mainly if sufficient time and effort are engaged, facilitating creative achievements at a professional level (i.e., transition from little-c creativity to pro-c creativity) (Simonton, 2000). Overall, creativity seems to peak around 30–40 before declining in older age (Sternberg & Lubart, 1991). However, this peak age varies across domains: for instance, mathematicians tend to peak much earlier than novelists, although the general pattern of a rise and decline remains consistent (Simonton, 2000). An explanation can be found in the increasingly competitive atmosphere in most fields over one's professional lifespan (Simonton, 1977), which is not an ideal condition for creativity. Another explanation lies in the decrease of some conative components, such as willingness to take risks (Kurnianingsih et al., 2015), tolerance of ambiguity (Liebherr et al., 2017), motivation (Swirsky et al., 2023), as well as the decline of certain cognitive abilities like memory, executive functions, and fluid intelligence (Alexander et al., 2012; Kievit et al., 2014). However, it should be noted that an important interpersonal variance exists: people with a more extensive educational background and in better health conditions decline less than others (Zhang & Niu, 2013). In all cases, personal characteristics (including cognitive functioning and personality) change over the years, impacting creative potential.

Charles Darwin's major work, *On the Origin of Species*, which would ensure his lasting legacy, was published in 1859 when he was 50. However, we know from his autobiography that his theory was inspired by his reading of *An Essay on the Principle of Population* by Malthus in 1838 when he was 29, and his theory of evolution by natural selection was firmly developed by 1839. Besides, he detailed it in a non-published 35-page paper in 1842, which was extended to 230 pages two years later. Consistent with creativity research and theory, Darwin's trajectory illustrates that the notion of a "creative peak" does not necessarily align with the moment of public recognition. Darwin appears to embody a hybrid profile that combines both conceptual and experiential aspects of creative work. Within this framework (Galenson, 2009), conceptual creators are characterized by their ability to generate novel ideas and theoretical insights early in their lives. In contrast, experiential creators tend to develop their work gradually over time, through continuous experimentation and refinement. Consequently, conceptual creators often reach their creative peak earlier than experiential ones. On the one hand, Darwin can be viewed as a conceptual creator, having conceived a groundbreaking theoretical framework early in life. On the other hand, he postponed its publication for nearly two decades, choosing instead to accumulate empirical evidence and refine his arguments, which is a hallmark of the experiential approach.

What this sequence also illustrates is perhaps that a creativity "peak" does not solely rely on accumulated knowledge. Why did it take so long for Darwin to eventually release his paradigm shifting theory, which was essentially ready 20 years earlier? What did it take *him* to finally release it? In addition to the time needed to transform the idea into a fully developed theory, this delay highlights how creativity may also be a matter of individual readiness, ability to take risks, perfectionism, or going beyond one's comfort zone; all of which may be linked to personal identity and developmental factors. This suggests that creativity is not only about idea generation, but also about the conditions that allow an idea to be expressed, shared, and ultimately accepted.

Source of Individual Differences in Creativity Development

Impact of Environmental Factors on the Development of Creative Potential

Environmental factors impacting the development of creative individuals include the family environment, the presence of eminent creative role models, and the spirit of the time (i.e., Zeitgeist). Unsurprisingly, those factors can be found to equally impact identity and individual development as a whole. Specifically, these factors impact resources (i.e., cognitive, conative, and emotional factors) linked with creativity (and identity) and, in turn, produce individual differences in creativity (and identity) development.

Regarding the family environment, studies have shown that parenting styles have a critical impact on children's creative abilities, with beneficial effects of an autonomy-supportive parenting style and detrimental implications of a controlling parenting style (e.g., Han et al., 2024). Likewise, earlier research has shown that children raised by parents who foster psychological safety and freedom are more likely to fully develop their creative potential than those who do not benefit from such conditions (Harrington et al., 1987; Rogers, 1954). Similarly, a family climate supporting conative factors like risk-taking and openness to new experiences fosters creative thinking (Deng et al., 2016). The role of socioeconomic status has also been highlighted (Acar et al., 2023; Lu et al., 2024) as it determines access to resources facilitating the development of creative potential. Indeed, a high socioeconomic status provides tools, opportunities, and experiences that nurture creative potential (Ritter et al., 2012). Here, though we highlighted a scientific literature showing the impact of environmental factors on creativity, at least as much evidence exist on how these factors influence one's identity development.

Concerning his familial environment, Charles Darwin was raised by his father and eldest sister after his mother's passing when he was eight. In his autobiography, he wrote that he did not remember much about the latter, but he gave much information about his father, brother, and four sisters. Regarding the influence of his family members on his development, Charles Darwin suggested in his autobiography that he did not owe much to them intellectually:

> *I am inclined to agree with Francis Galton*[1] *in believing that education and environment produce only a small effect on the mind of any one, and that most of our qualities are innate.* (Darwin, 1887, p. 22)

However, Charles Darwin seemed to underestimate the impact that his family members had on him. For example, his father, who was an esteemed medical doctor and a fellow of the Royal Society, provided him the opportunity to study medicine and theology at university and financed his five-year journey aboard the HMS Beagle (a Royal Navy ship that embarked him as a naturalist on a journey around the world), without which Charles Darwin could not have collected the necessary information to conceive his theory. He also wrote in his bibliography about his brother Erasmus:

> *Towards the close of my school life, my brother worked hard at chemistry, and made a fair laboratory with proper apparatus in the tool-house in the garden, and I was allowed to aid him as a servant in most of his experiments. He made all the gases and many compounds, and I read with care several books on chemistry, such as Henry and Parkes' 'Chemical Catechism.' The subject interested me greatly, and we often used to go on working till rather late at night. This was the best part of my education at school, for it showed me practically the meaning of experimental science.* (Darwin, 1887, p. 35)

This quote shows that Charles Darwin's interest in natural sciences was partly shaped by his brother. The same goes for his knowledge and his practice of experimental science, which are all determinant elements of his success. Finally, it is worth mentioning Charles Darwin's grandfather, Erasmus Robert Darwin, who passed away in 1802, seven years before Charles was born. Erasmus R. Darwin was a physician, botanist, and inventor. He is notably remembered for writing *Zoonomia, or the Laws of Organic Life* between 1794 and 1798, a work in which he anticipated some ideas later found in modern evolutionary theory. Reflecting on *Zoonomia*, Charles Darwin noted:

> *I had previously read the 'Zoonomia' of my grandfather, in which similar views are maintained, but without producing any effect on me. Nevertheless, it is probable that the hearing rather early in life such views maintained and*

[1] English polymath, first cousin of Charles Darwin, considered the father of behavioral genetics and a pioneer of differential (individual differences) psychology.

> *praised may have favoured my upholding them under a different form in my 'Origin of Species'.* (Darwin, 1887, p. 38)

This quote demonstrates that even a family member he never met played a significant role in shaping his intellectual curiosity and inspiring the work for which he would ultimately become renowned. In sum, it seems clear that Charles Darwin's familial environment had a vastly more significant impact on his creative achievements than he thought.

Regarding the influence of creative role models (akin to Darwin's grandfather), studies have shown that the presence of creative supervisors influences subordinate creativity (Collins & Cooke, 2013). However, a colleague who is not a hierarchical superior can also play the mentor role for a younger one, assisting him in being more creative, perceiving solutions to problems, thinking more critically, and analyzing situations from different perspectives (Shaughnessy, 1995). Charles Darwin rubbed shoulders with several renowned scientists who inspired his work, such as the geologists Charles Lyell and Adam Sedgwick. At some points, they could be viewed as creative role models for Darwin, but the one who was the most like a mentor to him was his botanic teacher at university: John Stevens Henslow. They quickly became friends and spent much time together debating natural sciences, to such an extent that Charles Darwin was nicknamed "the man who walks with Henslow". Although Charles Darwin did not consider Henslow someone particularly creative, he learned from him some crucial skills for his future creative achievements, as he wrote in his autobiography:

> *His knowledge was great in botany, entomology, chemistry, mineralogy, and geology. His strongest taste was to draw conclusions from long-continued minute observations. His judgment was excellent, and his whole mind well balanced; but I do not suppose that any one would say that he possessed much original genius.* (Darwin, 1887, p. 52)

Finally, there is much to say about the impact of the Zeitgeist on Charles Darwin's creative work. Through certain perspectives, scientific creativity arises from emerging social needs or contemporary scientific progress and interest. From this point of view, innovations are contextually determined, like innovative ideas were in the air, waiting for someone to pick them. With more nuances, Simonton (2004) argues that the Zeitgeist creates a sociocultural environment that can either foster or constrain the expression of creative eminence even if other factors like chance, logic, and genius are involved in eminent scientific creativity. The XIXe century's Zeitgeist was characterized by an increasing interest in natural history. In particular, the evolution of species has been debated since the advent of Lamarckism at the beginning of the century. Moreover, another biologist, Alfred Russel Wallace, developed almost the same evolutionary theory as Darwin in 1858, when Darwin had not yet published his own theory developed 16 years earlier. This synchronicity demonstrates that the Zeitgeist favored this discovery, even if we cannot summarize Charles Darwin's genius as an inevitable product of his time (Gould, 2002).

A Focus on School Environment

Another environmental factor that influences the creative individual deserves particular attention: school. Indeed, its impact on creativity development is a controversial issue. A popular opinion is that school kills creativity (Kim, 2011; Robinson, 2006), which would probably have been shared by Charles Darwin. It is the context for many creative contradictions (Beghetto & Sriraman, 2017). This opinion states that the general school climate fails to support student's creativity because of a lack of time devoted to it and a competitive atmosphere (Ahmadi et al., 2019). Along the same lines, supervision and evaluation expectations have been shown to impact creativity (e.g., Amabile, 1979, Camarda et al., 2021; Eisenberger & Rhoades, 2001; Silvia & Phillips, 2004; Yuan & Zhou, 2008). School is also blamed for promoting sameness instead of the diversity needed for creativity development (Glăveanu & Beghetto, 2017) and not leaving enough room for making mistakes and exploring (Gajda et al., 2017).

Nevertheless, these ideas are increasingly contested (e.g., Barbot & Said-Metlawy, 2021; Karwowski, 2022) with evidence of reciprocal relationships between creative skills and school achievement, over and beyond the effects of intelligence and personality traits. Therefore, adapting the school environment to a creativity-friendly development space is a growing area of research interest (e.g., Antonietti et al., 2020; Kettler et al., 2021; Khalid et al., 2020; Luna et al., 2018). In sum, the school environment is far from neutral in many ways (Rubenstein et al., 2018) and can impact individual factors involved in creativity development.

Cognitive Factors

From a cognitive standpoint, school contributes to intellectual development (Ritchie & Tucker-Drob, 2018). As a result, reforms extending compulsory education benefit intelligence (Brinch & Galloway, 2012), which is related to divergent thinking (Gerwig et al., 2021). There is also evidence that creativity and intelligence are both positively correlated with some executive functions, such as attention control (Frith et al., 2021) and inhibition (Benedek et al., 2012), emphasizing the relatedness of these constructs (Silvia, 2015). Moreover, executive functions are malleable, so environments, including schools, can support their development (Serpell & Esposito, 2016). Of course, school is also an important source of knowledge development, which is a necessary, yet not sufficient condition to be highly creative in a specific domain (Karwowski et al., 2020). Nevertheless, some cognitive skills, such as defining and redefining problems, may not be trained enough and developed at school. Indeed, students do not often formulate the problems to be resolved and are not encouraged to question established ways to tackle them (Sternberg & Lubart, 1991).

Charles Darwin was skeptical about the benefits his mind gained from his educational career. About the school he attended from 9 to 16 years, he wrote: "*Nothing could have been worse for the development of my mind than Dr. Butler's school, as it was strictly classical, nothing else being taught, except a little ancient geography and history*" (Darwin, 1887, pp. 31–32). He was not more enthusiastic about his university career, which initially took him to Edinburgh to study medicine for two years before he abandoned it to pursue theology at Cambridge: "*During the three years which I spent at Cambridge my time was wasted, as far as the academical studies were concerned, as completely as at Edinburgh and at school*" (Darwin, 1887, p. 46). However, it is difficult to conceive that he did not learn anything at school and university that was necessary for his scientific work. For instance, he learned crucial observation skills and scientific knowledge from his Cambridge professor, John Stevens Henslow. More broadly, Darwin learned a lot of essential skills to work as scientist by organizing expeditions when he was a student. Even if he did not consider it part of his formal education, it was allowed thanks to the opportunities of his universities and support from his professors (Gruber & Barrett, 1974). Charles Darwin was, in fact, aware of the beneficial role of schooling in skills and knowledge transmission and regretted not having benefited more from it. For example, he wrote about his time in Edinburg:

> *I was not urged to practice dissection, for I should soon have got over my disgust; and the practice would have been invaluable for all my future work. This has been an irremediable evil, as well as my incapacity to draw.* (Darwin, 1887, p. 36)

Conative Factors

School plays a role in shaping conative factors relevant to creativity development in two ways: unintentionally, resulting from teaching strategies, teachers' expectations, and peer norms; and intentionally, by organizing experiences such as in-breadth, in-depth, and reflective exploration (Verhoeven et al., 2019). For instance, creativity-related constructs such as self-regulation and metacognition (Schunk, 2008) are trained at school. That being said, there are many theoretical reasons to assume that several other components of the conative sphere can be impacted by the school environment, especially personality traits (Jirásek & Sudzina, 2020), motivation (Bonnardel, 2009), self-esteem (Barbot, 2020), or creative self-beliefs (Karwowski et al., 2019).

For instance, school environment could strengthen some personality traits involved in creativity, such as perseverance (Sternberg & Lubart, 1995). Indeed, perseverant people tend to persist through obstacles and actively mobilize their intellectual skills to generate creative ideas (Capron et al., 2018). Students who want to achieve academic success will likely be perseverant. Conversely, school could inhibit risk-taking and tolerance for ambiguity, which are also linked to creativity (Graciano et al., 2023; Mahmoud et al., 2020; Zenasni et al., 2008). People with a high level of tolerance for ambiguity generally accept ambiguous situations without stressing out or reacting abruptly and hastily. They can thus respond effectively to more situations, perceive more problems, and solve them creatively (Grégoire & Vlieghe, 2010). In a school context, such a situation can be viewed as a threat to academic success and so be avoided or not well tolerated. Relatedly, risk-takers fear less than others making a fool of themselves or losing time/money by proposing uncommon ideas (Capron Puozzo & Cavalla, 2018). According to Besançon et al. (2015), this behavior is not encouraged in school because students are often expected to follow predetermined learning paths, with limited agency over their goals.

The school environment can also provide opportunities to improve intrinsic motivational and self-regulatory skills (Huitt & Cain, 2018). Intrinsic motivation and creativity correlate positively (e.g., de Jesus et al.,

2013). In contrast, extrinsic motivation is often seen as unfavorable for creativity because it undermines intrinsic motivation (Amabile, 2011). However, rewards can benefit creativity by demonstrating or signaling to people their work is valued and by confirming their competencies (Amabile & Pratt, 2016). In a school context, such rewards can be good grades and social gratification that result from it. Ultimately, the most critical aspect of motivational orientation and creative performance is staying focused on the creative task. If someone is intrinsically motivated to achieve a creative task, they will focus on it. If they are extrinsically motivated, they will likely focus on the reward (Hennessey, 2019). As students quickly learn the "rat race for grades" and consider their grades as their salary (Pannier, 2005), school is not the best environment to express one's creativity and develop it. Nevertheless, intrinsic motivation-related constructs such as students' learning goal orientation, task value, self-efficacy, and self-regulation are determined by other factors, such as task orientation (i.e., the degree of importance placed on completing planned activities and maintaining focus on the subject matter) and perceived cohesiveness among students, emphasizing that school plays a role in shaping intrinsic motivation (Velayutham & Aldridge, 2013).

Conative factors that describe the creative person also include creative self-beliefs, which are people's convictions about their own creative capacities and the nature of creativity (Karwowski & Barbot, 2016). It is a broad concept encompassing several facets that impact creative performance, such as creative self-efficacy (Haase et al., 2018; Tierney & Farmer, 2011), creative personal identity (Karwowski, 2016), creative role identity (Kim, 2019), creative mindset (Hass et al., 2016; Karwowski, 2014), as well as creative metacognition (e.g., people's ability to monitor and evaluate their creative functioning, Anderson & Haney, 2021; Kaufman & Beghetto, 2013; Lebuda & Benedek, 2023). According to Barbot and Lubart (2012), the latter can be negatively impacted by school context because adolescents inhibit their own creative abilities to foster academic achievement. School is an environment where creative ideas are not always valued (Cropley, 2010). Finally, school can decrease self-esteem if the student anticipates academic failure. However, self-esteem positively correlates with creativity (Barbot, 2020) and is particularly fragile during adolescence (Boyd & Bee, 2017).

As previously mentioned, Charles Darwin was critical of school's impact on him and did not elaborate on how school shaped him on a conative level. However, his informal contacts with his professors and fellow students allowed him to share his passion for nature and engage in associated activities like shooting birds, collecting insects, and discussing science. Gruber and Barrett (1974, p. 74) describe their attitude toward nature as "*at once playful, reverent, analytical, and inquisitive—in short, enthusiastic*" fostering Charles Darwin's intrinsic motivation for this field. Moreover, it was at university that he met his mentor, his botanic professor John Henslow, who recommended him as a naturalist on board the HMS Beagle and significantly impacted his motivation to pursue a scientific career, as he prefaced in his travel journal: "*I must be here allowed to return my most sincere thanks to the Reverend Professor Henslow, who, when I was an undergraduate at Cambridge, was one chief means of giving me a taste for Natural History*" (Darwin, 1845, p. VII).

Emotional Factors

Finally, the school environment can influence emotional factors linked with creativity and generate stress, especially in evaluation context (Moyne et al., 2018; Prokofieva et al., 2017), which is known to impact cognitive functioning like attention abilities (Ferreri et al., 2004) and memory retrieval (Wolf, 2017). As stated by the emotion activation theory, according to which memories are related to our emotional state (Lubart & Getz, 1997), a stressed individual will tend to associate the task they are doing with concepts linked with stress in their memories, which may limit the number of possible associations. In this context, students may also overlook concepts associated with other emotions.

Moreover, many aspects of the school climate impact students' well-being over time (Bosacki et al., 2023) and can play a key role in emotional development (Pan & Zhang, 2023). For example, teacher relationships and disciplinary style impact students' well-being. Indeed, an authoritative school environment, which is supportive and highly structured, enhances students' grit and self-efficacy and decreases depression, hopelessness, and stress (Wong et al., 2021). In line with this, Ivcevic et al. (2022) highlight that supportive teacher-student relationships and positive peer interactions contribute to a nurturing emotional climate, which encourages students to take creative risks. When students feel emotionally secure and valued, they are more likely to actively participate in creative thinking tasks, as creativity is closely tied to emotional regulation and expression.

Asynchronicity in the Development of Resources Involved in Creative Potential

Several theories explain cognitive development by a succession of developmental phases. It suggests that not all components of the mind develop simultaneously, notably those involved in creativity development. For example, verbal divergent thinking and insight abilities continue to improve into early adulthood, whereas visuo-spatial divergent thinking peaked earlier, around mid-adolescence, suggesting asynchronous development of different creativity-related abilities (Kleibeuker et al., 2012). Moreover, a body of research implies that the emergence of new cognitive skills could be detrimental to other attributes involved in creative processes (Barbot et al., 2016). For example, Lubart (1996) noted a decrease in divergent thinking abilities, in parallel within (expected) increase in logical reasoning during Piaget's concrete operations stage (7–11 years old). Another example lies in temporal gap between the development of the socioemotional and cognitive control systems in adolescence, which can lead to the emergence of maladaptive behaviors such as impulsivity and risk-taking (Barbot & Hunter, 2012), but could also be a favorable context for creative thinking. Indeed, this developmental asynchrony is associated with heightened sensation-seeking, which may increase traits often conducive to creativity, such as exploration, openness, and risk-taking (Barbot & Tinio, 2015).

A specific dimension can be added to the equation regarding scientific creativity. Indeed, according to Gruber and Barrett (1974), science is the fusion of two distinguishing elements: an existing body of knowledge and a set of methods for creating new ones. However, these two components do not always evolve in synchrony. Excessive respect for established knowledge can hinder the questioning process for developing new theories. At the same time, innovative methods may remain underutilized or unrecognized if they do not align with current knowledge. Scientific creativity emerges when these two elements move from being potentially antagonistic to becoming mutually supportive.

In Darwin's case, this last point can explain why he made his great discovery at the time he made it. Indeed, his method for creating new knowledge, based on observations followed by deducing new general laws, had already been developed during his university years and further refined during his journey on board of the HMS Beagle. Nevertheless, he still lacked fundamental knowledge necessary for his main discovery: Thomas

Malthus' theories, which are exposed in *An Essay on the Principle of Population*, in which the concept of "struggle for existence" is debated. It was only two years after returning from his five-year voyage that he discovered this work, providing the missing conceptual framework that allowed him to integrate his observations into a coherent and highly creative evolutionary theory. This illustrates how different resources involved in his scientific creativity did not develop simultaneously. His ability to observe and deduce general principles emerged early, but his theoretical understanding of population dynamics came much later. On the *existing knowledge* side, we can cite those from his observations around the world, economic theories from Adam Smith and Thomas Malthus, and geological theories from James Hutton (Gould, 2010). On the *creation of knowledge* side, Darwin could rely on his deduction abilities, his ability to make analogies, and his convergent thinking skills. However, it was only when these two sets of resources aligned that his creative breakthrough became possible.

Converting Creative Potential into Creative Achievements

One's high creative potential is not a guarantee for creative achievement. Several factors are involved in creative accomplishments, and individual differences in these factors can explain whether an individual will fulfill (or not) their full potential.

According to the investment theory of creativity (Sternberg & Lubart, 1991), individual resources are not strictly additive: it is not sufficient to reach a high level on each factor to make performances of high creative value. First, these resources determine a creative potential, a necessary but insufficient condition to become a highly creative person. Second, these resources interact with each other, and their ideal level is not necessarily as high as possible. A dynamic interaction of a particular combination of these resources, instead of a maximum level, is necessary for creativity. The investment theory of creativity also implies that people decide the intensity with which they mobilize their resources when engaging in a creative project. The key to creative success is to be able to determine how this investment can lead to genuinely creative performance. From a definitional point of view, investing massively in an already popular idea is not profitable to creativity because of a lack of novelty. In contrast, investing heavily in an unconventional idea is relevant because, if this idea ends up being accepted and seen as valuable, its creator will be recognized as a creative person (Sternberg & Lubart, 1991). Nevertheless, although individuals express appreciation for creative ideas, they often opt for conventional ones in practice (Mueller et al., 2012), leading to the emergence of a "happy medium" where ideas are sufficiently original to be considered novel, yet not so radical as to hinder their likelihood of acceptance and implementation.

Another explanation for how creative potential is (or is not) converted into creative achievements can be found in the model of Creative Behavior as Agentic Action (CBAA) (Karwowski & Beghetto, 2019). According to this model, creative potential will turn into creative behavior only under two conditions: the individual must be confident about their creative abilities and perceive creativity's value. More precisely, creative self-confidence mediates the link between creative potential and creative behavior, while the perceived value of creativity moderates it.

Furthermore, each creative potential corresponds to a unique profile of creative resources. Some profiles are suitable for a particular creative task but not for another one requiring a different set of resources. Hence, the output produced by the same individual can differ in creative quality depending on the fit between one's profile of creative resources and the demands of a given creative task (Barbot et al., 2016). Accordingly, two people with equally high creative potential can produce two outputs of different creative value because one's creative profile fits with the task's features while the other does not. Extended to a developmental perspective, the asynchronous development of key creativity resources within individual can lead to variable creative "success" over time: the configuration of resources recruited for that given creative work might vary as individuals develop (developmental asynchronicity) resulting in profiles of resources more or less "fit" to the task requirements at a given moment (Barbot et al., 2016).

Charles Darwin is a great example of converting creative potential into high creative achievements. First, he invested much time in developing his theory of evolution by natural selection. Twenty years passed between developing the precepts of his theory and publishing *On the Origin of Species* because Darwin was concerned with presenting a detailed and well-argued theory. The sheer amount of time Darwin dedicated to refining his theory reflects his confidence in the strength of his ideas and his determination to ensure their validity. Nevertheless, another factor could explain this long delay in addition to his substantial investment. According to Gould (1991), it is possible that Darwin was afraid to compromise his career with such a revolutionary idea, explaining why he devoted so much time to providing proof of his theory but also why he worked on side projects simultaneously. For instance, he devoted 8 of these 20 years to writing four volumes on the taxonomy and development of cirripedes. It is surprising to have invested so much time in this work while the most significant discovery in biology history awaited publication. Charles Darwin admitted on this subject: "*Nevertheless, I doubt whether the work was worth the consumption of so much time*" (Darwin, 1887, pp. 81–82). Moreover, there is evidence that he feared negative outcomes that could follow the publication of his ideas. He wrote to his friend Joseph Hooker that "*telling the secret of his evolutionary ideas was like confessing a murder*" (Gruber & Barrett, 1974, p. 44). This illustrates that Charles Darwin was aware of the importance of his discovery and its revolutionary aspect, not only for the immense value it held for scientific progress but also its potentially explosive impact on society at large. According to the CBAA model (Karwowski & Beghetto, 2019), Darwin's unwavering commitment to refining his theory demonstrates his creative confidence, while his deep concern about the potential backlash against his theory reveals how highly he perceived its value. His fear of controversy did not stem from doubt about his ideas, but from an awareness of their groundbreaking nature and the resistance they could trigger. These two conditions together created the ideal environment for him to fully realize his creative potential. Finally, his profile of creative resources was perfectly fit to his creative field. Regarding the qualities that allowed him to achieve success, he wrote:

> *I think that I am superior to the common run of men in noticing things which easily escape attention, and in observing them carefully. My industry has been nearly as great as it could have been in the observation and collection of facts.* (Darwin, 1887, p. 103)

He also attributed his success to his ability to make the most of his observations: "*My mind seems to have become a kind of machine for grinding general laws out of large collections of facts*" (Darwin, 1887, p. 101). However, Charles Darwin knew his weakness, notably in drawing and mathematics: "*I attempted mathematics. [...] But I do not believe that I should ever have succeeded beyond a very low grade*" (Darwin, 1887, p. 46). With these weaknesses, it seems challenging to imagine Charles Darwin succeeding in other scientific domains such as engineering or physics.

Identity Development as a Creative Process

Through this brief review of factors that shape creativity development and excerpts from Darwin's life, the lines between creativity development and identity development have blurred. Indeed, although self-selected for the purpose of this chapter, a narrative of Darwin's creativity and success has indirectly told us much about his identity formation. When Darwin asserts that he is essentially low performing in mathematics—reflecting not only low self-efficacy in that domain but perhaps also an accurate evaluation of his own limitations—while perceiving his superiority in observation abilities, we have a fine illustration of how particular self-beliefs, that populate one's identity, might influence our own creative work. The temporal gap between the formulation of his groundbreaking theory and its actual delivery to the world also illustrates how the enactment of creative "potential" into "achievement" may be a matter of identity.

Reciprocally, critical aspects of creativity influence one's identity formation. For example, in various excerpts from his biography and the Beagle report, Darwin's illustrates how his religious identity progressively shifted from a form of *foreclosed* identity (Marcia, 1966) whereby strong commitments are "inherited" from parental and societal values to a ***moratorium*** status (time of intense exploration for alternative considerations) and eventually ending up in an ***achieved*** identity configuration (i.e., agnosticism):

> *After having spent two sessions in Edinburgh, my father perceived, or he heard from my sisters, that I did not like the thought of being a physician, so he proposed that I should become a clergyman.* (Darwin, 1887, p. 45)

> *I asked for some time to consider, as from what little I had heard or thought on the subject I had scruples about declaring my belief in all the dogmas of the Church of England.* (Darwin, 1887, p. 45)

I gradually came to disbelieve in Christianity as a divine revelation. [...] I found it more and more difficult, with free scope given to my imagination, to invent evidence which would suffice to convince me. Thus disbelief crept over me at a very slow rate, but was at last complete. (Darwin, 1958, p. 86)

Interestingly, Darwin attributed this shift in religious identity to the increased freedom given to his "imagination". Although this illustration is not directly tied to Darwin's scientific creativity as it taps more into ideological domains of identity development, it points up to a key mechanism of identity development: exploration—an identity process closely linked to divergent thinking (Barbot, 2008). Indeed, creativity and identity development are deeply intertwined processes that unfold across the lifespan (Barbot, 2021). As individuals engage in creative activities, they not only generate novel and meaningful ideas but also construct and refine their sense of self. Reciprocally, one's identity development greatly shapes the type of creative activity they invest in and the creative outcomes resulting from this investment. Conceptually, identity development may be viewed as a creative process involving self-exploration, integration of disparate self-representations, and resulting in a "product" that is both unique (selfhood) and acknowledged by others (feeling of belongingness) (Barbot, 2008). But the links between identity and creativity go beyond the metaphorical level.

Early Theories: Humanistic Perspective

The links between creativity and identity development have been discussed for a long time. Early works on that topic include the humanistic perspective from Maslow (1943), according to which creativity is necessary for self-actualization (i.e., the fulfillment of personal potential), which is at the top of his model of the hierarchy of needs. Accordingly, human needs are hierarchical and pyramidally organized, and those needs lying at the bottom of the pyramid must be fulfilled before attempting to satisfy those on higher levels. People fulfill their physiological needs (at the very bottom of the pyramid), then their safety needs, belongingness and love needs, esteem needs, and finally, try to reach their full potential through self-actualization (top of the pyramid). The latter corresponds to the need to accomplish oneself and is closely related to identity development. According to Maslow (1962), creativity and self-realization are interdependent: individuals need creative abilities to create their best version, and self-actualization facilitates creativity.

With his client-centered therapy, Rogers (1951) supports this idea. From his point of view, everyone owns the necessary resources to overcome difficulties and to reach their full potential. Creativity is important in this process as Rogers considers the creative act to be an expression of self-actualization (Rogers, 1951). Later, May (1975) added an existentialist component to this perspective, arguing that courage is needed to reach self-actualization through creativity. Indeed, it is necessary to embrace uncertainty, overcome fear, and face personal anxieties to engage in this process. This idea resonates with Csikszentmihalyi's (2009) concept of flow, as creative individuals tend to enter a state of deep immersion and intrinsic motivation, overcoming external distractions and self-doubt to fully actualize their potential.

In sum, early humanistic perspectives highlight the role of creativity in personal development. Creativity is seen as a way to reach self-accomplishment (process), and as a self-accomplishment itself (product). This idea is significant in Charles Darwin's mind. During his five-year journey aboard the HMS Beagle, he wrote in his autobiography:

> *As far as I can judge of myself, I worked to the utmost during the voyage from the mere pleasure of investigation, and from my strong desire to add a few facts to the great mass of facts in Natural Science. But I was also ambitious to take a fair place among scientific men,—whether more ambitious or less so than most of my fellow-workers, I can form no opinion.* (Darwin, 1887, p. 65)

In the same line, he adds:

> *This pure love* [in natural sciences] *has, however, been much aided by the ambition to be esteemed by my fellow naturalists. From my early youth, I have had the strongest desire to understand or explain whatever I observed—that is, to group all facts under some general laws.* (Darwin, 1887, p. 103)

These quotes highlight Charles Darwin's pleasure in being creative in his field (i.e., the intrinsic motivation to discover new facts and general laws) and the self-accomplishment it procured (i.e., creativity as a self-accomplishment itself), which was likely conducive of a "flow state". However, they also shed light on how Darwin's creativity was driven by extrinsic motivation, as it served to achieve another goal: being recognized as a great scientist (i.e., creativity as a way to self-actualization). This integration (intrinsic and extrinsic motivational orientation) is consistent with the motivational drivers of Pro-C creativity (Kaufman & Beghetto, 2009).

Developmental Perspective

In earlier work anchored in developmental psychology, three key mechanisms through which creativity and identity development interact have been highlighted (Barbot, 2008, 2020; Barbot & Heuser, 2017; Barbot & Lubart, 2012):

1. Creativity and identity development may share common cognitive processes; theoretical assumption and empirical evidence suggest that both creativity and identity development rely on overlapping cognitive functions, including divergent thinking, cognitive flexibility, or integrative / synthetic thinking. During adolescence and early adulthood, when identity formation is particularly salient, these cognitive processes support individuals in exploring multiple perspectives, generating potential self-concepts, integrating self-representations that may be experienced as contradictory, or experimenting with various "possible selves" (e.g., Barbot & Heuser, 2017). It is therefore not surprising that some empirical links exist between aspects of creative cognition and identity processes—such as divergent thinking and identity exploration (e.g., Barbot, 2008; Dollinger et al., 2005; Dollinger & Dollinger, 2017)—with the hypothesis of a bi-directional, reciprocal relationship.
2. Commitments to creative outlets provide the individual with some means for self-definition. In fact, any arena in which the individual is strongly committed contributes to building a personal narrative and positive self-esteem. Indeed, commitments have a social meaning in that they contribute to the definition of self. Darwin may only define himself as a biologist if he is sufficiently committed as such (e.g. "I am a biologist"). Further, one will remain committed to a given creative outlet only if this commitment is a source of satisfaction and positive self-esteem, thereby reinforcing creative commitment (Barbot, 2020; Karwowski & Barbot, 2016).
3. Creativity is often an outlet for self-expression and personal growth, including in everyday manifestations (Ivcevic, 2007; Ivcevic & Mayer, 2009). Creativity also plays a role in expressing aspects of identity that may not be easily articulated through "conventional" means (e.g., verbalization) and therefore contribute to the sense of self. Creative endeavors allow individuals to externalize emotions, not just in the process of "doing" creativity (e.g., experience of flow), but also in the resulting creative outcomes (e.g., an artist's piece of art, a composer's new symphony, a biologist's theory, or inventing a bedtime story). This expressive function of creativity is especially relevant in expressive domains—though still heavily "colored" by one's sense of Self in any domain—and for individuals who experience identity distress, as it provides a space for expression outside of societal constraints.

Conclusion

This chapter explored the development of creative individuals from two complementary perspectives: the role of individual differences in the development of creative potential, and the dynamic interplay between creativity and identity formation. Creative potential refers to the extent to which an individual possesses the capacity to produce highly creative outputs. This multifaceted concept relies on a constellation of cognitive, conative, and emotional resources that evolve over the lifespan. Beyond individual characteristics, the broader environment plays a crucial role in shaping these resources, with well-documented influences of family background, educational experiences, and sociocultural context that can either constrain or foster creativity. The development of creativity is often marked by asynchronicities in the development of these resources, which contribute to individual differences at certain stages and significantly affect the timing and expression of high-level creative behaviors. In sum, having tremendous creative potential does not guarantee outstanding creative achievement. Conditions such as creative self-confidence, perceived value of creativity, personal investment, and the fit between individual creative resources and task demands must be met in order to effectively translate potential into creative accomplishments. Finally, the development of (creative) individuals is inextricably linked to the broader process of identity formation. Through shared cognitive mechanisms, creative commitments that provide a definition of the self, and as a channel for self-expression, creativity provides a means for individuals to explore, refine, and solidify their sense of self. Understanding this dynamic interplay not only enriches our knowledge of creativity but also offers insights into the psychological processes that shape identity across the lifespan.

References

Acar, S., Tadik, H., Uysal, R., Myers, D., & Inetas, B. (2023). Socio-economic status and creativity: A meta-analysis. *The Journal of Creative Behavior, 57*(1), 138–172. https://doi.org/10.1002/jocb.568

Ahmadi, N., Peter, L., Lubart, T., & Besançon, M. (2019). School environments: Friend or foe for creativity education and research? In C. A. Mullen (Ed.), *Creativity under duress in education? Resistive theories, practices, and actions* (pp. 255–266). Springer International Publishing. https://doi.org/10.1007/978-3-319-90272-2_14

Alexander, G. E., Ryan, L., Bowers, D., Foster, T. C., Bizon, J. L., Geldmacher, D., & Glisky, E. L. (2012). Characterizing cognitive aging in humans with links to animal models. *Frontiers in Aging Neuroscience, 4.* https://doi.org/10.3389/fnagi.2012.00021

Amabile, T. M. (1979). Effects of external evaluation on artistic creativity. *Journal of Personality and Social Psychology, 37*(2), 221–233. https://doi.org/10.1037/0022-3514.37.2.221

Amabile, T. (2011). *Componential theory of creativity.* Harvard Business School Boston MA.

Amabile, T. M., & Pratt, M. G. (2016). The dynamic componential model of creativity and innovation in organizations: Making progress, making meaning. *Research in Organizational Behavior, 36,* 157–183. https://doi.org/10.1016/j.riob.2016.10.001

Anderson, R. C., & Haney, M. (2021). Reflection in the creative process of early adolescents: The mediating roles of creative metacognition, self-efficacy, and self-concept. *Psychology of Aesthetics, Creativity, and the Arts, 15*(4), 612. https://doi.org/10.1037/aca0000324

Antonietti, A., Pizzingrilli, P., & Valenti, C. (2020). *Enhancing creativity through story-telling: Innovative training programs for school settings.* Springer Nature. https://doi.org/10.1007/978-3-030-63013-3

Barbot, B. (2008). Le paradigmede Marcia: Variabilitéinter etintra-individuelle dans la formation de l'identité. In *Perspectives différentielles en psychologie* (pp. 507–510). Presses Universitaires deRennes.

Barbot, B. (2020). Creativity and self-esteem in adolescence: A study of their domain-specific, multivariate relationships. *The Journal of Creative Behavior, 54*(2), 279–292. https://doi.org/10.1002/jocb.365

Barbot, B. (2021). The intertwined development of identity and creativity: Immersing in the digital self. In S. W. Russ, J. D. Hoffmann, & J. C. Kaufman (Eds.), *The Cambridge handbook of lifespan development of creativity* (pp. 159–175). Cambridge University Press. https://doi.org/10.1017/9781108755726.011

Barbot, B., & Eff, H. (2019). The genetic basis of creativity: A multivariate approach. In J. C. Kaufman & R. J. Sternberg (Eds.), *The Cambridge handbook of creativity* (2nd ed., pp. 132–147). Cambridge University Press. https://doi.org/10.1017/9781316979839.009

Barbot, B., & Heuser, B. (2017). Chapter 5—Creativity and identity formation in adolescence: A developmental perspective. In M. Karwowski & J. C. Kaufman (Eds.), *The creative self* (pp. 87–98). Academic Press. https://doi.org/10.1016/B978-0-12-809790-8.00005-4

Barbot, B., & Hunter, S. R. (2012). Developmental changes in adolescence and risks for delinquency. In E. L. Grigorenko (Ed.), *Handbook of juvenile forensic psychology and psychiatry* (pp. 11–34). Springer US. https://doi.org/10.1007/978-1-4614-0905-2_2

Barbot, B., & Lubart, T. (2012). Adolescence, créativité et transformation de Soi. *Enfance, 3*(3), 299–312. https://doi.org/10.3917/enfl.123.0299

Barbot, B., & Rogh, W. (2020). Developmental trends in creative abilities and potentials. In S. Pritzker & M. Runco (Eds.), *Encyclopedia of creativity* (3rd ed., pp. 323–326). Academic Press. https://doi.org/10.1016/B978-0-12-809324-5.06167-8

Barbot, B., & Tinio, P. P. L. (2015). Where is the "g" in creativity? A specialization–differentiation hypothesis. *Frontiers in Human Neuroscience, 8*. https://www.frontiersin.org/articles/10.3389/fnhum.2014.01041

Barbot, B., Tan, M., & Grigorenko, E. L. (2013). *The Genetics of Creativity: The Generative and Receptive Sides of the Creativity Equation*. https://doi.org/10.7551/mitpress/9747.003.0008

Barbot, B., Lubart, T. I., & Besançon, M. (2016). "Peaks, slumps, and bumps": Individual differences in the development of creativity in children and adolescents. *New Directions for Child and Adolescent Development, 2016*(151), 33–45. https://doi.org/10.1002/cad.20152

Beghetto, R. A. (2014). Creative mortification: An initial exploration. *Psychology of Aesthetics, Creativity, and the Arts, 8*(3), 266–276. https://doi.org/10.1037/a0036618

Beghetto, R. A., & Sriraman, B. (2017). Introduction: Creative contradictions in education. In *Creative contradictions in education* (pp. xi–xiii). Springer International Publishing. https://doi.org/10.1007/978-3-319-21924-0

Benedek, M., Franz, F., Heene, M., & Neubauer, A. C. (2012). Differential effects of cognitive inhibition and intelligence on creativity. *Personality and Individual Differences, 53*(4), 480–485. https://doi.org/10.1016/j.paid.2012.04.014

Besançon, M., Fenouillet, F., & Shankland, R. (2015). Influence of school environment on adolescents' creative potential, motivation and well-being. *Learning and Individual Differences, 43*, 178–184. https://doi.org/10.1016/j.lindif.2015.08.029

Bijvoet-van den Berg, S., & Hoicka, E. (2014). Individual differences and age-related changes in divergent thinking in toddlers and preschoolers. *Developmental Psychology, 50*(6), 1629–1639. https://doi.org/10.1037/a0036131

Bonnardel, N. (2009). Activités de conception et créativité: De l'analyse des facteurs cognitifs à l'assistance aux activités de conception créatives. *Le travail humain, 72*(1), 5–22. https://doi.org/10.3917/th.721.0005

Bosacki, S., Talwar, V., & Lecce, S. (2023). Critical review: Secondary school climate and adolescents' emotional well-being. Adolescents, *3*(3), Article 3. https://doi.org/10.3390/adolescents3030036.

Boyd, D., & Bee, H. (2017). *Les âges de la vie* (5e éd ed.). ERPI.

Brinch, C. N., & Galloway, T. A. (2012). Schooling in adolescence raises IQ scores. *PNAS Proceedings of the National Academy of Sciences of the United States of America, 109*(2), 425–430. https://doi.org/10.1073/pnas.1106077109

Camarda, A., Bouhours, L., Osmont, A., Le Masson, P., Weil, B., Borst, G., & Cassotti, M. (2021). Opposite effect of social evaluation on creative idea generation in early and middle adolescents. *Creativity Research Journal, 33*(4), 399–410. https://doi.org/10.1080/10400419.2021.1902174

Capron Puozzo, I., & Cavalla, C. (2018). Le lâcher-prise, un microprocessus conatif nécessaire à la créativité dans l'apprentissage ? In F. Berdal-Masuy (Ed.), *Emotissage—Les émotions dans l'apprentissage des langues (pp. 129–139)*. Presses Universitaire de Louvain. https://hal.science/hal-01890668

Collins, J., & Cooke, D. K. (2013). Creative role models, personality and performance. *Journal of Management Development, 32*(4), 336–350. https://doi.org/10.1108/02621711311326347

Csikszentmihalyi, M. (2009). *Flow: The psychology of optimal experience*. Harper Collins.

Darwin, C. (1845). *The voyage of H.M.S.* Beagle. John Murray.

Darwin, C. (1887). *The life and letters of Charles Darwin: Including an autobiographical chapter*. D. Appleton.

Darwin, C. (1958). *The autobiography of Charles Darwin 1809–1882: With the original omissions restored* (N. Barlow, Ed.). Collins.

de Jesus, S. N., Rus, C. L., Lens, W., & Imaginário, S. (2013). Intrinsic motivation and creativity related to product: A meta analysis of the studies published between 1990–2010. *Creativity Research Journal, 25*(1), 80–84. https://doi.org/10.1080/10400419.2013.752235

Deng, L., Wang, L., & Zhao, Y. (2016). How creativity was affected by environmental factors and individual characteristics: A cross-cultural comparison perspective. *Creativity Research Journal, 28*(3), 357–366. https://doi.org/10.1080/10400419.2016.1195615

Dobzhansky, T. (1973). Nothing in biology makes sense except in the light of evolution. *American Biology Teacher, 35*, 125–129. https://doi.org/10.2307/4444260

Dollinger, S. J., & Dollinger, S. C. (2017). Creativity and identity. In M. Karwowski & J. C. Kaufman (Eds.), *The creative self* (pp. 49–64). Elsevier Academic Press. https://doi.org/10.1016/B978-0-12-809790-8.00003-0

Dollinger, S. J., Clancy Dollinger, S. M., & Centeno, L. (2005) Identity and creativity. *Identity, 5*(4), 315–339. https://doi.org/10.1207/s1532706xid0504_2

Eisenberger, R., & Rhoades, L. (2001). Incremental effects of reward on creativity. *Journal of Personality and Social Psychology, 81*(4), 728–741. https://doi.org/10.1037/0022-3514.81.4.728

Ferreri, F., Peretti, C., & Mattei, P. (2004). Stress et cognition. *Act. Méd. Int. Psychiatr, 21*, 9–10.

Frith, E., Kane, M. J., Welhaf, M. S., Christensen, A. P., Silvia, P. J., & Beaty, R. E. (2021). Keeping creativity under control: Contributions of attention control and fluid intelligence to divergent thinking. *Creativity Research Journal, 33*(2), 138–157. https://doi.org/10.1080/10400419.2020.1855906

Gajda, A., Beghetto, R. A., & Karwowski, M. (2017). Exploring creative learning in the classroom: A multi-method approach. *Thinking Skills and Creativity, 24*, 250–267. https://doi.org/10.1016/j.tsc.2017.04.002

Galenson, D. W. (2009). Old masters and young geniuses: The two life cycles of human creativity. *Journal of Applied Economics, 12*(1). https://doi.org/10.1016/s1514-0326(09)60002-7

Gerwig, A., Miroshnik, K., Forthmann, B., Benedek, M., Karwowski, M., & Holling, H. (2021). The Relationship between Intelligence and Divergent Thinking—A Meta-Analytic Update. *Journal of Intelligence, 9*(2), Article 2. https://doi.org/10.3390/jintelligence9020023.

Glăveanu, V. P., & Beghetto, R. A. (2017). The difference that makes a 'creative' difference in education. In R. A. Beghetto & B. Sriraman (Eds.), *Creative contradictions in education: Cross disciplinary paradoxes and perspectives* (pp. 37–54). Springer International Publishing. https://doi.org/10.1007/978-3-319-21924-0_3

Gould, S. J. (1991). *Ever since Darwin: Reflections in natural history*. WW Norton & Company.

Gould, S. J. (2002). The structure of evolutionary theory. *Harvard University Press*. https://doi.org/10.4159/9780674417922

Gould, S. J. (2010). *The panda's thumb: More reflections in natural history*. WW Norton & Company.

Graciano, P., Lermen, F. H., Reichert, F. M., & Padula, A. D. (2023). The impact of risk-taking and creativity stimuli in education towards innovation: A systematic review and research agenda. *Thinking Skills and Creativity, 47*, 101220. https://doi.org/10.1016/j.tsc.2022.101220

Grégoire, J., & Vlieghe, M. (2010). Haut potentiel, créativité et personnalité. *Enfance, 1*(1), 85–98. https://doi.org/10.3917/enf1.101.0085

Gruber, H. E., & Barrett, P. H. (1974). *Darwin on man: A psychological study of scientific creativity*. E. P. Dutton.

Haase, J., Hoff, E. V., Hanel, P. H. P., & Innes-Ker, Å. (2018). A meta-analysis of the relation between creative self-efficacy and different creativity measurements. *Creativity Research Journal, 30*(1), 1–16. https://doi.org/10.1080/10400419.2018.1411436

Han, W., Zhang, M., Feng, X., Gong, G., Peng, K., & Zhang, D. (2018). Genetic influences on creativity: An exploration of convergent and divergent thinking. *PeerJ, 6*. https://doi.org/10.7717/peerj.5403

Harrington, D. M., Block, J. H., & Block, J. (1987). Testing aspects of Carl Rogers's theory of creative environments: Child-rearing antecedents of creative potential in young adolescents. *Journal of Personality and Social Psychology, 52*(4), 851–856. https://doi.org/10.1037/0022-3514.52.4.851

Hass, R. W., Katz-Buonincontro, J., & Reiter-Palmon, R. (2016). Disentangling creative mindsets from creative self-efficacy and creative identity: Do people hold fixed and growth theories of creativity? *Psychology of Aesthetics, Creativity, and the Arts, 10*(4), 436. https://doi.org/10.1037/aca0000081

Hennessey, B. A. (2019). Motivation and creativity. In J. C. Kaufman & R. J. Sternberg (Eds.), *The Cambridge handbook of creativity* (2nd ed., pp. 374–395). Cambridge University Press. https://doi.org/10.1017/9781316979839.020

Hui, A. N. N., He, M. W. J., & Wong, W. (2019). Understanding the development of creativity across the life span. In J. C. Kaufman & R. J. Sternberg (Eds.), *The Cambridge handbook of creativity* (2nd ed., pp. 69–87). Cambridge University Press. https://doi.org/10.1017/9781316979839.006.

Ishiguro, C., Sato, Y., Takahashi, A., Abe, Y., Kato, E., & Takagishi, H. (2022). Relationships among creativity indices: Creative potential, production, achievement, and beliefs about own creative personality. *PLoS One, 17*(9), e0273303. https://doi.org/10.1371/journal.pone.0273303

Ivcevic, Z. (2007). Artistic and everyday creativity: An act-frequency approach. *The Journal of Creative Behavior, 41*(4), 271–290. https://doi.org/10.1002/j.2162-6057.2007.tb01074.x

Ivcevic, Z., & Mayer, J. D. (2009). Mapping dimensions of creativity in the life-space. *Creativity Research Journal, 21*(2–3), 152–165. https://doi.org/10.1080/10400410902855259

Ivcevic, Z., Hoffmann, J. D., & McGarry, J. A. (2022). Scaffolding positive creativity in secondary school students. *Education Sciences, 12*(4), Article 4. https://doi.org/10.3390/educsci12040239

Jirásek, M., & Sudzina, F. (2020). *Big Five personality traits and creativity*. 24(3). https://www.muni.cz/vyzkum/publikace/1693136

Karwowski, M. (2014). Creative mindsets: Measurement, correlates, consequences. *Psychology of Aesthetics, Creativity, and the Arts, 8*(1), 62. https://doi.org/10.1037/a0034898

Karwowski, M. (2016). The dynamics of creative self-concept: Changes and reciprocal relations between creative self-efficacy and creative personal identity. *Creativity Research Journal, 28*(1), 99–104. https://doi.org/10.1080/10400419.2016.1125254

Karwowski, M. (2022). School does not kill creativity, *27*(3), 263–275. https://doi.org/10.1027/1016-9040/a000449

Karwowski, M., & Barbot, B. (2016). Creative self-beliefs: Their nature, development, and correlates. In J. C. Kaufman & J. Baer (Eds.), *Creativity and reason in cognitive development* (2nd ed.) (1775388232; 2016-09475-016; 2nd ed., pp. 302–326, 394 pages). Cambridge University Press; APA PsycInfo®. https://doi.org/10.1017/CBO9781139941969.016.

Karwowski, M., & Lebuda, I. (2014). Digit ratio predicts eminence of Polish actors. *Personality and Individual Differences, 64*, 30–34. https://doi.org/10.1016/j.paid.2014.02.014

Karwowski, M., Lebuda, I., & Beghetto, R. A. (2019). Creative self-beliefs. In *The Cambridge handbook of creativity* (2nd ed., pp. 396–417). Cambridge University Press. https://doi.org/10.1017/9781316979839.021

Karwowski, M., Jankowska, D. M., Brzeski, A., Czerwonka, M., Gajda, A., Lebuda, I., & Beghetto, R. A. (2020). Delving into creativity and learning. In V. P. Glăveanu, I. J. Ness, & C. de Saint Laurent (Eds.), *Creative learning in digital and virtual environments: Opportunities and challenges of technology-enabled learning and creativity* (pp. 7–29). Routledge. https://doi.org/10.4324/9781003094630-2

Kaufman, J. C., & Beghetto, R. A. (2009). Beyond big and little: The four c model of creativity. *Review of General Psychology, 13*(1), 1–12. https://doi.org/10.1037/a0013688

Kaufman, J. C., & Beghetto, R. A. (2013). In praise of Clark Kent: Creative metacognition and the importance of teaching kids when (not) to be creative. *Roeper Review, 35*(3), 155–165. https://doi.org/10.1080/02783193.2013.799413

Kettler, T., Lamb, K. N., & Mullet, D. R. (2021). Developing creativity in the classroom: Learning and innovation for 21st-century schools. *Routledge*. https://doi.org/10.4324/9781003234104

Khalid, M., Saad, S., Hamid, S. R. A., Abdullah, M. R., Ibrahim, H., & Shahrill, M. (2020). Enhancing creativity and problem solving skills through creative problem solving in teaching mathematics. *Creativity Studies, 13*(2), Article 2. https://doi.org/10.3846/cs.2020.11027.

Kievit, R. A., Davis, S. W., Mitchell, D. J., Taylor, J. R., Duncan, J., & Henson, R. N. A. (2014). Distinct aspects of frontal lobe structure mediate age-related differences in fluid intelligence and multitasking. *Nature Communications, 5*(1), 5658. https://doi.org/10.1038/ncomms6658

Kim, K. H. (2011). The creativity crisis: The decrease in creative thinking scores on the Torrance tests of creative thinking. *Creativity Research Journal, 23*(4), 285–295. https://doi.org/10.1080/10400419.2011.627805

Kim, J.-E. (2019). The impact of creative role identity and creative self-efficacy on employee creativity in the hotel business. *The Journal of Asian Finance, Economics and Business, 6*(2), 123–133. https://doi.org/10.13106/jafeb.2019.vol6.no2.123

Kleibeuker, S. W., Dreu, C. K. W. D., & Crone, E. A. (2012). The development of creative cognition across adolescence: Distinct trajectories for insight and divergent thinking. *Developmental Science, 16*(1). https://doi.org/10.1111/j.1467-7687.2012.01176.x

Kurnianingsih, Y. A., Sim, S. K. Y., Chee, M. W. L., & Mullette-Gillman, O. A. (2015). Aging and loss decision making: Increased risk aversion and decreased use of maximizing information, with correlated rationality and value maximization. *Frontiers in Human Neuroscience, 9*. https://doi.org/10.3389/fnhum.2015.00280

Lebuda, I., & Benedek, M. (2023). A systematic framework of creative metacognition. *Physics of Life Reviews, 46*, 161–181. https://doi.org/10.1016/j.plrev.2023.07.002

Liebherr, M., Schiebener, J., Averbeck, H., & Brand, M. (2017). Decision making under ambiguity and objective risk in higher age—A review on cognitive and emotional contributions. *Frontiers in Psychology, 8*. https://doi.org/10.3389/fpsyg.2017.02128

Lu, Z., Ding, Y., & Nie, Y. (2024). How does family socioeconomic status affect creativity? The role of creative self-efficacy and critical thinking disposition. *Current Psychology, 43*(6), 5674–5681. https://doi.org/10.1007/s12144-023-04768-x

Lubart, T. (1996). The development of creativity in 9-to 10-year-old children. *International Journal of Psychology, 31*(3–4), 4176–4176.

Lubart, T. I., & Getz, I. (1997). Emotion, metaphor, and the creative process. *Creativity Research Journal, 10*(4), 285–301. https://doi.org/10.1207/s15326934crj1004_1

Lubart, T., & Guignard, J.-H. (2004). The generality-specificity of creativity: A multivariate approach. In *Creativity: From potential to realization* (pp. 43–56). American Psychological Association. https://doi.org/10.1037/10692-004

Lubart, T., & Thornhill-Miller, B. (2020). *Creativity: An overview of the 7C's of creative thought* (pp. 277–305). https://doi.org/10.17885/heiup.470.c6678

Luna, E., Ernst, J., Clark, A., DeLuca, V. W., & Kelly, D. (2018). Enhancing classroom creativity. *Technology and Engineering Teacher, 77*(6), 26–31.

Mahmoud, N. E., Kamel, S. M., & Hamza, T. S. (2020). The relationship between tolerance of ambiguity and creativity in architectural design studio. *Creativity Studies, 13*(1), Article 1. https://doi.org/10.3846/cs.2020.9628.

Maslow, A. H. (1943). A theory of human motivation. *Psychological Review, 1*, 943. https://doi.org/10.1037/h0054346

Maslow, A. H. (1962). Creativity in self-actualizing people. In *Toward a psychology of being* (pp. 127–137). D Van Nostrand. https://doi.org/10.1037/10793-010

May, R. (1975). *The courage to create*. WW Norton &Company.

Moyne, A., Barthod-Malat, Y., & Kubiszewski, V. (2018). Stress scolaire des collégiens et des lycéens: Effet de l'appréhension de l'orientation et de la pression de la note. *Pratiques Psychologiques, 24*(2), 177–194. https://doi.org/10.1016/j.prps.2017.07.001

Mueller, J. S., Melwani, S., & Goncalo, J. A. (2012). The bias against creativity: Why people desire but reject creative ideas. *Psychological Science, 23*(1), 13–17. https://doi.org/10.1177/0956797611421018

Pan, H., & Zhang, Y. (2023). Understanding the emotional development of school-aged children: A critical review. *Journal of Education, Humanities and Social Sciences, 8*, 1860–1866. https://doi.org/10.54097/ehss.v8i.4597

Pannier, I. (2005). Pour en finir (ou presque) avec les notes—Évaluer par les compétences. *Les Cahiers pédagogiques, 438*, 15–16.

Prokofieva, V., Brandt-Pomares, P., Velay, J.-L., Hérold, J.-F., & Kostromina, S. (2017). Stress de l'évaluation scolaire: Un nouveau regard sur un problème ancien. *Recherches & éducations, 18*, Article 18. https://doi.org/10.4000/recherchesedu cations.4657.

Ritchie, S. J., & Tucker-Drob, E. M. (2018). How much does education improve intelligence? A meta-analysis. *Psychological Science, 29*(8), 1358–1369. https://doi.org/10.1177/0956797618774253

Ritter, S. M., Damian, R. I., Simonton, D. K., van Baaren, R. B., Strick, M., Derks, J., & Dijksterhuis, A. (2012). Diversifying experiences enhance cognitive flexibility. *Journal of Experimental Social Psychology, 48*(4), 961–964. https://doi.org/10.1016/j.jesp.2012.02.009

Robinson, S. K. (2006). *Sir Ken Robinson: Do schools kill creativity? | TED Talk.* https://www.ted.com/talks/sir_ken_robinson_do_schools_kill_creativity

Rogers, C. R. (1951). *Client-centered therapy: Its current practice, implications and theory.* Houghton Mifflin.

Rogers, C. R. (1954). Toward a theory of creativity. *ETC: A Review of General Semantics, 11*(4), 249–260.

Rubenstein, L. D., Ridgley, L. M., Callan, G. L., Karami, S., & Ehlinger, J. (2018). How teachers perceive factors that influence creativity development: Applying a social cognitive theory perspective. *Teaching and Teacher Education, 70*, 100–110. https://doi.org/10.1016/j.tate.2017.11.012

Said-Metwaly, S., Fernández-Castilla, B., Kyndt, E., Van den Noortgate, W., & Barbot, B. (2021). Does the fourth-grade slump in creativity actually exist? A meta-analysis of the development of divergent thinking in school-age children and adolescents. *Educational Psychology Review, 33*(1), 275–298. https://doi.org/10.1007/s10648-020-09547-9

Said-Metwaly, S., Taylor, C. L., Camarda, A., & Barbot, B. (2022). Divergent thinking and creative achievement—How strong is the link? An updated meta-analysis. *Psychology of Aesthetics, Creativity, and the Arts*, No Pagination Specified-No Pagination Specified. https://doi.org/10.1037/aca0000507.

Schunk, D. H. (2008). Metacognition, self-regulation, and self-regulated learning: Research recommendations. *Educational Psychology Review, 20*(4), 463–467. https://doi.org/10.1007/s10648-008-9086-3

Serpell, Z. N., & Esposito, A. G. (2016). Development of executive functions: Implications for educational policy and practice. *Policy Insights from the Behavioral and Brain Sciences, 3*(2), 203–210. https://doi.org/10.1177/2372732216654718

Shaughnessy, M. F. (1995). *Creativity in mentoring*. https://eric.ed.gov/?id=ED387718.

Silvia, P. J. (2015). Intelligence and creativity are pretty similar after all. *Educational Psychology Review, 27*(4), 599–606. https://doi.org/10.1007/s10648-015-9299-1

Silvia, P. J., & Phillips, A. G. (2004). Self-awareness, self-evaluation, and creativity. *Personality and Social Psychology Bulletin, 30*(8), 1009–1017. https://doi.org/10.1177/0146167204264073

Simonton, D. K. (1977). Creative productivity, age, and stress: A biographical time-series analysis of 10 classical composers. *Journal of Personality and Social Psychology, 35*(11), 791–804. https://doi.org/10.1037/0022-3514.35.11.791

Simonton, D. K. (2000). Creative development as acquired expertise: Theoretical issues and an empirical test. *Developmental Review, 20*(2), 283–318. https://doi.org/10.1006/drev.1999.0504

Simonton, D. K. (2004). *Creativity in science: Chance, logic, genius, and zeitgeist*. Cambridge University Press. https://doi.org/10.1017/CBO9781139165358

Sternberg, R. J., & Lubart, T. I. (1991). An investment theory of creativity and its development. *Human Development, 34*(1), 1–31. https://doi.org/10.1159/000277029

Sternberg, R. J., & Lubart, T. I. (1995). *Defying the crowd. Cultivating creativity in a culture of conformity*. Free Press.

Swirsky, L. T., Sparrow, E. P., Sullivan, M. D., Valenzano, S. L., Chowdhury, S., & Spaniol, J. (2023). Age differences in motivated cognition: A meta-analysis. *The Journals of Gerontology: Series B, 78*(7), 1169–1181. https://doi.org/10.1093/geronb/gbad049

Tierney, P., & Farmer, S. M. (2011). Creative self-efficacy development and creative performance over time. *The Journal of Applied Psychology, 96*(2), 277–293. https://doi.org/10.1037/a0020952

Velayutham, S., & Aldridge, J. M. (2013). Influence of psychosocial classroom environment on students' motivation and self-regulation in science learning: A structural equation modeling approach. *Research in Science Education, 43*(2), 507–527. https://doi.org/10.1007/s11165-011-9273-y

Verhoeven, M., Poorthuis, A. M. G., & Volman, M. (2019). The role of School in Adolescents' identity development. A literature review. *Educational Psychology Review, 31*(1), 35–63. https://doi.org/10.1007/s10648-018-9457-3

Wolf, O. T. (2017). Stress and memory retrieval: Mechanisms and consequences. *Current Opinion in Behavioral Sciences, 14*, 40–46. https://doi.org/10.1016/j.cobeha.2016.12.001

Wong, M. D., Dosanjh, K. K., Jackson, N. J., Rünger, D., & Dudovitz, R. N. (2021). The longitudinal relationship of school climate with adolescent social and emotional health. *BMC Public Health, 21*(1), 207. https://doi.org/10.1186/s12889-021-10245-6

Yuan, F., & Zhou, J. (2008). Differential effects of expected external evaluation on different parts of the creative idea production process and on final product creativity. *Creativity Research Journal, 20*(4), 391–403. https://doi.org/10.1080/10400410802391827

Zenasni, F., Besançon, M., & Lubart, T. (2008). Creativity and tolerance of ambiguity: An empirical study. *The Journal of Creative Behavior, 42*(1), 61–73. https://doi.org/10.1002/j.2162-6057.2008.tb01080.x

Zhang, W., & Niu, W. (2013). Creativity in the later life: Factors associated with the creativity of the Chinese elderly. *The Journal of Creative Behavior, 47*(1), 60–76. https://doi.org/10.1002/jocb.23

CHAPTER 8

The Creativity and Mental Health Debate Through the Lens of the Creative Person

Molly Holinger and Lakshmi Sithambaram

The idea of the "mad genius" or "tortured artist" has pervaded both the scientific study of creativity and general perceptions of creativity for decades (Kaufman, 2014). This is, perhaps, unsurprising as we can all, no doubt, name creative geniuses who suffered from severe mental illness. Watching Woody Allen's *Midnight in Paris,* for example, which introduces a string of artistic geniuses living in the city in the 1920s, one cannot help but ask: *what was in the water (or rather, the cocktails)?* Some of the iconic figures include Earnest Hemingway, Zelda and F. Scott Fitzgerald, and Pablo Picasso. More recent examples (not in the film) include David Foster Wallace, Robin Williams, and Anthony Bourdain.

As *Midnight in Paris* and more modern celebrities demonstrate, the mad genius stereotype makes for a compelling narrative, though an incomplete one. In truth, existing research shows a *positive* correlation between creativity and mental health, on average (Acar et al., 2021). With the possible exception of eminent (or "Big-C") creators, the majority of people creating for personal or professional means lead lives of greater well-being.

M. Holinger (✉) • L. Sithambaram
Department of Creativity and Change Leadership, State University of New York, SUNY, Buffalo State, Buffalo, NY, USA
e-mail: holingml@buffalostate.edu

Z. Ivcevic (ed.), *Creators*, The Seven C's of Creativity,
https://doi.org/10.1007/978-3-032-09225-0_8

That being said, current research has yet to catch up to long-standing beliefs. According to Benedek et al. (2021), about 40 percent of individuals across six different countries, believed that "exceptional creativity is usually accompanied by mental health disorders" (p. 4). While this myth can be harmless, it can also lead those who desire to be more creative to decide against treatment of their mental health issues as this may lessen their creative *edge*, so to speak. There is growing evidence to suggest that mental health interventions for certain conditions increase cognitive flexibility that is linked to creative thinking (Baas et al., 2008; Richards, 2007). Richards (2007) argues that individuals who actively cultivate mental well-being are better equipped to engage in creative activities.

The Current Chapter

This chapter outlines the existing research on the relationship between creativity, mental health and well-being, as it pertains to the creative person. Importantly, we take into account five essential considerations:

1. Level of creativity
2. Domain
3. Personality
4. Type of assessment/measure
5. Type and clinical level of disease/mental illness

We break down the current literature in this way for the sake of capturing the nuances of this topic. Moreover, given that this volume focuses on the creative *person*, it seems only fitting to take individual differences into account. We hope to provide the reader with a current, accurate, and nuanced picture of the research, from which they can draw their own conclusions.

Level of Creativity and Domain

In connection to creativity, mental illnesses such as depression are not necessarily counter to creativity and have even been found in higher levels in certain domains, and at certain levels of creativity, such as in eminent women poets (Kaufman, 2001).

The Four C's

Kaufman and Beghetto (2009) identified four levels of creativity: mini-c, little-c, Pro-c, and Big-C. They define mini-c creativity as the novel and personally meaningful interpretation of experiences, actions, and events that may not be visible to outsiders and may consist purely of ideas and connections that the learner creates. As Vygotsky (1967, p. 7) explains: "Any human act that gives rise to something new is referred to as a creative act, regardless of whether what is constructed is a physical object or some mental or emotional construct that lives within the person who created it and is known only to him."

Next, the term little-c pertains to non-expert creativity that is about "acting with flexibility, intelligence, and novelty in the everyday" (Craft, 2005, p. 43). This results in creating something new that has "originality and meaningfulness" (Richards, 2007, p. 5). This type of everyday creativity can manifest in various individuals, from those with a passion for gardening or those who take creative photographs and share them on online platforms.

Pro-c creativity bridges the gap between everyday creativity (little-c) and the esteemed recognition of Big-C creativity. These individuals advance beyond amateur levels of creativity, dedicating substantial effort and utilizing advanced expertise to make innovate inroads within specific creative domains (Kaufman & Beghetto, 2009). They are skilled professionals who excel in problem-solving and the creation of original applications often in the context of work, though have not yet achieved the highest levels of acclaim associated with Big-C creativity (Kaufman & Beghetto, 2009).

Finally, Big-C is the highest level of creative accomplishment within a specific domain, focusing on the originality, practicality, and societal acceptance of ideas. Big-C creativity involves well-defined, highly recognized creative achievements (Kaufman & Beghetto, 2009). A key factor in determining whether a contribution is considered Big-C or little-c isn't how it was created, but rather how it is evaluated within a social context (Csikszentmihalyi, 2014).

The literature on creativity and mental health focuses on little-c, Pro-c, and Big-C.

Little-c

Both theory and research suggest that little-c creativity, self-actualization/personal growth, and well-being are interwoven. One study showed that people who engaged in everyday creativity often did so as a means of self-expression (Ivcevic & Mayer, 2009) and, in another study, reported experiencing personal growth (Ivcevic, 2007). The theoretical connections between personal growth and creativity date back to humanistic psychology and have re-emerged more recently within positive psychology. Maslow (1971), for example, emphasized the role of creativity in self-actualization; Peterson and Seligman (2004) included creativity among their classification of character strengths under the broader umbrella of wisdom and knowledge. Furthermore, individuals who believed that their creativity contributed to their short-term (hedonic) and long-term (hedonic) well-being also had higher creative self-efficacy, or confidence in their ability to accomplish creative tasks (Holinger & Kaufman, 2024).

A daily diary study (Conner et al., 2018) found that individuals who performed creative activities displayed more energy, enthusiasm, and excitement the following day. These residual effects also pertained to flourishing, or a sense of meaning, social connectedness, and zest for life. Neither positive affect nor flourishing led to increased creativity the subsequent day, indicating that creativity may lead to increased positive affect and flourishing but the relationship may not be reciprocal from one day to the next.

Pro-C

Smith et al. (2022) examined the everyday creative behavior of Pro-c individuals (creative professionals, students in creative domains, and hobbyists involved in 20 or more hours of creative activity per week) over the course of two weeks. Results showed higher levels of creativity and activated positive emotions on the same day and decreased creativity on days marked by negative emotion. These findings are consistent with the stream of research linking creativity to high-arousal, positive emotion in general (e.g., Baas et al., 2008) and at work (e.g., Amabile et al., 2005; Diener et al., 2020). Similarly, vitality or the extent to which an individual experiences positive arousal (encompassing such emotions as excitement and enthusiasm) appears to enhance creative performance in a psychologically safe environment (Kark & Carmeli, 2009).

Amabile and Kramer (2011) identified a third factor connecting positive emotion with creativity: progress. Using daily diary methods, they discovered that making progress was the strongest predictor of workplace happiness and engagement. Not only did progress enhance positive emotions, but those emotions, in turn, fueled further progress—an effect they termed the "progress loop." Even minor achievements were found to trigger positive feelings, which then encouraged continued productivity, including creative productivity. Both this workplace study and the aforementioned everyday creativity studies indicate that cycles and residual effects can play an important role in creative engagement and productivity.

Forgeard (2024b) examined the conscious motivations of professional artists and scientists to create. Emotional motivations constituted one significant reason, as well as prosocial and intellectual motivators. For example, individuals reported pursuing creative work "because it makes me feel better mentally," and "because it somehow helps me deal with difficult personal experiences" (p. 230). Importantly, emotional motivations differed from intellectual motivations, despite their shared emphasis on the positive emotions and gratification associated with intellectual engagement.

Emotion regulation appears to play an important intervening role in stimulating creative performance according to a study (Parke et al., 2015) that examined various workplace scenarios related to cognitive demands. When information processing requirements were high, individuals with higher emotion regulation abilities were better able to cope and maintain positive affect. This positive affect, in turn, resulted in higher creativity. Second, when creative processing demands were low, individuals who were able to emotionally regulate to make their work more engaging, experienced increased positive affect and, subsequently, greater creativity.

In terms of more long-term mental health markers—as opposed to momentary affect—Ivcevic et al. (2022) found that Pro-c artists had both more psychological vulnerabilities and psychological resources as compared to the general population. They discovered a unique profile that professional creative artists exhibited greater ego-resilience, psychological well-being, and hope, while also reporting higher levels of anxiety, stress, and depression.

Big-C

The vast majority of research on creativity and mental health has focused on historiometric methods and Big-C creators until a shift in recent decades toward little-c and Pro-c. These studies can be problematic for a few reasons: first, most of this research is based on anecdotal evidence or biographical accounts of highly eminent creators. Another concern is that eminent creators tend to exaggerate when reporting on their psychopathology/mental illness. Older studies often used dichotomous measures (whether a creator had mental illness or was sufficiently eminent) and sometimes lacked independent assessments (Simonton, 2014b). Finally, it may be the case that these individuals were accomplished *despite* their disease and if they may have been more productive in the absence of mental illness. As Carl Jung argued,

> It is, of course, an unanswerable question what an artist would have created if he had not been neurotic. Nietzsche's syphilitic infection undoubtedly exerted a strongly neuroticizing influence on his life. But one could imagine a *sound* Nietzsche possessed of creative power without hypertension—something like Goethe. He would have written much the same as he did, but less strident, less shrill—i.e., less German—more restrained, more responsible, more reasonable and reverent. (1984, p. 333)

Though flawed, these studies nevertheless provide some valuable insight into patterns of well-being of creativity at the *Big-C level* when examined *within specific domains*. For example, Simonton (2014b), in a study of 204 eminent creative individuals, found that as writers and artists approached Big-C, they were more likely to have a mental illness. Scientists, composers, and thinkers, conversely, were more creative up to a threshold. Interestingly, the "peak" differed for each domain: the most eminent scientists exhibited psychopathology a bit more than mild, composers increased to marked, and thinkers were much closer to severe. Finally, scientists were the only group where those with severe psychopathology were worse off in terms of eminence than those with none at all. Similar findings emerged from a re-examination of data from Cox's earlier work on 282 Big-C creators, showing that imaginative writers displayed inferior mental health compared to the group's average, while politicians and composers displayed superior mental health (Simonton & Song, 2009).

These sources address the apparent contradiction that creative people, at the little-c and Pro-c levels, seem more mentally healthy than non-creative people, while highly creative people appear more prone to mental illness (Simonton, 2014a). To reiterate, when examining this research, it is important to recognize that both eminence and psychopathology are quantitative variables that exist on a spectrum, must be independently quantified, and their relationship can be linear or curvilinear depending on the domain.

Type of Assessment/Measure

A few meta-analyses strongly suggest that how creativity is measured/operationalized significantly moderates its relationship with mental health. Across studies, it appears that a stronger link exists when looking at creative behavior versus creative cognition. For example, one meta-analysis (Acar & Runco, 2012) reported greater effect sizes for creative behavior ($r = .22$) and self-report measures ($r = .17$), as compared to divergent thinking ($r = .06$). Similarly, varying results were also found in a comprehensive meta-analysis on mood disorder (Taylor, 2017), in which case "only creativity assessments of accomplishment and behavior demonstrated significant associations with mood disorder" (p. 1062). But why this discrepancy? As put by Acar et al. (2021),

> Divergent thinking is primarily a cognitive measure, whereas the measures of creative activity and behavior are more behavioral, goal oriented, and motivational … Well-being is more likely to be achieved when someone takes concrete steps toward their goals and witnesses the outcome of their own creative activity. The stronger relation of creative activity or behavior to well-being than creative ideation has implications for organizations because engaging in creative activities benefits to the organizations through enhancing innovation and effective problem-solving behaviors as well as the well-being of the organization's people. (p. 746)

Personality

In the last two decades, the Big Five trait model has become the predominant framework in psychology for describing personality traits. These traits are often referred to as dispositional or core traits, distinguishing them from other facets of individuals' personalities, such as their values, attitudes, interests (characteristic adaptations), self-esteem, identity (self concepts), and career backgrounds (objective biography) (McAdams &

Pals, 2006; McCrae & Costa, 1996). This distinction underscores the comprehensive scope of personality research encompassed by the Big Five model. The Big Five personality traits—Neuroticism, Extraversion, Openness, Agreeableness, and Conscientiousness—are widely accepted as fundamental factors of adult personality (Costa & McCrae, 1992; Goldberg, 1990).

Extraversion reflects an energetic engagement with the social and material environment. Agreeableness contrasts a prosocial, cooperative orientation with tendencies toward antagonism. Conscientiousness involves socially regulated impulse control that supports goal-directed behaviors. Openness to experience encompasses the breadth, originality, and complexity of an individual's mental and experiential life (adapted from John et al., 2008). Neuroticism indicates a propensity for emotional instability, characterized by experiencing negative emotions like anger, anxiety, and depression (Costa & McCrae, 1992; McCrae & John, 1992).

Openness to Experience

Openness to experience refers to an individual's willingness to actively seek out and appreciate diverse experiences, as well as their ability to tolerate and explore novel situations (Pervin, 2003). Openness to experience is a broad dimension that encompasses traits such as originality, curiosity, broadmindedness, and imaginativeness (Costa & McCrae, 1992). Other related concepts include aesthetic experience, intellectual curiosity, and a preference for non-traditional or original things (Costa and McCrae, 1992; Ingram et al., 2013). McCrae (1996) noted that individuals who score high on openness tend to have a fascination with ambiguity and open-ended tasks, possess strong cognitive abilities that are necessary for creativity, and are inclined toward seeking out novel and diverse experiences. These skills of curiosity, flexibility (Guilford, 1950), and tolerance for ambiguity and complexity are fundamental to creativity (Puccio et al., 2011).

There is a significant amount of literature that has shown a consistent and positive correlation between creativity and openness to experience (e.g., Feist, 1998; Feist & Barron, 2003; Silvia et al., 2009). Openness to experience has also been shown to enable more flexible coping with adverse events (Kocjan et al., 2021), allowing the individual to be resilient. According to a study by Kocjan et al. (2021), openness had an indirect negative impact on stress through resilience. Recent research supports the usefulness of everyday creative problem-solving and personal characteristics such as openness, non-defensiveness, and bravery as facilitators in responding to adversity (Gruber, 1993; Richards, 2007; Runco, 1996; Runco & Richards, 1997). Importantly, longitudinal research indicates that openness to experience remains relatively stable across time, even in the presence of stressors (e.g., Forgeard et al., 2022).

Openness-Related Constructs

Tolerance for Ambiguity

Tolerance for ambiguity, which is the ability to deal with uncertainty and avoid jumping to conclusions (Puccio et al., 2011), is believed to facilitate creativity and flexibility (Dollinger et al., 1995). Resilience, similarly, is characterized by the ability to tolerate long periods of ambiguity and to thrive and even grow despite the lack of clarity, as argued by Boss (2013). Kellerman and Seligman (2023) also emphasize the importance of embracing ambiguity as a key trait for creativity and one that is crucial for resilience to flourish in times of uncertainty, connecting creativity and resilience.

Tolerance for Risk and Adventure-Seeking

Adventure-seeking (often interchangeably used with sensation-seeking; Zuckerman, 1994) involves willingness to take risks of various types (Zuckerman, 1994). Individuals who exhibit a tendency to seek adventure typically have lower levels of need for closure and avoidance of fear-inducing experiences (Kaufman, 2020). Furthermore, adventure-seeking has been associated with increased resilience (McKay et al., 2018), mapping the indirect role that creativity could play in resilience. High adventure seekers often use problem-focused coping strategies (Carroll, 2013), which involve managing stress by confronting the source of the stress and exploring potential solutions (Kaufman, 2020). It is important to note, however, that while sensation seeking has been shown to be correlated with beneficial and prosocial behaviors, it has also been associated with substance use, risky sex, and antisocial behavior when fueled by maladaptive traits such as emotional volatility, impulsivity, and self-absorption (Maples-Keller, 2016).

Neuroticism

Neuroticism represents a dimension of personality that reflects variations in individuals' tendencies to perceive and feel negative emotions and thoughts (Perkins et al., 2015). Eysenck (1990) suggests that neuroticism may facilitate creativity by reducing cognitive and behavioral inhibition. This reduction is thought to enhance conceptual fluency, originality, and the propensity for independent and norm-challenging behavior. Simonton proposed an "optimal level" of psychopathology (Simonton, 2014b, p. 54) may exist in that a degree of neuroticism can fuel creativity but eventually becomes detrimental at higher levels. The research on diversifying experiences (Goclowksa et al., 2018), or rare and unforeseen experiences or situations, is relevant to this claim. Diversifying experiences vary in intensity, which can affect whether they are experienced as positive or negative. For example, an individual may percieve living abroad as positive or negative depending on the demands of situation and their ability to adjust. Goclowski et al. proposed that at lower levels of intensity, diversifying experiences are associated with enhanced cognitive flexibility; however, beyond a certain level, such experiences cease to be beneficial and may even hinder flexibility. Furthermore, they argued that the degree to which individuals possess adequate adaptive resources to navigate a diversifying experience and have the capacity to deploy those resources affects their perception of such experiences as threatening or non-threatening which moderates the impact—positive or negative—on creativity.

Neuroticism-Related Constructs

Negative affect

Creativity is not solely the outcome of cognitive processes, as it is also influenced by emotions and affective states (Puccio et al., 2011). Emotions, whether positive or negative, contain valuable information that can contribute to the creative process, as different types of emotions can be more or less conducive to specific stages of the creative process (Ivevic & Hoffman, 2019). For example, Kaufmann and Vosburg (2002) found that positive mood led to superior scores in early idea generation, and negative mood led to superior scores in late idea generation. Similarly, studies have shown that experiencing negative moods can lead to increased problem-solving abilities in creative tasks, especially those involving focused attention, precise execution, divergent thinking, and analogical problem-solving

(Abele, 1992; Jausovec, 1989; Kaufmann & Vosburg, 1997). According to De Dreu et al. (2008) in their dual pathway model of creativity, negative moods characterized by low hedonic tone, or unpleasantness, are suggested to increase creative fluency and originality by promoting greater perseverance. Conversely, positive moods with high activation are proposed to enhance creative fluency and originality by fostering improved cognitive flexibility.

In other words, creativity does not depend on a particular type of emotion. While most creativity research stresses benefits from positive, high activation emotions, it is equally true that creativity calls for a range of emotions to be utilized and regulated. The key factor is the individual's ability to effectively harness and utilize those emotions in a productive manner. Throughout the creative process, emotions play a significant role, starting from the decision to take on a challenging project to the creation and presentation of the final product. Emotions are not mere impositions on individuals; rather, people have agency over their emotions and can utilize this agency to enhance their creativity (Ivcevic et al., 2023). Individuals who possess both high creative abilities and mastery over their emotions are more likely to be viewed as more creative by others and display greater persistence in overcoming challenges (Ivcevic & Brackett, 2015).

Rumination

Rumination is a form of cognitive processing and is linked to creative thinking when used constructively (Forgeard, 2013). Research suggests that when rumination focuses on negative emotional states, it can lead to poor problem-solving, self-criticism, and reduced self-confidence (Lyubomirsky et al., 1999). This type of rumination is also associated with decreased cognitive flexibility (Davis & Nolen-Hoeksema, 2000), which is important for creative thinking. On the other hand, self-reflective rumination can enhance creativity by allowing individuals to engage in deeper processing of their experiences, thoughts, and emotions. This deeper processing and the level of seriousness that individuals report while engaging in creative activities has a positive effect on their creative fluency, the originality of their ideas, and the degree of elaboration of these ideas. Additionally, this seriousness also influences the number of hours that individuals dedicate to creative endeavors (Cohen & Ferrari, 2010; Verhaeghen et al., 2014; Verhaeghen et al., 2005).

Emotional Stability

Emotional stability, neuroticism's polar opposite, describes individuals who tend to react calmly and resiliently when facing difficulties (Soto, 2018). There is evidence that personal and social creativity may play a supporting role in well-being in the wake of adversity. Vanada (2018) states, "As a problem-solving venture that requires known traits associated with creativity—flexibility, openness to experience, tolerance of ambiguity, and ingenuity—it makes sense that resilience (rising above adversity) draws upon creative thinking. We need imagination to overcome and rise above unintended circumstances" (p. 31).

Emotional Stability-Related Constructs

Creative Adaptability and Stress Tolerance
Based on emerging research, it appears that creative individuals may be better equipped to deal with adverse life circumstances. Orkibi (2021, 2023) introduced the concept of creative adaptability, defined as "the cognitive–behavioral-emotional ability to respond creatively and adaptively to stressful situations" (2021, p. 1).

Notably, CA is distinct from the closely related concept of resilience. While resilience generally involves enduring or recovering from trauma or significant adversity, creative adaptability specifically entails generating *novel* responses to stress or change. In essence, originality is a core component of CA but not a necessary feature of resilience. Although research on creative adaptability is nascent, emerging evidence points to a link with well-being. For instance, a study conducted during the initial phase of the COVID-19 pandemic assessed stress levels at two separate points in time, during which lockdown restrictions escalated. Findings revealed that individuals with higher levels of creative adaptability experienced lower stress across this period, suggesting that creative adaptability may play a beneficial role in coping with challenging circumstances (Orkibi, 2023).

Post-traumatic Growth
Roepke and Seligman (2015) found that the ability to engage with new possibilities and perceive new opportunities emerging after adversity was a strong predictor of personal growth; however, the relationship between post-traumatic growth and *creativity* is less clear. A notable longitudinal study (Forgeard et al., 2022) compared individuals across three groups:

those who experienced a recent major stressor and had low clinical symptoms; those without a recent major stressor who had low clinical symptoms; and those with a recent major stressor and serious symptoms. No significant differences in terms of identifying new possibilities for one's life, one of the five factors of post-traumatic growth, were found. Rather, all groups, regardless of whether or not they had experienced a major stressor reported discovering new possibilities for their lives over the course of the study. Looking at this body of research as a whole, Forgeard (2024a) comments,

> If longitudinal assessments fail to capture changes in constructs closely related to creativity, it may be necessary to reconsider the relationship between adversity and creativity ... A more plausible explanation is that individuals employ creativity as a coping mechanism to navigate the effects of adversity. This perspective can help resolve debates surrounding the adversity- creativity link, as well as the link between mental illness and creativity. (p. 3)

Type and Clinical Level of Disease

Next, we examine the trends identified between psychopathology-related traits (e.g., schizotypy) and specific mental health diagnoses (e.g., mood disorders) and creativity. Personality scholars have identified traits theoretically and empirically related to clinical disorders that can present in individuals to varying degrees, but do not raise to clinical diagnoses (e.g., psychoticism; Eysenck, 1995). In the last two decades, most research has focused on trait schizotypy and clinical categories of mood disorders.

Schizotypy

Meta-analytic findings indicate a general link between creativity and schizotypy (Acar & Sen, 2013), however, the relationship is not uniform and manifests differently depending on the specific schizotypal traits and the creative domain being considered. Most existing studies have examined how profiles/pairings of schitzotypical traits within non-clinical samples can enhance or impede creativity. For example, schizotypy has been conceptualized according to four dimensions (O-LIFE Schizotypy Scales; Mason et al., 1995):

1. Unusual Experiences: hallucinatory, irrational, or "magical" (Nettle, 2006, p. 885) thinking; generally considered positive
2. Cognitive Disorganization: challenges with focus and concentration, accompanied by feelings of purposelessness and emotional instability
3. Introvertive Anhedonia: lack of enjoyment; generally considered negative
4. Impulsive Nonconformity: aggressive, impulsive, and self-destructive behaviors

Individuals with symptoms such as "magical ideation, odd beliefs, ideas of reference, and unusual perceptual experiences" (Acar & Sen, 2013, p. 222) displayed higher creativity, whereas those with symptoms including "social isolation and anxiety, odd speech and behavior, and limited affect" (p. 222) were less creative, based on both self-report and performance-based measures. Nettle (2006) found high levels of these same symptoms in artists and poets as compared to controls though mathematicians, by contrast, displayed fewer symptoms as compared to controls. In terms of implications, Schuldberg suggests, "if positive and negative symptoms are considered as behavioral or psychological excess and deficits rather than as symptoms per se, the distinction becomes a useful one for classifying health process of resilience, resourcefulness, and creativity" (1990, p. 226).

Mood Disorder

In a systematic review, Taylor (2017) investigated the relationship between creativity and various types of mood disorder (e.g., Bipolar I, Bipolar II, cyclothymia, etc.). Multiple meta-analyses were carried out to explore (1) whether creative individuals are more prone to mood discorders as compared to the general population, and (2) whether individuals with mood disorders demonstrate higher creativity.

In response to the first question, analyses revealed that creative individuals, as compared to their non-creative counterparts, showed a higher overall incidence of mood disorders. This pattern was consistent across all mood disorder types, with the exception of dysthymic disorder, in which case creative individuals exhibited significantly fewer occurrences of dysthymia than the control group.

In response to the second query, Taylor (2017) found that only individuals with cyclothymic and unspecified bipolar disorders (i.e., those on the milder end of the spectrum of mood disorders) showed enhanced creativity compared to controls. These findings align with the inverted-U hypothesis (Richards et al., 1988) which proposes that sub-clinical or mild psychopathy may benefit creativity, but creative gains decrease as psychopathy increases and once reaching clinical levels, psychopathy has a harmful effect.

Conclusion

In conclusion, the relationship between creativity and mental health is far more intricate than the "mad genius" stereotype suggests. By comprehensively examining this connection across five approaches—creativity level, domain, personality traits, type of assessment, and type and severity of mental illness—this chapter highlights the multifaceted nature of the creativity's relationship to mental health. While some evidence supports an association between elevated creativity and certain psychopathological traits, particularly among Big-C creators in artistic fields, the majority of creative individuals—particularly at the little-c and Pro-c levels—demonstrate positive associations between creative engagement and well-being. Any accurate interpretation of the creativity–mental illness relationship must move beyond simple binaries and instead take an individualized and context-specific perspective.

References

Abele, A. (1992). Positive and negative mood influences on creativity: Evidence for asymmetrical effects. *Polish Psychological Bulletin, 23*, 203–221.

Acar, S., & Runco, M. (2012). Psychoticism and creativity: A meta-analytic review. *Psychology of Aesthetics, Creativity, and the Arts, 6*, 341–350. https://doi.org/10.1037/a0f027497

Acar, S., & Sen, S. (2013). A multilevel meta-analysis of the relationship between creativity and schizotypy. *Psychology of Aesthetics, Creativity, and the Arts, 7*, 214–228. https://doi.org/10.1037/a0031975

Acar, S., Tadik, H., Myers, D., Sman, C., & Uysal, R. (2021). Creativity and well-being: A meta-analysis. *The Journal of Creative Behavior, 55*(3), 738–751. https://doi.org/10.1002/jocb.485

Amabile, T., & Kramer, S. (2011). *The progress principle: Using small wins to ignite joy, engagement, and creativity at work*. Harvard Business Press

Amabile, T. M., Barsade, S. G., Mueller, J. S., & Staw, B. M. (2005). Affect and creativity at work. *Administrative Science Quarterly, 50*, 367–403. https://doi.org/10.2189/asqu.2005.50.3.367

Baas, M., De Dreu, C. K., & Nijstad, B. A. (2008). A meta-analysis of 25 years of mood- creativity research: Hedonic tone, activation, or regulatory focus? *Psychological Bulletin, 134*, 779–806. https://doi.org/10.1037/a0012815

Benedek, M., Karstendiek, M., Ceh, S. M., Grabner, R. H., Krammer, G., Lebuda, I., Silvia, P. J., Cotter, K. N., Li, Y., Hu, W., Martskvishvili, K., & Kaufman, J. C. (2021). Creativity myths: Prevalence and correlates of misconceptions on creativity. *Personality and Individual Differences, 182*, Article 111068. https://doi.org/10.1016/j.paid.2021.111068

Boss, P. (2013). Resilience as tolerance for ambiguity. In D. S. Becvar (Ed.), *Handbook of family resilience* (pp. 285–297). Springer Science + Business Media. https://doi.org/10.1007/978-1-4614-3917-2_17

Carroll, L. (2013). Problem-focused coping. In M. D. Gellman & J. R. Turner (Eds.), *Encyclopedia of behavioral medicine* (pp. 1540–1541). Springer Science + Business. https://doi.org/10.1007/978-1-4419-1005-9_1171

Cohen, J. P., & Ferrari, J. R. (2010). Take some time to think this over: The relation between rumination, indecision, and creativity. *Creativity Research Journal, 22*(1), 68–73. https://doi.org/10.1080/10400410903579601

Conner, T. S., DeYoung, C. G., & Silvia, P. J. (2018). Everyday creative activity as a path to flourishing. *The Journal of Positive Psychology, 13*, 181–189. https://doi.org/10.1080/17439760.2016.1257049

Costa, P. T., Jr., & McCrae, R. R. (1992). Four ways five factors are basic. *Personality and Individual Differences, 13*(6), 653–665. https://doi.org/10.1016/0191-8869(92)90236-I

Craft, A. (2005). *Creativity in schools: Tensions and dilemmas.* Routledge. https://doi.org/10.4324/9780203357965

Csikszentmihalyi, M. (2014). *The systems model of creativity: The collected works of Mihaly Csikszentmihalyi.* Springer. https://doi.org/10.1007/978-94-017-9085-7

Davis, R. H., & Nolen-Hoeksema, S. (2000). Cognitive inflexibility among ruminators and non-ruminators. *Cognitive Therapy and Research, 24*(6), 699–711. https://doi.org/10.1023/a:1005591412406

De Dreu, C. K. W., Baas, M., & Nijstad, B. A. (2008). Hedonic tone and activation level in the mood–creativity link: Towards a dual pathway to creativity model. *Journal of Personality and Social Psychology, 94*, 739–756. https://doi.org/10.1037/0022-3514.94.5.739

Diener, E., Thapa, S., & Tay, L. (2020). Positive emotions at work. *Annual Review of Organizational Psychology and Organizational Behavior, 7*, 451–477. https://doi.org/10.1146/annurev-orgpsych-012119-044908

Dollinger, M. J., Saxton, T., & Golden, P. A. (1995). Intolerance of ambiguity and the decision to form an alliance. In *Psychological reports* (Vol. 77, Issue 3_suppl, pp. 1197–1198). SAGE Publishing. https://doi.org/10.2466/pr0.1995.77.3f.1197

Eysenck, H. J. (1990). Genetic and environmental contributions to individual differences: The three major dimensions of personality. *Journal of Personality, 58*, 245–261. https://doi.org/10.1111/j.1467-6494.1990.tb00915.x
Eysenck, H. J. (1995). *Genius: The natural history of creativity.* Cambridge University Press. https://doi.org/10.1017/CBO9780511752247
Feist, G. J. (1998). A meta-analysis of personality in scientific and artistic creativity. *Personality and Social Psychology Review, 2*(4), 290–309. https://doi.org/10.1207/s15327957pspr0204_5
Feist, G. J., & Barron, F. (2003). Predicting creativity from early to late adulthood: Intellect, potential, and personality. *Journal of Research in Personality, 37*(2), 62–88. https://doi.org/10.1016/s0092-6566(02)00536-6
Forgeard, M. J. (2013). Perceiving benefits after adversity: The relationship between self reported posttraumatic growth and creativity. *Psychology of Aesthetics, Creativity, and the Arts, 7*, 245–264. https://doi.org/10.1037/a0031223
Forgeard, M. (2024a). Creativity and resilience: Creativity from, or through adversity? *Creativity Research Journal. Advance online publication.* https://doi.org/10.1080/10400419.2023.2299639
Forgeard, M. (2024b). Prosocial motivation and creativity in the arts and sciences: Qualitative and quantitative evidence. *Psychology of Aesthetics, Creativity, and the Arts, 18*(2), 222–244. https://doi.org/10.1037/aca0000435
Forgeard, M., Roepke, A. M., Atlas, S., Bayer-Pacht, E., Björgvinsson, T., & Silvia, P. J. (2022). Openness to experience is stable following adversity: A case-control longitudinal investigation. *European Journal of Personality, 36*(4), 483–506. https://doi.org/10.1177/08902070221076902
Gocłowska, M. A., Damian, R. I., & Mor, S. (2018). The diversifying experience model: Taking a broader conceptual view of the multiculturalism–creativity link. *Journal of Cross-Cultural Psychology, 49*(2), 303–322. https://doi.org/10.1177/0022022116650258
Goldberg, L. R. (1990). An alternative 'description of personality': The Big-Five factor structure. *Journal of Personality and Social Psychology, 59*(6), 1216–1229. https://doi.org/10.1037/0022-3514.59.6.1216
Gruber, H. E. (1993). Creativity in the moral domain: Ought implies can implies create. *Creativity Research Journal, 6*(1–2), 3–15. https://doi.org/10.1080/10400419309534462
Guilford, J. P. (1950). Creativity. *American Psychologist, 5*(9), 444 454. https://doi.org/10.1037/h0063487
Holinger, M., & Kaufman, J. C. (2024). Measuring self-beliefs of creativity and well-being. *Thinking Skills and Creativity, 53*, Article 101604. https://doi.org/10.1016/j.tsc.2024.101604

Ingram, P., Boan-Lenzo, C., & Vuyk, M. A. (2013). Openness/intellect in a 50-Item IPIP instrument. *Journal of Psychoeducational Assessment*. https://doi.org/10.1177/0734282913481448

Ivcevic, Z. (2007). Artistic and everyday creativity: An act-frequency approach. *The Journal of Creative Behavior, 41*(4), 271–290. https://doi.org/10.1002/j.2162-6057.2007.tb01074.x

Ivcevic, Z., & Hoffmann, J. D. (2019). Emotions and creativity: From process to person and product. In J. C. Kaufman & R. S. Sternberg (Eds.), *Cambridge handbook of creativity* (pp. 273–295). Cambridge University Press. https://doi.org/10.1017/9781316979839.015

Ivcevic, Z., & Brackett, M. A. (2015). Predicting creativity: Interactive effects of openness to experience and emotion regulation ability. *Psychology of Aesthetics, Creativity, and the Arts, 9*(4), 480–487. https://doi.org/10.1037/a0039826

Ivcevic, Z., & Mayer, J. D. (2009). Mapping dimensions of creativity in the life-space. *Creativity Research Journal, 21*(2–3), 152–165. https://doi.org/10.1080/10400410902855259

Ivcevic, Z., Grossman, E., & Ranjan, A. (2022). Patterns of psychological vulnerabilities and resources in artists and nonartists. *Psychology of Aesthetics, Creativity, and the Arts, 16*(1), 3–15. https://doi.org/10.1037/aca0000309

Ivcevic, Z., Lin, S., Kaufman, J. C., & Hoffmann, J. D. (2023). Creativity and emotion: Connecting the dots. In Z. Ivcevic, J. D. Hoffmann, & J. C. Kaufman (Eds.), *Cambridge handbook of creativity and emotions* (pp. 620–640). Cambridge University Press. https://doi.org/10.1017/9781009031240

Jausovec, N. (1989). Affect in analogical transfer. *Creativity Research Journal, 2*, 255–266. https://doi.org/10.1080/10400418909534322

John, O. P., Naumann, L. P., & Soto, C. J. (2008). Paradigm shift to the integrative Big-Five trait taxonomy: History, measurement, and conceptual issues. In O. P. John, R. W. Robins, & L. A. Pervin (Eds.), *Handbook of personality: Theory and research* (pp. 114–158). Guilford Press.

Jung, C. G. (1984). *Selected letters of C.G. Jung, 1909–1961*. Princeton Legacy Library.

Kark, R., & Carmeli, A. (2009). Alive and creating: The mediating role of vitality and aliveness in the relationship between interpersonal work climate and creative work involvement. *Journal of Organizational Behavior, 30*, 785–804. https://doi.org/10.1002/job.571

Kaufman, J. C. (2001). The Sylvia Plath effect: Mental illness in eminent creative writers. *Journal of Creative Behavior, 35*, 37–50. https://doi.org/10.1002/j.2162-6057.2001.tb01220.x

Kaufman, J. C. (Ed.). (2014). *Creativity and mental illness*. Cambridge University Press. https://doi.org/10.1017/CBO9781139128902

Kaufman, S. B. (2020). *Transcend: The new science of self-actualization*. Tarcher Perigee.

Kaufman, J. C., & Beghetto, R. A. (2009). Beyond big and little: The four-c model of creativity. *Review of General Psychology, 13*(1), 1–12. https://doi.org/10.1037/a0013688

Kaufmann, G., & Vosburg, S. K. (1997). "Paradoxical" mood effects on creative problem-solving. *Cognition and Emotion, 11*, 151–170.

Kaufmann, G., & Vosburg, S. K. (2002). The effects of mood on early and late idea production. *Creativity Research Journal, 14*(3–4), 317–330. https://doi.org/10.1207/s15326934crj1434_3

Kellerman, G. R., & Seligman, M. E. (2023). *Tomorrowmind: Thriving at work with resilience, creativity, and connection—Now and in an uncertain future.* Simon Element/Simon Acumen.

Kocjan, G. Z., Kavčič, T., & Avsec, A. (2021). Resilience matters: Explaining the association between personality and psychological functioning during the COVID-19 pandemic. *International Journal of Clinical and Health Psychology, 21*(1), 100198. https://doi.org/10.1016/j.ijchp.2020.08.002

Lyubomirsky, S., Tucker, K. L., Caldwell, N. W., & Berg, K. A. (1999). Why ruminators are poor problem solvers: Clues from the phenomenology of dysphoric rumination. *Journal of Personality and Social Psychology, 77*(5), 1041–1060. https://doi.org/10.1037/0022-3514.77.5.1041

Maples-Keller, J. L., Berke, D. S., Few, L. R., & Miller, J. D. (2016). A review of sensation seeking and its empirical correlates: Dark, bright, and neutral hues. In V. Zeigler-Hill & D. K. Marcus (Eds.), *The dark side of personality: Science and practice in social, personality, and clinical psychology* (pp. 137–156). American Psychological Association. https://doi.org/10.1037/14854-008

Maslow, A. H. (1971). *The further reaches of human nature.* Arkana/Penguin Books.

Mason, O., Claridge, G., & Jackson, M. (1995). New scales for the assessment of schizotypy. *Personality and Individual Differences, 1*, 7–13. https://doi.org/10.1016/0191-8869(94)00132-C

McAdams, D. P., & Pals, J. L. (2006). A new Big Five: Fundamental principles for an integrative science of personality. *American Psychologist, 61*(3), 204–217. https://doi.org/10.1037/0003-066X.61.3.204

McCrae, R. R. (1996). Social consequences of experiential openness. *Psychological Bulletin, 120*(3), 323–337. https://doi.org/10.1037/0033-2909.120.3.323

McCrae, R. R., & Costa, P. T., Jr. (1996). Toward a new generation of personality theories: Theoretical contexts for the Five-Factor model. In J. S. Wiggins (Ed.), *The Five-Factor Model of personality: Theoretical perspectives* (pp. 51–87). Guilford.

McCrae, R. R., & John, O. P. (1992). An introduction to the five-factor model and its applications. *Journal of Personality, 60*(2), 175–215. https://doi.org/10.1111/j.1467-6494.1992.tb00970.x

McKay, S., Skues, J., & Williams, B. A. (2018). With risk may come reward: Sensation seeking supports resilience through effective coping. In *Personality and individual differences.* https://doi.org/10.1016/j.paid.2017.09.030

Nettle, D. (2006). Schizotypy and mental health amongst poets, visual artists, and mathematicians. *Journal of Research in Personality, 40*(6), 876–890. https://doi.org/10.1016/j.jrp.2005.09.004

Orkibi, H. (2021). Creative adaptability: Conceptual framework, measurement, and outcomes in times of crisis. *Frontiers in Psychology, 11*(3695). https://doi.org/10.3389/fpsyg.2020.588172

Orkibi, H. (2023). Creative adaptability: A measurable personal resource. *Creativity Research Journal.* Advance online publication. https://doi.org/10.1080/10400419.2023.2223448

Parke, M. R., Seo, M.-G., & Sherf, E. N. (2015). Regulating and facilitating: The role of emotional intelligence in maintaining and using positive affect for creativity. *Journal of Applied Psychology, 100*(3), 917–934. https://doi.org/10.1037/a0038452

Perkins, A. M., Arnone, D., Smallwood, J., & Mobbs, D. (2015). Thinking too much: Self-generated thought as the engine of neuroticism. *Trends in Cognitive Sciences, 19*(9), 492–498. https://doi.org/10.1016/j.tics.2015.07.003

Pervin, L. A. (2003). *The science of personality.* Oxford University Press.

Peterson, C., & Seligman, M. E. P. (2004). *Character strengths and virtues: A handbook and classification.* Oxford University Press; American Psychological Association.

Puccio, G. J., Mance, M., & Murdock, M. C. (2011). *Creative leadership: Skills that drive change.* SAGE Publications.

Richards, R. (2007). *Everyday creativity and new views of human nature: Psychological, social, and spiritual perspectives.* American Psychological Association EBooks. https://doi.org/10.1037/11595-000

Richards, R., Kinney, D. K., Lunde, I., Benet, M., & Merzel, A. P. (1988). Creativity in manic depressives, cyclothymes, their normal relatives, and control subjects. *Journal of Abnormal Psychology, 97*, 281–288. https://doi.org/10.1037/0021-843X.97.3.281

Roepke, A. M., & Seligman, M. E. P. (2015). Doors opening: A mechanism for growth after adversity. *The Journal of Positive Psychology, 10*(2), 107–115. https://doi.org/10.1080/17439760.2014.913669

Runco, M. A. (1996). Personal creativity: Definition and developmental issues. *New Directions for Child and Adolescent Development, 1996*(72), 3–30. https://doi.org/10.1002/cd.23219967203

Runco, M. A., & Richards, R. (Eds.). (1997). *Eminent creativity, everyday creativity, and health.* Greenwood Publishing Group.

Schuldberg, D. (1990). Schizotypal and hypomanic traits, creativity, and psychological health. *Creativity Research Journal, 3*(3), 218–230. https://doi.org/10.1080/10400419009534354

Silvia, P. J., Nusbaum, E. C., Berg, C. J., Martin, C., & O'Connor, A. M. (2009). Openness to experience, plasticity, and creativity: Exploring lower-order, high-order, and interactive effects. *Journal of Research in Personality, 43*(6), 1087–1090. https://doi.org/10.1016/j.jrp.2009.04.015

Simonton, D. K. (2014a). The mad-genius paradox: Can creative people be more mentally healthy but highly creative people more mentally ill? *Perspectives on Psychological Science, 9*, 470–480. https://doi.org/10.1177/1745691614543973

Simonton, D. K. (2014b). More method in the mad-genius controversy: A historiometric study of 204 historic creators. *Psychology of Aesthetics, Creativity, and the Arts, 8*, 53. https://doi.org/10.1037/a0035367

Simonton, D. K., & Song, A. V. (2009). Eminence, IQ, physical and mental health, and achievement domain: Cox's 282 geniuses revisited. *Psychological Science, 20*(4), 429–434. https://doi.org/10.1111/j.1467-9280.2009.02313.x

Smith, K., Pickering, A., & Bhattacharya, J. (2022). The creative life: A daily diary study of creativity, affect, and well-being in creative individuals. *Creativity Research Journal, 34*(4), 460–479. https://doi.org/10.1080/10400419.2022.2122371

Soto, C. J. (2018). Big Five personality traits. In M. H. Bornstein, M. E. Arterberry, K. L. Fingerman, & J. E. Lansford (Eds.), *The SAGE encyclopedia of lifespan human development* (pp. 240–241). Sage. https://doi.org/10.4135/9781506307633

Taylor, C. L. (2017). Creativity and mood disorder: A systematic review and meta-analysis. *Perspectives on Psychological Science, 12*(6), 1040–1076. https://doi.org/10.1177/1745691617699653

Vanada, D. I. (2018). Danish creativity and resilience in the face of adversity. *The Bridge, 41*(2), Article 6. https://scholarsarchive.byu.edu/thebridge/vol41/iss2/6

Verhaeghen, P., Joorman, J., & Khan, R. (2005). Why we sing the blues: The relation between self-reflective rumination, mood, and creativity. *Emotion, 5*(2), 226–232. https://doi.org/10.1037/1528-3542.5.2.226

Verhaeghen, P., Joormann, J., & Aikman, S. N. (2014). Creativity, mood, and the examined life: Self-reflective rumination boosts creativity, brooding breeds dysphoria. *Psychology of Aesthetics, Creativity, and the Arts, 8*(2), 211–218. https://doi.org/10.1037/a0035594

Vygotsky, L. S. (1967). Play and its role in the mental development of the child. *Soviet Psychology, 5*(3), 6–18. https://doi.org/10.2753/rpo1061-040505036

Zuckerman, M. (1994). *Behavioral expressions and biosocial bases of sensation seeking*. Cambridge University Press.

CHAPTER 9

Knowing the Creative Person

Zorana Ivcevic

Creativity scholars commonly consider J.P. Guilford's address to the American Psychological Association in 1950 as the birthday of the modern psychology of creativity (Guilford, 1950). Scholars quickly realized that creativity is best conceptualized as an umbrella term that includes multiple aspects. Rhodes (1961) distinguished the creative person, process, product, and press, and more recently, Lubart (2017) added collaborations, consumptions, and curricula to the mix, reflecting advances in the

Author Note
I have no known conflict of interests to disclose.
The work on this chapter and editing of this book was funded by the Fundación Botín, Santander, Spain (Emotions, Creativity and the Arts grant; Principal investigator: Zorana Ivcevic).
Correspondence concerning this article should be addressed to: Zorana Ivcevic, Yale Center for Emotional Intelligence, Yale University, 350 George St., New Haven, CT 06511, United States.

Z. Ivcevic (✉)
Yale Center for Emotional Intelligence, Yale University, New Haven, CT, USA
e-mail: Zorana.ivcevic@yale.edu

Z. Ivcevic (ed.), *Creators*, The Seven C's of Creativity,
https://doi.org/10.1007/978-3-032-09225-0_9

intervening decades. The study of the creative person—or creators—might be the most complex of endeavors because it has to draw on multiple of the other aspects. Creators employ processes by which they devise and develop creations, they engage in collaborations, and work in contexts that support or put barriers on their efforts. Some develop their creative potential through training programs and curricula teaching about creativity and teaching creatively.

Chapters in this volume acknowledge this complexity in understanding creators. Razaei and Kapoor (Chap. 2) provide a big picture view of research and theorizing on creative individuals. They situate the study of creators within broader debates in creativity research—levels of creativity, domain generality vs. specificity, myth of lone genius, and the role of social and environmental factors in shaping creative individuals. Two chapters address traditional topics in the study of creative people—personality traits describing creators (Rodriguez-Boerwinkle; Chap. 3) and the creative self (Pretz; Chap. 4). Another two chapters discuss attributes of specific functional areas within a person: motivation (Lin; Chap. 5) and cognition (Dumas & Kagan; Chap. 6). These chapters ask big questions about how creators typically think, feel, and act, how they perceive themselves and their creative capacities, what drives their creative action, and how their cognitive abilities support action and achievement. These questions are as old as creativity studies. For instance, scholarship on personality traits goes back to foundational research at the Institute of Personality Assessment and Research at the University of California at Berkeley in the 1950s and 1960s (Ivcevic, in press). Similarly, investigations into the nature of cognitive abilities go back to the theory of intellect formulated by the father of modern creativity studies J. P. Guilford (1975), which were expanded by Wallach and Kogan (1965) and Torrance (1988).

Although traditional topics in the study of creative individuals remain relevant, especially as research questions become more complex and incorporate areas of overlap with other aspects of creativity (e.g., environmental and socio-cultural influences), this volume also draws attention to emerging areas. Urbaniak and Barbot (Chap. 7) discuss development of creative individuals. This chapter explicitly adds the component of time to the study of creators, filling a specific gap identified by contemporary theorists (Kaufman & Beghetto, 2023). Finally, although the study of creative individuals is usually approached as an outcome (Forgeard & Kaufman, 2016)—we aim to predict which traits or motivations distinguish creators (e.g., artists from non-artists, more or less creative scientists; Feist,

1998)—there is growing interest in creativity as input for other outcomes. Hollinger and Sithambaram (Chap. 8) discuss health and well-being of creative individuals.

Who Are the Creators? Or, What Do We Mean When We Talk About a Creative Person?

How we identify creators might appear obvious and the question itself irrelevant. Creators are those who create. Yet, when we consider that scholars use the terms creators and creative individual/person interchangeably, the complexities of identification become clearer. Whereas a creator is someone who creates (emphasis on action, behavior, and achievement), creative person can be taken to imply internal attributes and traits (such as measures by various scales of creative personality; e.g., Gough, 1979, 1992). To address this discrepancy, it is helpful to go back to the definition of creativity as an umbrella term.

Plucker et al. (2004) defined creativity as "the interaction among aptitude, process and environment by which an individual or group produces a perceptible product that is both novel and useful as defined within a social context" (p. 90). According to this definition, creative individuals are agents who transform potential into actual products and achievements. The full definition involves multiple key aspects: individuals (or groups), potential (evident in aptitude), observable outcomes of thinking and action, processes by which they are built, and the social context which both supports these processes and assigns value to them. The question of identifying creative individuals asks where we should place the emphasis on the continuum between creative potential and achievement. If we take to heart the full definition of creativity, I argue that we should focus on manifest behavior and achievement. This view defines creative individuals as those who act and achieve something creative, regardless of the level of those actions or achievements, rather than those who have creative potential according to some metrics (e.g., performance on divergent thinking tests), but do not necessarily put that potential to use in everyday or professional action.

Creativity studies have converged on the 4c model of levels of creative contributions (Kaufman & Beghetto, 2009). The same levels can be distinguished as types of creative individuals if we consider the modal or maximal level of creative attainment (Razaei & Kapoor; Chap. 2). We can thus talk about mini-c creators as those who primarily manifest creativity in the learning process, such as devising personally meaningful mnemonics or using personal experience to enrich understanding of new material they are learning. Mini-c creators can also come up with inventive strategies to regulate their own emotions (i.e., generate original and meaningful reappraisals of emotionally triggering situations; Weber et al., 2014). Little-c creators would be those who primarily show creativity in everyday actions and interactions. They might devise original and effective ways to enliven close relationships or solve everyday problems. Pro-c creators show creativity in ways that require expertise in one or more specific domains. Whereas mini-c and little-c creators are likely to cross domains, Pro-c creators are best described in the context of their domains of expertise. They could be creative designers, artists, scientists, entrepreneurs, or professionals in virtually any other domain of human endeavor. A special class of Pro-c creators can be considered polymaths and demonstrate interest, expertise, and activity in multiple distinct domains (Araki, 2018). Finally, Big-C creators are those who have achieved eminence and continued influence in one or more fields (Ivcevic & Kaufman, 2024). Those who are considered Big-C creators might be influential for some of their work and accomplishment and not other.

Contemporary scholars have added to the definition the issue of values, and theorized about positive or transformational creativity on one end (Sternberg, 2021) and dark or malevolent creativity on the other (Cropley et al., 2010; Kapoor, 2025). This discussion could be interpreted as echoing in the context of creativity the broader debate in psychology about human nature as either good or bad. This research has made it clear that creative individuals are not inherently heroic figures as they might have been traditionally assumed to be (Helson, 1996). We are at a point of being able to ask questions that go beyond a simple dichotomy about whether creativity is good or bad. For instance, approximately 10% of people refuse to even engage with test questions soliciting unethical ideas, even if they know that these ideas would not be enacted, and researchers are investigating their personality attributes (Kapoor et al., 2025; Kapoor & Khan, 2020). Whereas this research focuses on dark creative potential, Hunter et al. (2022) developed a framework to address how some people move from darkly creative ideas to implementing and enacting them, at which point we talk about darkly creative individuals in the sense adopted in this chapter. In terms of understanding the darkly creative person, research will have to engage with the notion of character "as those characteristics that are descriptive of actions, cognitions, emotions, and motivations that are considered to be relevant to right and wrong according to a relevant moral standard" (Fleeson et al., 2014, p. 181).

What Do We Know When We Know a Creative Person?

The Life-Story Model

McAdams (1995) rethought and reconceptualized personality by starting with a simple, yet profound question: *What do We Know When We Know a Person?* His answer includes attributes organized at three levels with increasing degrees of contextualization. At the most basic level, we learn about a person by studying their traits. These are broad descriptors of typical behavior across time and situations. On the second level are attributes that he calls personal concerns, which are contextual and often domain-specific. These could be personal strivings, emotion regulation strategies, or work orientations. Finally, on the third level is narrative identity, which is a unique individual reconstruction of one's past, interpretation of the present, and possible futures that collectively provide a coherent sense of purpose and meaning. Whereas the first two levels in personality can be described as nearly universal, the third level of life-stories might be specific to adulthood and possibly limited to cultures that place a high value on individualism.

This model of personality and understanding the person was not explicitly widely adopted in creativity research, but the emphases on traits and dynamic motivational constructs have been traditionally central topics in the research on creative individuals (Helson, 1996) and the level of life-stories overlaps with the study of lives (Policastro & Gardner, 1999; White, 1963). Helson (1996) reviewed four decades of studies aiming to describe and understand creative individuals at the University of California at Berkeley, which primarily focused on personality traits and motivational constructs (interests, needs). This research tradition was influenced by personological theory of Henry Murray (1936) and shaped by developments in personality assessment, including measures of personality traits like the California Psychological Inventory (CPI; Gough, 1956) and the Adjective Check List (ACL; Gough, 1960). With the changes in the psychology Zeitgeist, the emphasis in research changed too. The rise of social psychology replaced interest in intrapsychic needs such as power and achievement (McClelland, 1962, 1975) with socially shaped intrinsic vs.

extrinsic motivation (Amabile, 1979, 1983, 1996). Similarly, the rise of the Big Five model of personality traits (Digman, 1990) spurred an interest in broad description of personality and provided a way to compare previous findings (Feist, 1998).

The Big Five Theory of Personality

The Big Five model of personality traits emerged from multiple independent factor analyses of large sets of individual trait ratings (Digman, 1990) and gained popularity with the development of assessment tools like the adjective marker scales (Goldberg, 1992), revisions of existing personality inventories (Costa & McCrae, 1992), and development of new ones (Big Five Inventory, BFI; John & Srivastava, 1999; Big Five Aspects Scale, De Young et al., 2007). Consensus that emerged about the major dimensions of inter-individual differences spurred research relating these dimensions to various aspects of creative self, creative process, and creative behavior and achievement.

As the Big Five was firmly established as a structural model of broad personality dimensions, there was also an effort to situate it in a comprehensive framework for understanding personality. McCrae and Costa (1999) formulated the Big Five Theory of personality, which conceptualized the five broad traits as biologically based tendencies. These basic tendencies shape attributes that they called characteristic adaptations and which were defined as including culturally conditioned personal strivings, values, and attitudes. The model defined self-concept as the special aspect of characteristic adaptations reflecting a cognitive-affective view of oneself that is consistent with one's personality traits and which serves as a lens through which people see the world and their place within it. Characteristic adaptations were posited to influence objective biography, from micro-acts such as emotional reactions, to one's everyday activities, to major life choices (e.g., educational and career decisions), and finally significant life achievements. The model explicitly acknowledged reciprocal influence between objective biography and external influences, such as historical events, cultural norms, and specific life events and situations.

Core and Surface Personality Attributes

Asendorpf and van Aken (2003) accepted the distinction between largely stable personality traits (such as the Big Five) and more dynamic attributes of the self-concept. However, they questioned the view of broad trait dimensions as biological entities, pointing to evidence that personality traits are susceptible to socio-cultural influences and individual life experiences. They also did not find the term "characteristic adaptations" helpful because of its functional implications. Instead, they proposed terms core and surface personality attributes.

Concepts of core and surface aspects of personality have been directly examined in creativity research. Lebuda et al. (2021) measured Big Five traits and cognitive abilities (core attributes) along with the creative self-concept (combination of creative self-efficacy and creative personal identity) and found that incremental validity of surface attributes over the core ones depends on the domain (and is observed for artistic and everyday creative behavior, but not science). Lebuda (2025) argued that the next generation of research on creative personality should combine individual difference perspectives focused primarily on personality traits with socio-cultural approaches that examine how surface attributes such as creative self-beliefs and attitudes arise in the interaction of individuals and environment. She proposed that this approach can help elucidate how creative individuals transform potential into behavior and ultimately achievement.

A set of chapters in this volume reviewed advancements in these traditional topics in personality and understanding of creative individuals. The chapter on personality traits (Rodriguez-Boerwinkle, Chap. 3) reflects a full circle in creativity studies, starting from the study of many narrower traits, to grouping of those traits into five broad dimensions, to a renewed interest and focus on single traits and their facets. Broad Big Five dimensions made it possible to integrate and create a high-level outline of the creative personality. A meta-analysis of 188 samples (Puryear et al., 2017) showed that Openness to Experience is the Big Five dimension associated with all aspects of creativity, from creative thinking to creative behavior and achievement. Although the broad trait dimensions were useful in providing a way to synthesize findings from many studies of different trait collections, the picture of creative individuals based on just five traits was too devoid of detail and richness. As McAdams (1995) put it, this is a "psychology of a stranger" portrait.

A number of narrower traits have been examined as descriptors of creative personality. Curiosity, for instance, has been defined as including five subdimensions (Kashdan et al., 2018): (1) joyous exploration—pleasure stemming from seeking out and engaging with new experiences, (2) deprivation sensitivity—discomfort of not knowing and the associated desire to reduce it by seeking information, (3) stress tolerance—willingness to accept distress when engaging with something new or unexpected, (4) social curiosity—interest in others and their experiences, and (5) thrill-seeking—enjoyment of perceived risk when exploring something unknown. Although different aspects of curiosity are related to creative achievement in the arts and science (Lin et al., 2024), it remains unclear whether this association stays significant after controlling for Big Five traits, particularly Openness, which includes curiosity.

Another line of research on narrower traits examines risk-taking as a higher order trait that includes domain-specific aspects pertaining to social, recreational, financial, health, and ethical risk (Weber et al., 2002). Creativity is by its very nature uncertain and this uncertainty is psychologically experienced as risk, making descriptions of creative individuals as willing to take risks common. Emerging research shows that specific aspects of risk matter. Tyagi et al. (2017) found that social risk-taking was related to measures of creative personality and behavior, whereas other aspects were not. Items describing social risk-taking—for example, admitting that one's tastes differ from a friend, willingness to disagree about a major issue with an authority figure, speaking one's mind about an unpopular issue in a work meeting—suggest nonconformity and independence which are associated with Openness to Experience. If we are to demonstrate that social risk is in fact a more specific descriptor of creative personality than Openness, researchers will have to demonstrate that it has incremental validity beyond the broad personality dimension.

The study of the creative self has seen a great surge after Tierney and Farmer (2002) applied the concept of self-efficacy to self-evaluations of creativity. Research has examined the predictive power of creative self-efficacy in relation to multiple aspects of creativity (meta-analysis: Haase et al., 2018), as well as its dynamic changes in a micro-longitudinal design (before, during, and after a task; Karwowski et al., 2019; Puente-Díaz & Cavazos-Arroyo, 2022), and over six months in a real-life work context (Tierney & Farmer, 2011). These empirical studies have been accompanied by theoretical considerations of the role creative self plays in the relationship between creative potential (evidenced in cognitive abilities of creative thinking) and creative behavior and achievement. Karwowski and Beghetto (2019) in their model of creative behavior as agentic action posited and provided evidence that creative self-efficacy mediates and value of creativity moderates this relationship. According to this model, the creative person is best understood as an active agent who, if interested in creativity, builds their confidence based on observations of their creative thinking abilities and uses that confidence to motivate behavior.

By placing the creative individual as an active observer of their own thinking and past behavior, the model of creativity as agentic action focuses on the mechanism of personal experience in developing creative self-efficacy. As general self-efficacy, creative self-efficacy can also be based on three other sources: vicarious learning, verbal persuasion, and feelings. In vicarious learning, people observe creative actions of others (e.g., leaders; Newman et al., 2018), especially those with whom they identify, and reason about their own abilities in the "if they can do it, I can do it too" manner. In verbal persuasion, people reason that expectations of others have meaning in the "if they think I can be creative, I suppose I could" way. Evidence for this mechanism comes from research showing that creative self-efficacy is predicted by creative job demands (Mathisen, 2011; Shalley et al., 2000; Zhou et al., 2012) and leader expectations of creativity (Hunter & Cushenbery, 2011; Tierney & Farmer, 2004). Finally, creative self-efficacy can be built by noting one's physiological and emotional reactions when working on creative tasks, what Puente-Diaz and Cavazos-Arroyo (2017, 2022) termed metacognitive feelings. This is "if it feels good, I must be good at it" route to creative self-efficacy.

Pretz (Chap. 4) focused on a different question about acquisition of creative self-efficacy–accuracy of self-evaluations. She identified sources of challenges to accurate self-assessment of creative capacity, including misleading beliefs about creativity (e.g., art bias, eminence bias, fixed mindset bias) and limited personal experiences with creativity. This discussion poses an important question: To what extent do self-beliefs have to be objectively accurate to motivate behavior? Lebuda et al. (2021) found that creative self predicted creative activity, but was only indirectly related to creative achievement. They concluded that, "while surface characteristics play an essential role in behaving creatively, they do not necessarily say who will be socially recognized and appreciated by the field" (p. 8). One possible reason is that even inaccurate self-assessment can inspire self-congruent action.

Functional Approaches to Personality

Instead of asking what kinds of personality attributes exist in terms of their pervasiveness and stability (e.g., core vs. surface), functional approaches ask about the purpose of different categories of personality attributes. According to these approaches, we know a person when we have knowledge to describe each of the functional areas of personality. Feist (1998) adopted the tripartite division and applied it to interpret results of his meta-analysis of studies of personality traits of artists and scientists. He identified personality functions as (1) motivational and affective, (2) cognitive, and (3) social, and found that artists can be described as driven and sensitive, open and imaginative, and nonconforming and aloof, whereas scientists are driven, open and flexible, arrogant, and self-confident. Each of these sets of attributes describes something that the personality does. Personality affectively colors one's outlook and energizes action, shapes thinking, and shapes action in the social world.

Mayer (2005, 2015) described a systems framework for the study of personality and distinguished four functional areas of personality attributes, which he named the systems set: (1) Energy development, including attributes of emotions and motivation; (2) Knowledge guidance, consisting of attributes such as general intelligence, specific cognitive abilities, and typical ways of thinking (e.g., curiosity); (3) Executive management, comprising attributes of self-awareness and self-regulation; and (4) Action implementation in the social world, describing action planning, social skills, and social styles (e.g., social intelligence, dominance).

Scholars have examined attributes of creative individuals in each of these areas. The study of the energy development area warranted its own handbook, reviewing and integrating more than four decades of intensive scholarship (Ivcevic et al., 2023). Research in areas of knowledge guidance and social action has been summarized by multiple meta-analyses, addressing, for instance, intelligence of creative individuals (Karwowski et al., 2021), divergent thinking abilities (Said-Metwaly et al., 2024), and unethicality (Storme et al., 2021). There is growing interest in self-regulation, with recent theoretical and empirical work relating self-regulation of creative action to personality traits and related constructs, as well as creative behavior and achievement across domains (Ivcevic, 2024; Ivcevic et al., 2023; Ivcevic & Nusbaum, 2017; Zielińska et al., 2022, 2025).

One study explicitly adopted the functional model of personality and used it as a basis for selecting personality attributes to describe different types of creative individuals (Ivcevic & Mayer, 2006). The authors identified five creativity types based on extensive assessments of everyday behavior: conventional, everyday creative individuals, artists, scholars, and renaissance individuals (showing creativity across multiple domains). To describe these groups of creative individuals, they selected a set of attributes in each functional area, as well as assessing Openness to Experience (which includes traits across functional areas, e.g., openness to feelings, curiosity, tolerance of ambiguity, independence). For energy development these included intrinsic motivation and hypomanic trait; for knowledge guidance, divergent thinking and evaluation abilities; for executive management, intellectual persistence and risk-taking; and for social action, nonconformity and creative role. The results of a discriminant function analysis using these traits to differentiate among creative types pointed to both domain-general and -specific descriptions of creative individuals. One set of personality attributes, including Openness to Experience, creative role, intellectual persistence, trait hypomania, and intrinsic motivation, distinguished between conventional and all types of creative individuals. Another set of personality attributes, including risk-taking, divergent thinking, nonconformity, and evaluation ability, differentiated scholars (those showing creative behavior in intellectual domains) from other types. The authors concluded that the general description of creative individuals paints them as imaginative; having high energy, self-uniqueness beliefs, and broad interests; seeing oneself as creative; and being enduringly inquisitive. Domain-specific descriptions would likely benefit from domain-specific considerations in selecting attributes for study.

Although there is ample research in creativity studies about each of the functional areas of personality described above, two areas deserved special attention, considering the richness of existing work focused on describing creative individuals (as opposed to, for instance, momentary states, such as affect, Baas et al., 2008): motivation and cognition.

Lin (Chap. 5) addressed what motivates creative individuals through the lens of major contemporary theories of motivation, including intrinsic vs. extrinsic motivation, achievement goal orientation model, self-determination theory, and the theory of basic values. Furthermore, he discussed the application of concepts from motivation science in the specific context of creativity, including research on the creative self (stemming from Bandura's socio-cognitive theory, 1997) and creativity-related attitudes and values. Distinction between intrinsic and extrinsic motivation has proved fruitful in creativity studies. We can now confidently describe creative individuals as intrinsically motivated and we are gaining understanding about circumstances under which extrinsic motivation becomes an asset to creative individuals and can act synergistically with their intrinsic motivation (Amabile, 1993; Amabile & Pratt, 2016). Research adopting the achievement goal orientation theory shows that creative individuals are most strongly described by a learning/mastery goal orientation and weakly by performance approach (positively) and performance avoid orientations (negatively; meta-analysis: Nandi & Watts, 2025). Furthermore, research based on the model of basic values showed evidence of some likely domain-general values as relevant to creative individuals. Results showed that creative individuals have a tendency to be self-directed, have universalist concerns, and value novelty, as well as holding non-traditional values, and not placing great value on life stability (Kasof et al., 2007). These values echo the central finding from research based on the self-determination theory about the key role of satisfaction of autonomy needs and importance of contextual autonomy supports for creativity (e.g., Li et al., 2018; Liu et al., 2011).

Although creative self-efficacy has been theoretically and empirically posited as a general descriptor of creative individuals (Karwowski & Beghetto, 2019), scholars have also argued that it should be both conceived and assessed as a dynamic attribute, which would by necessity have to be domain (or task)-specific (Karwowski et al., 2019). Emerging creativity-native motivational constructs, such as attitudes toward creativity, echo this need for context or domain-specific research. For instance, Ivcevic and Hoffmann (2022) identified three creativity-relevant attitudes in a sample of high school students—anticipating negative social consequences of creativity, anxious risk avoidance, and valuing creativity—and showed that they have incremental validity over Openness to Experience in predicting creative behavior specifically at school (and not outside of the school context).

When we ask what it takes to know creative individuals, it is unavoidable to consider their intellectual abilities. There is a long tradition of research on divergent thinking abilities (Torrance, 1988). These abilities were theoretically defined by Guilford (1956) in his model of intelligence and they became the central construct of creative potential, with tests measuring these abilities most commonly used criteria in gifted identification (Lee et al., 2024) and in evaluating interventions aiming to build creative skills (Haase et al., 2025). In addition to divergent thinking, more recently developed test battery, Evaluation of Potential Creativity (EPoC; Lubart et al., 2013) has added convergent integrative thinking and this approach was also adopted by the influential Programme for International Student Assessment (PISA) in their creative thinking assessments. Meta-analytic evidence supports the conceptualization of divergent thinking as an attribute of creative potential that is related to creative behavior and achievement (Said-Metwaly et al., 2024).

Dumas and Kagan discuss cognitive attributes of highly creative individuals (Chap. 6). They acknowledge the importance of divergent thinking to the creative process more broadly. In studying it, we have learned much about the micro-dynamics of creativity-relevant thinking, such as that it is influenced by momentary mood (Baas et al., 2008) or that people expect their first ideas to be most original, but later ideas tend to be more original by objective measures (Lucas & Nordgren, 2020). However, Dumas and Kagan note that these abilities and their typical measures are disconnected from real-world adult creativity. Such enacted creativity is expressed within specific domains and social contexts and influenced by cognitive attributes that include (1) domain-relevant knowledge; (2) epistemic cognition that is the basis for critical thinking; (3) relational reasoning and associative thinking; (4) problem-finding; and (5) ability to evaluate and select ideas that are worth investing in. This is not an exhaustive list of cognitive attributes of creative individuals, but they cover the whole course of the creative process necessary to actualize creative potential, from identification of areas or questions that provide opportunities for real-world creativity and innovation, to acquiring and critically examining existing knowledge that is the jumping point for creative work, to making new connections, and finally evaluating generated ideas.

Directions for Future Research

As we look forward toward a new generation of research on the creative person, it is important to pause and acknowledge our past. When Helson (1996) did the same in looking back at the past of her own and work of others in the early decades of research on creative individuals, she concluded, "Creativity takes place in diverse contexts, and we cannot expect the personalities of people who create in different domains to be the same, or to differ in the same ways from comparison subjects" (p. 303). Almost three decades later, conclusions of all chapters in this book have a version of this statement. This message is now loud and clear.

However, studies that explicitly acknowledge and examine different contexts for creativity, whether we are talking about domains or socio-cultural contexts, are not common enough. An early meta-analysis of personality traits and creativity was domain specific, focusing on traits in artists and (more or less) creative scientists (Feist, 1998). Yet, a more recent meta-analysis of personality traits and creativity was primarily domain-general (Puryear et al., 2017). Even research on creativity at work, which is inherently domain-specific—people work in particular industries and have specific job roles—tends to be domain agnostic and talk about creativity in general. Perhaps two exceptions are research on design and designers and entrepreneurship and entrepreneurs, possibly because they are the focus of their respective academic fields (design studies, entrepreneurship) and scholars often publish in specialized journals (e.g., *Design Studies*, *Journal of Business Venturing*). Although creativity scholars are aware of the need to study real-life creativity in the contexts in which it happens, more focused action evident in the questions we ask and how we address them in our studies is needed.

Research benefits from theory. Developments in personality theory provide a blueprint that we can follow. I will argue that two such developments are especially useful for creativity studies: functional approach to personality and distinction between core and surface attributes. These approaches do not stand in opposition; rather, they complement each other.

Scholars have long acknowledged that creativity requires a confluence of multiple resources (Amabile, 1996; Mumford & Gustafson, 1988; Sternberg & Lubart, 1995). The question is what resources. Functional models of personality provide a useful tool for addressing this question—sample attributes from each of the main functional areas. If we adopted Mayer's (2005, 2015) model, for instance, this would include attributes of emotion and motivation, cognition, social action, and self-regulation. Which specific attributes within each of those areas we should focus on if our goal is to understand creative individuals across different domains is a question for scholars who focus on each of the functional areas. Contributors to this volume have discussed possible candidate attributes. Dumas and Kagan (Chap. 6) explicitly provided a list of five attributes describing cognition of creative individuals and included domain knowledge to stay grounded in real-world domain-specific creativity. Similar lists could be created for other functional areas and research using profile analysis or exploratory network analysis (Chen et al., 2023) can then identify different groups of individuals based on their personality attributes.

Functional approaches tell us where to look for attributes to study. They do not necessarily tell us which kinds of attributes to choose. There, a distinction between core and surface attributes is helpful (Lebuda, 2025). For each functional area, research is likely to benefit from a combination of core attributes and surface attributes. Table 9.1 shows a sample of such attributes. This example is not meant as an exhaustive list describing the creative person (or creative people), but only as an illustration of possible attributes across functional areas of personality that include both

Table 9.1 Sample creativity-relevant core and surface personality attributes

Functional area	*Core attributes (Big Five domain)*	*Surface attributes*
Emotion and motivation	Positive emotions (Extraversion)	Attitudes toward creativity
Cognition	Curiosity (Openness)	Domain knowledge
Social action	Nonconformity (Openness)	Self-uniqueness
Self-regulation	Persistence (Conscientiousness)	Tolerance of ambiguity

core and surface attributes. Depending on samples under investigation, this list can (and should) be expanded. For instance, intellect (aspect of the Big Five Openness to Experience dimension) is relevant to describing personality of scientists, but not artists (Kaufman et al., 2016). Therefore, in studies that include scientists, it would be important to have this core trait represented.

Selecting core personality attributes to study is likely to be an easier task than selecting surface attributes. Research under the umbrella of the Big Five model has provided much information on core traits and their relevance for creativity across domains. The conceptual space for surface attributes within each functional area is much broader and selection therefore more challenging. For instance, for the functional area of emotion and motivation, there is rich tradition of research on intrinsic motivation (which is relevant to specific domain, such as one's professional setting; de Jesus et al., 2013), research on specific motives (e.g., emotion regulation, prosocial; Forgeard, 2024), and context-specific attitudes toward creativity (Ivcevic & Hoffmann, 2022). Choice of key variables will depend on the samples under investigation.

Another crucial area for future research concerns developmental emergence of creativity-relevant surface attributes. Scholars have proposed that mature creativity we observe in adulthood (e.g., in Pro-c creators) emerges from earlier forms of little-c creativity (Ivcevic & Mayer, 2006) and is based on specialization-differentiation processes (Barbot & Tinio, 2015). Mechanisms by which some surface attributes emerge have been theoretically proposed and empirically studied. This is most prominently the case for creative self-efficacy. For other attributes, this is less the case. For instance, we can ask how attitudes toward creativity emerge from both core personality traits and early experiences. We might hypothesize a person (core traits) x developmental situation (e.g., experiences of harsh criticism) interaction in shaping the attitude of anticipating negative social consequences of creativity.

In concluding the final chapter of this volume about creators, it is worthwhile to reach into history of the field of creativity studies once again. In their influential *Annual Review of Psychology* article, Barron and Harrington (1981, p. 455) asked:

> Which of these "core" personality characteristics facilitate effective social behavior of almost any form? Which specifically facilitate creative behavior? Which are by products of social achievement and recognition of almost any form? Which are specifically by-products of creative achievement and recognition? Which are merely noncausally related correlates of creative achievement?

Although the field of creativity studies has made much progress in more than 40 years since the publication of this review, these questions remain relevant. We can be confident that the core traits of Openness to Experience indeed facilitate enacted creativity and creative achievement. Yet, we should be less confident what is the meaning of the observed relationships between measures of creativity and Extraversion. Are these at the heart of who creators are (what helps them become creators and continually create) or are they a byproduct of creativity-irrelevant behavior that assists in selling ideas and products and thus making them more likely to be acknowledged and socially accepted? These are questions for the next generation of research on creative individuals.

References

Amabile, T. M. (1979). Effects of external evaluation on artistic creativity. *Journal of Personality and Social Psychology, 37*(2), 221–233. https://doi.org/10.1037/0022-3514.37.2.221

Amabile, T. M. (1983). The social psychology of creativity: A componential conceptualization. *Journal of Personality and Social Psychology, 45*(2), 357–376. https://doi.org/10.1037/0022-3514.45.2.357

Amabile, T. M. (1993). Motivational synergy: Toward new conceptualizations of intrinsic and extrinsic motivation in the workplace. *Human Resource Management Review, 3*(3), 185–201. https://doi.org/10.1016/1053-4822(93)90012-S

Amabile, T. M. (1996). *Creativity in context.* Westview Press.

Amabile, T. M., & Pratt, M. G. (2016). The dynamic componential model of creativity and innovation in organizations: Making progress, making meaning. *Research in Organizational Behavior, 36*, 157–183. https://doi.org/10.1016/j.riob.2016.10.001

Araki, M. E. (2018). Polymathy: A new outlook. *Journal of Genius and Eminence, 3*(1), 66–82. https://doi.org/10.18536/jge.2018.04.3.1.06

Asendorpf, J. B., & van Aken, M. A. G. (2003). Personality-relationship transaction in adolescence: Core versus surface personality characteristics. *Journal of Personality, 71*(4), 629–666. https://doi.org/10.1111/1467-6494.7104005

Baas, M., De Dreu, C. K. W., & Nijstad, B. A. (2008). A meta-analysis of 25 years of mood-creativity research: Hedonic tone, activation, or regulatory focus? *Psychological Bulletin, 134*(6), 779–806. https://doi.org/10.1037/a0012815

Bandura, A. (1997). *Self-efficacy: The exercise of control.* W.H. Freeman.

Barbot, B., & Tinio, P. P. L. (2015). Where is the "g" in creativity? A specialization–differentiation hypothesis. *Frontiers in Human Neuroscience, 8*, Article 1041. https://doi.org/10.3389/fnhum.2014.01041

Barron, F., & Harrington, D. M. (1981). Creativity, intelligence, and personality. *Annual Review of Psychology, 32*, 439–476. https://doi.org/10.1146/annurev.ps.32.020181.002255

Chen, Q., Christensen, A. P., Kenett, Y. N., Ren, Z., Condon, D. M., Bilder, R. M., Qiu, J., & Beaty, R. E. (2023). Mapping the creative personality: A psychometric network analysis of highly creative artists and scientists. *Creativity Research Journal, 35*(3), 455–470. https://doi.org/10.1080/10400419.2023.2184558

Costa, P. T., & McCrae, R. R. (1992). Normal personality assessment in clinical practice: The NEO Personality Inventory. *Psychological Assessment, 4*(1), 5–13. https://doi.org/10.1037/1040-3590.4.1.5

Cropley, D. H., Cropley, A. J., Kaufman, J., & Runco, M. (2010). *The dark side of creativity.* Cambridge University Press.

De Jesus, S. N., Rus, C. L., Lens, W., & Imaginário, S. (2013). Intrinsic motivation and creativity related to product: A meta-analysis of the studies published between 1990–2010. *Creativity Research Journal, 25*(1), 80-84. https://doi.org/10.1080/10400419.2013.752235.

De Young, C. G., Quilty, L. C., & Peterson, J. B. (2007). Between facets and domains: 10 aspects of the Big Five. *Journal of Personality and Social Psychology, 93*(5), 880–896. https://doi.org/10.1037/0022-3514.93.5.880

Digman, J. M. (1990). Personality structure: Emergence of the five-factor model. *Annual Review of Psychology, 41*, 417–440. https://doi.org/10.1146/annurev.ps.41.020190.002221

Feist, G. J. (1998). A meta-analysis of personality in scientific and artistic creativity. *Personality and Social Psychology Review, 2*(4), 290–309. https://doi.org/10.1207/s15327957pspr0204_5

Fleeson, W., Furr, R. M., Jayawickreme, E., Meindl, P., & Helzer, E. G. (2014). Character: The prospects for a personality-based perspective on morality. *Social and Personality Psychology Compass, 8*(4), 178–191. https://doi.org/10.1111/spc3.12094

Forgeard, M. (2024). Prosocial motivation and creativity in the arts and sciences: Qualitative and quantitative evidence. *Psychology of Aesthetics, Creativity, and the Arts, 18*(2), 222–244. https://doi.org/10.1037/aca0000435

Forgeard, M. J. C., & Kaufman, J. C. (2016). Who cares about imagination, creativity, and innovation, and why? A review. *Psychology of Aesthetics, Creativity, and the Arts, 10*(3), 250–269. https://doi.org/10.1037/aca0000042

Goldberg, L. R. (1992). The development of markers for the Big-Five factor structure. *Psychological Assessment, 4*(1), 26.

Gough, H. G. (1956). *California psychological inventory.* Consulting Psychologists Press.

Gough, H. G. (1960). The adjective check list as a personality assessment research technique. *Psychological Reports, 6*, 107–122. https://doi.org/10.2466/PR0.6.1.107-122

Gough, H. G. (1979). A creative personality scale for the Adjective Check List. *Journal of Personality and Social Psychology, 37*(8), 1398–1405. https://doi.org/10.1037/0022-3514.37.8.1398

Gough, H. G. (1992). Assessment of creative potential in psychology and the development of a creative temperament scale for the CPI. In J. C. Rosen & P. McReynolds (Eds.), *Advances in psychological assessment* (pp. 225–257). Plenum.

Guilford, J. P. (1950). Creativity. *The American Psychologist, 9*(5), 444–454.

Guilford, J. P. (1956). The structure of intellect. *Psychological Bulletin, 53*(4), 267–293. https://doi.org/10.1037/h0040755

Guilford, J. P. (1975). Creativity: A quarter of century of progress. In I. A. Taylor & J. W. Getzels (Eds.), *Perspectives in creativity* (pp. 37–59). Aldine Publishing Company.

Haase, J., Hoff, E. V., Hanel, P. H. P., & Innes-Ker, Å. (2018). A meta-analysis of the relation between creative self-efficacy and different creativity measurements. *Creativity Research Journal, 30*(1), 1–16. https://doi.org/10.1080/10400419.2018.1411436

Haase, J., Hanel, P. H. P., & Gronau, N. (2025). Creativity enhancement methods for adults: A meta-analysis. *Psychology of Aesthetics, Creativity, and the Arts, 19*(4), 708–736. https://doi.org/10.1037/aca0000557

Helson, R. (1996). In search of the creative personality. *Creativity Research Journal, 9*(4), 295–306. https://doi.org/10.1207/s15326934crj0904_1

Hunter, S. T., & Cushenbery, L. (2011). Leading for innovation: Direct and indirect influences. *Advances in Developing Human Resources, 13*(3), 248–265.

Hunter, S. T., Walters, K., Nguyen, T., Manning, C., & Miller, S. (2022). Malevolent creativity and malevolent innovation: A critical but tenuous linkage. *Creativity Research Journal, 34*(2), 123–144. https://doi.org/10.1080/10400419.2021.1987735

Ivcevic, Z. (2024). The continuum of regulatory processes in creativity: Comment on "A systematic framework of creative metacognition" by Lebuda, Izabela & Benedek, Mathias. *Physics of Life Reviews, 48*, 99–100. https://doi.org/10.1016/j.plrev.2023.10.020

Ivcevic, Z. (in press). Laying foundation to creativity studies: The legacy and lessons of IPAR and Donald MacKinnon. In G. Puccio, V. Glaveanu, J. A. Yudess, & M. Schwartz (Eds.), *The mid-century creativity reader*. Oxford University Press.

Ivcevic, Z., & Hoffmann, J. D. (2022). The creativity dare: Attitudes toward creativity and prediction of creative behavior in school. *The Journal of Creative Behavior, 56*(2), 239–257. https://doi.org/10.1002/jocb.527

Ivcevic, Z., & Kaufman, J. C. (2024). Inside the box: Considering the role of task-appropriateness for creativity. *Psychology of Aesthetics, Creativity, and the Arts*. Advance online publication. https://doi.org/10.1037/aca0000703

Ivcevic, Z., & Mayer, J. D. (2006). Creative types and personality. *Imagination, Cognition and Personality, 26*(1–2), 65–86. https://doi.org/10.2190/0615-6262-G582-853U

Ivcevic, Z., & Nusbaum, E. C. (2017). From having an idea to doing something with it: Self-regulation for creativity. In M. Karwowski & J. C. Kaufman (Eds.), *The creative self: How our beliefs, self-efficacy, mindset, and identity impact our creativity* (pp. 343–365). Academic Press. https://doi.org/10.1016/B978-0-12-809790-8.00020-0

Ivcevic, Z., Lin, S., Kaufman, J. C., & Hoffmann, J. D. (2023). Creativity and emotion: Connecting the dots. In Z. Ivcevic, J. D. Hoffmann, & J. C. Kaufman (Eds.), *Cambridge handbook of creativity and emotions* (pp. 620–640). Cambridge University Press. https://doi.org/10.1017/9781009031240

John, O. P., & Srivastava, S. (1999). The Big Five Trait taxonomy: History, measurement, and theoretical perspectives. In L. A. Pervin & O. P. John (Eds.), *Handbook of personality: Theory and research* (2nd ed., pp. 102–138). Guilford Press.

Kapoor, H. (2025). Shining a light on dark creativity. *Creativity Research Journal, 37*(2), 236–241. https://doi.org/10.1080/10400419.2023.2224689

Kapoor, H., & Khan, A. (2020). Creators and presses: The person–situation interaction in negative creativity. *The Journal of Creative Behavior, 54*(1), 75–89. https://doi.org/10.1002/jocb.346

Kapoor, H., Mahadeshwar, H., Rezaei, S., Reiter-Palmon, R., & Kaufman, J. C. (2025). The ties that bind: Low morals, high deception, and dark creativity. *Creativity Research Journal, 37*(3), 452–471. https://doi.org/10.1080/10400419.2024.2306447

Karwowski, M., & Beghetto, R. A. (2019). Creative behavior as agentic action. *Psychology of Aesthetics, Creativity, and the Arts, 13*(4), 402–415. https://doi.org/10.1037/aca0000190

Karwowski, M., Han, M.-H., & Beghetto, R. A. (2019). Toward dynamizing the measurement of creative confidence beliefs. *Psychology of Aesthetics, Creativity, and the Arts, 13*(2), 193–202. https://doi.org/10.1037/aca0000229

Karwowski, M., Czerwonka, M., Wisniewska, E., & Forthmann, B. (2021). How is intelligence test performance associated with creative achievement? A meta-analysis. *Journal of Intelligence, 9*, Article 28. https://doi.org/10.31234/osf.io/fm7hr

Kashdan, T. B., Stiksma, M. C., Disabato, D. J., McKnight, P. E., Bekier, J., Kaji, J., & Lazarus, R. (2018). The Five-Dimensional Curiosity Scale: Capturing the bandwidth of curiosity and identifying four unique subgroups of curious people. *Journal of Research in Personality, 73*, 130–149. https://doi.org/10.1016/j.jrp.2017.11.011

Kasof, J., Chen, C., Himsel, A., & Greenberger, E. (2007). Values and creativity. *Creativity Research Journal, 19*(2–3), 105–122. https://doi.org/10.1080/10400410701397164

Kaufman, J. C., & Beghetto, R. A. (2009). Beyond big and little: The four c model of creativity. *Review of General Psychology, 13*(1), 1–12. https://doi.org/10.1037/a0013688

Kaufman, J. C., & Beghetto, R. A. (2023). Where is the when of creativity?: Specifying the temporal dimension of the four Cs of creativity. *Review of General Psychology, 27*(2), 194–205. https://doi.org/10.1177/10892680221142803

Kaufman, S. B., Quilty, L. C., Grazioplene, R. G., Hirsh, J. B., Gray, J. R., Peterson, J. B., & DeYoung, C. G. (2016). Openness to experience and intellect differentially predict creative achievement in the arts and sciences. *Journal of Personality, 84*(2), 248–258. https://doi.org/10.1111/jopy.12156

Lebuda, I. (2025). Broadening perspective on creative personality: Surface and core characteristics as predictors of creative achievements. *Creativity Research Journal., 37*(2), 250–256. https://doi.org/10.1080/10400419.2023.2300198

Lebuda, I., Zielińska, A., & Karwowski, M. (2021). On surface and core predictors of real-life creativity. *Thinking Skills and Creativity, 42*, Article 100973. https://doi.org/10.1016/j.tsc.2021.100973

Lee, L. E., Rinn, A. N., & Rambo-Hernandez, K. E. (2024). What happens after nomination? Evaluating the probability of gifted identification with the Torrance Test of Creative Thinking. *Gifted Child Quarterly, 68*(2), 119–136. https://doi.org/10.1177/00169862231222886

Li, H., Li, F., & Chen, T. (2018). A motivational–cognitive model of creativity and the role of autonomy. *Journal of Business Research, 92*, 179–188. https://doi.org/10.1016/j.jbusres.2018.07.025

Lin, S., Ivcevic, Z., Kashdan, T., & Kaufman, S. B. (2024). Curious and persistent, but not consistent: Self-regulation traits and creativity. *Journal of Creative Behavior*. Advance online publication. https://doi.org/10.1002/jocb.638

Liu, D., Chen, X. P., & Yao, X. (2011). From autonomy to creativity: A multilevel investigation of the mediating role of harmonious passion. *Journal of Applied Psychology, 96*(2), 294–309. https://doi.org/10.1037/a0021294

Lubart, T. (2017). The 7 C's of creativity. *Journal of Creative Behavior, 51*(4), 293–296. https://doi.org/10.1002/jocb.190

Lubart, T. I., Zenasni, F., & Barbot, B. (2013). Creative potential and its measurement. *International Journal of Talent Development and Creativity, 1*(2), 41–51.

Lucas, B. J., & Nordgren, L. F. (2020). The creative cliff illusion. *PNAS Proceedings of the National Academy of Sciences of the United States of America, 117*(33), 19830–19836. https://doi.org/10.1073/pnas.2005620117

Mathisen, G. E. (2011). Organizational antecedents of creative self-efficacy. *Creativity and Innovation Management, 20*(3), 185–195.

Mayer, J. D. (2005). A tale of two visions: Can a new view of personality help integrate psychology? *American Psychologist, 60*(4), 294–307. https://doi.org/10.1037/0003-066X.60.4.294

Mayer, J. D. (2015). The personality systems framework: Current theory and development. *Journal of Research in Personality, 56*, 4–14. https://doi.org/10.1016/j.jrp.2015.01.001

McAdams, D. P. (1995). What do we know when we know a person? *Journal of Personality, 63*(3), 365–396. https://doi.org/10.1111/j.1467-6494.1995.tb00500.x

McClelland, D. C. (1962). On the dynamics of creative physical scientists. In H. B. Gruber, G. Terrell, & M. Wertheimer (Eds.), *Contemporary approaches to creative thinking* (pp. 141–174). Atherton.

McClelland, D. C. (1975). *Power: The inner experience*. Wiley.

McCrae, R. R., & Costa, P. T., Jr. (1999). The five-factor theory of personality. In L. A. Pervin & O. P. John (Eds.), *Handbook of personality: Theory and research* (2nd ed., pp. 139–153). The Guilford Press.

Mumford, M. D., & Gustafson, S. B. (1988). Creativity syndrome: Integration, application, and innovation. *Psychological Bulletin, 103*(1), 27–43. https://doi.org/10.1037/0033-2909.103.1.27

Murray, H. A. (1936). Basic concepts for a psychology of personality. *The Journal of General Psychology, 15*(2), 241–268. https://doi.org/10.1080/00221309.1936.9917922

Nandi, S., & Watts, L. L. (2025). Achievement goal orientation and employee creativity: A meta-analysis. In *Psychology of aesthetics, creativity, and the arts.* Advance online publication. https://doi.org/10.1037/aca0000749

Newman, A., Herman, H. M., Schwarz, G., & Nielsen, I. (2018). The effects of employees' creative self-efficacy on innovative behavior: The role of entrepreneurial leadership. *Journal of Business Research, 89*, 1–9. https://doi.org/10.1016/j.jbusres.2018.04.001

Plucker, J. A., Beghetto, R. A., & Dow, G. T. (2004). Why isn't creativity more important to educational psychologists? Potentials, pitfalls, and future directions in creativity research. *Educational Psychologist, 39*(2), 83–96. https://doi.org/10.1207/s15326985ep3902_1

Policastro, E., & Gardner, H. (1999). From case studies to robust generalizations: An approach to the study of creativity. In R. J. Sternberg (Ed.), *Handbook of creativity* (pp. 213–225). Cambridge University Press.

Puente-Díaz, R., & Cavazos-Arroyo, J. (2017). Creative self-efficacy: The influence of affective states and social persuasion as antecedents and imagination and divergent thinking as consequences. *Creativity Research Journal, 29*(3), 304–312. https://doi.org/10.1080/10400419.2017.1360067

Puente-Díaz, R., & Cavazos-Arroyo, J. (2022). Creative self-efficacy and metacognitive feelings as sources of information when generating, evaluating, and selecting creative ideas: A metacognitive perspective. *The Journal of Creative Behavior, 56*(4), 647–658. https://doi.org/10.1002/jocb.557

Puryear, J. S., Kettler, T., & Rinn, A. N. (2017). Relationships of personality to differential conceptions of creativity: A systematic review. *Psychology of Aesthetics, Creativity, and the Arts, 11*(1), 59–68. https://doi.org/10.1037/aca0000079

Rhodes, M. (1961). An analysis of creativity. *The Phi Delta Kappan, 42*(7), 305–310. https://www.jstor.org/stable/20342603

Said-Metwaly, S., Taylor, C. L., Camarda, A., & Barbot, B. (2024). Divergent thinking and creative achievement—How strong is the link? An updated meta-analysis. *Psychology of Aesthetics, Creativity, and the Arts, 18*(5), 869–881. https://doi.org/10.1037/aca0000507

Shalley, C. E., Gilson, L. L., & Blum, T. C. (2000). Matching creativity requirements and the work environment: Effects on satisfaction and intentions to leave. *Academy of Management Journal, 43*, 215–223. https://doi.org/10.2307/1556378

Sternberg, R. J. (2021). Transformational creativity: The link between creativity, wisdom, and the solution of global problems. *Philosophies, 6*(3), 75. https://doi.org/10.3390/philosophies6030075

Sternberg, R. J., & Lubart, T. I. (1995). *Defying the crowd: Cultivating creativity in a culture of conformity.* The Free Press.

Storme, M., Celik, P., & Myszkowski, N. (2021). Creativity and unethicality: A systematic review and meta-analysis. *Psychology of Aesthetics, Creativity, and the Arts, 15*(4), 664–672. https://doi.org/10.1037/aca0000332

Tierney, P., & Farmer, S. M. (2002). Creative self-efficacy: Its potential antecedents and relationship to creative performance. *Academy of Management Journal, 45*(6), 1137–1148. https://doi.org/10.2307/3069429

Tierney, P., & Farmer, S. M. (2004). The Pygmalion process and employee creativity. *Journal of Management, 30*(3), 413–432. https://doi.org/10.1016/j.jm.2002.12.001

Tierney, P., & Farmer, S. M. (2011). Creative self-efficacy development and creative performance over time. *Journal of Applied Psychology, 96*(2), 277–293. https://doi.org/10.1037/a0020952

Torrance, E. P. (1988). The nature of creativity as manifest in its testing. In R. J. Sternberg (Ed.), *The nature of creativity* (pp. 43–75). Cambridge University Press.

Tyagi, V., Hanoch, Y., Hall, S. D., Runco, M., & Denham, S. L. (2017). The risky side of creativity: Domain specific risk taking in creative individuals. *Frontiers in Psychology, 8*, 145. https://doi.org/10.3389/fpsyg.2017.00145

Wallach, M. A., & Kogan, N. (1965). *Modes of thinking in young children: A study of the creativity-intelligence distinction*. Holt, Rinehart, and Winston.

Weber, E. U., Blais, A.-R., & Betz, N. E. (2002). A domain-specific risk-attitude scale: Measuring risk perceptions and risk behaviors. *Journal of Behavioral Decision Making, 15*(4), 263–290. https://doi.org/10.1002/bdm.414

Weber, H., Assunção, V. L., Martin, C., Westmeyer, H., & Geisler, F. C. M. (2014). Reappraisal inventiveness: The ability to create different reappraisals of critical situations. *Cognition and Emotion, 28*(2), 345–360. https://doi.org/10.1080/02699931.2013.835254

White, R. W. (Ed.). (1963). *The study of lives: Essays on personality in honor of Henry A. Murray*. Atherton Press. https://doi.org/10.1037/12238-000

Zhou, Q., Hirst, G., & Shipton, H. (2012). Promoting creativity at work: The role of problem-solving demand. *Applied Psychology, 61*(1), 56–80. https://doi.org/10.1111/j.1464-0597.2011.00455.x

Zielińska, A., Lebuda, I., Ivcevic, Z., & Karwowski, M. (2022). How adolescents develop and implement their ideas? On self regulation of creative action. *Thinking Skills and Creativity, 43*, 1–16. https://doi.org/10.1016/j.tsc.2022.100998

Zielińska, A., Forthmann, B., Lebuda, I., & Karwowski, M. (2025). Self-regulation for creative activity: The same or different across domains? *Psychology of Aesthetics, Creativity, and the Arts, 19*(2), 307–328. https://doi.org/10.1037/aca0000540

Index[1]

[1] Note: Page numbers followed by 'n' refer to notes.

Z. Ivcevic (ed.), *Creators*, The Seven C's of Creativity,
https://doi.org/10.1007/978-3-032-09225-0

The manufacturer's authorised representative in the EU is Springer Nature Customer Service Centre GmbH, Europaplatz 3, 69115 Heidelberg, Germany. If you have any concerns regarding our products, please contact ProductSafety@springernature.com

Printed and bound by CPI Group (UK) Ltd, Croydon, CR0 4YY
16/09/2026
02217786-0005